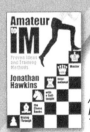

.

Andrew Soltis

THE
INNER GAME
OF CHESS

MONGOOSE
Press

Publisher: Mongoose Press
1005 Boylston Street, Suite 324
Newton Highlands, MA 02461
info@mongoosepress.com
www.MongoosePress.com

ISBN 978-1-936277-60-5

Distributed to the trade by National Book Network
custserv@nbnbooks.com, 800-462-6420
For all other sales inquiries please contact the publisher.

Editor: Jorge Amador
Technical Advisor: IM Grigory Bogdanovich
Layout: Andrey Elkov
Cover Design: Al Dianov
Printed in the United States of America

Revised edition
0 9 8 7 6 5 4 3 2 1

TABLE OF CONTENTS

Chapter 1

WHAT CALCULATION IS – AND ISN'T

"We think in generalities, we live in details."

–Alfred North Whitehead

Like the rest of us, chessplayers think in generalities – the value of centralizing pieces, the way to exploit doubled pawns and bad bishops, the strength of a rook or knight. But they also live in the details of a game – the "if I move my bishop there, he plays knight takes pawn check" details.

Entire libraries have been devoted to teaching the generalities of chess. These books use specific examples, of course, to illustrate when files should be opened or passed pawns pushed or queens exchanged. But then, in a real game, when you have to apply several of those general principles to a very specific situation, you may find that they contradict each other. In a typical middlegame position there may be two or three solid principles recommending, say 23.♖c6, and a couple more endorsing 23.exf5, and still others that seem to urge you to play 23.♘f6+. And the only way to figure out which is best is to wade into the details.

Ask a master what he actually does during a game and, if truthful, he'll answer: "I calculate variations." He looks a few moves ahead and makes a judgment about the various possibilities at his disposal.

He knows the old saying that, "Chess is 99 percent tactics," but he also knows it's inaccurate. Chess is really 99 percent calculation – the inner game of chess.

KAMSKY – MAMEDYAROV
World Cup 2013

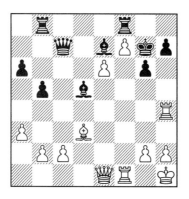

White to move

An amateur looking at this position would quickly count up material and realize that White has three extra pawns and Black has an extra bishop. That's roughly even.

He would see that White has two advanced passed pawns, at e6 and f7, an important asset. But he would also see that those pawns are firmly blockaded. Moreover, they could be quickly lost after ...♖b6 and ...♖xe6 or ...♗xe6.

The amateur would also realize that White's rook is aggressively placed at h4 but threatened by a bishop. He would look for a forcing way to make use of the rook. But 1.♕e5+?? just loses the queen and 1.♕c3+? ♕xc3 2.bxc3 ♗xh4 trades into a dead-lost endgame.

That's a lot to see. But a master would see something else. If the queen were to check on another square, such as d4 or h6, mate would follow immediately.

With that in mind, a master quickly calculates a promising line:

1.♕e3!!

What he saw was 1...♗xh4 2.♕d4+, which can lead to 2...♗f6 3.♕xf6+ ♔h6. (Or Black can play 2...♔h6 3.♕xh4+ ♔g7 4.♕f6+ ♔h6. The same position is reached.)

The master would see that far and realize he can force perpetual check. But he would look further, for a knockout. Then he would find 4.♖f4!. It threatens 5.♖h4#.

Black could avoid that with 4...♕xf4, but after 5.♕xf4+ ♔g7 White is now ahead in material and there is likely to be a way to win more of it. (It's there: 6.♕d4+ and 7.♕xd5.)

The master would also see that Black has one alternative after 1.♕e3. That's what happened in the game.

1...	h5!
2.♕d4+	♔h6

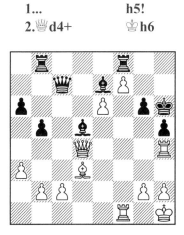

A master might only see this far when he began calculating 1.♕e3. But he appreciates that Black's king position has been weakened considerably since the position in the previous diagram.

A master "feels" that there should be a killer here. He knows it should be a forcing move, such as 3.♖f6. That threatens 4.♖xg6+. A quick look at 3...♗xf6 4.♕xf6 with a threat of 5.♕xg6# looks good. But he also finds:

3.♖xh5+!

A check is more forcing and its consequences are generally easier to calculate. White saw that 3...gxh5 4.♖f6+ leads to another quick mate (4...♗xf6 5.♕xf6#; 4...♔g5 5.h4#; or 4...♔g7 5.♖g6+).

Black saw that much – and also that 3...♔xh5 4.♕g7! ends resistance, with its threat of ♕xg6+ – so he **resigned**. Once again good calculation clinched the win.

Calculation may well be the most important skill a chessplayer can master. Yet more misinformation is circulated about calculating than about any other aspect of chess.

It is widely believed, for example, that you are born either with or without calculating ability, that it cannot be taught. Almost everyone agrees, furthermore, that computers calculate much more efficiently than humans. And it is stated with the utmost authority that there is one and only one correct method of counting out variations, which all masters follow rigorously.

None of these statements is true. Calculation is a skill that can be studied, learned, and sharpened. A player can calculate much more efficiently than any machine. And masters select moves and visualize and evaluate their consequences using a wide variety of methods.

We'll examine these claims in subsequent chapters, but right now let's consider a few more myths:

The Myth of the Long Variations

A popular view among amateurs is that grandmasters are grandmasters because they routinely see 10 moves ahead. There are, of course, examples of this by GMs, but they are relatively rare.

Much more common is the kind of calculation that calls for seeing *not more than two moves* into the future. And most of the time these two-move variations lead only to minor improvements in the position. But these improvements can add up.

When Mikhail Botvinnik lost on first board during the 1955 Soviet-American match, the world champion explained the result simply: "It shows I need to perfect my play of two-move variations."

Let's see what Botvinnik meant:

RESHEVSKY – BOTVINNIK
USA-USSR Match
Moscow 1955

1.d4 e6 2.c4 d5 3.♘c3 c6 4.e3 ♘f6 5.♘f3 ♘bd7 6.♗d3 dxc4 7.♗xc4 b5 8.♗d3 a6 9.e4 c5 10.e5 cxd4 11.♘xb5 ♘xe5 12.♘xe5 axb5 13.♕f3 ♕a5+ 14.♔e2 ♗d6 15.♕c6+ ♔e7 16.♗d2 b4 17.♕xd6+!? ♔xd6 18.♘c4+ ♔d7 19.♘xa5 ♖xa5 20.♖hc1 ♗a6 21.♗xa6 ♖xa6 22.♖c4 ♘d5 23.♖xd4 ♖b8 24.♔d3 h5 25.♔c4 b3 26.a4 ♖c6+ 27.♔d3 ♖c2 28.♖b1

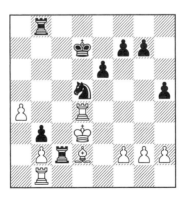

Because it was played in the depths of the Cold War, this game drew enormous attention and the news accounts made much of White's queen sacrifice at move 17. Actually, it was just a three-move combination designed to trade down to an equal-material endgame.

What do we have now? White has a passed a-pawn, a somewhat better-positioned king, and a minor piece (the bishop) with greater scope. But his pieces are temporarily tied to the defense of his second-rank pawns. Black's rooks and centralized knight should give him enough counterplay. Here, for example, Black has good winning chances with 28...♖b6!, threatening 29...♖d6, 30...e5, and a powerful discovered check once the d4-rook moves.

28...   **♖bc8?**

Botvinnik saw 28...♖b6 but talked himself out of it, thinking that 29.♖c4, threatening 30.♖xc2, was a strong reply. What he overlooked was 29...♖c6!, after which White's position is precarious (30.♖xc2 ♖xc2 31.a5 ♔c6 and White begins to run out of moves).

So Black prepares ...♖bc8-c6-d6, stopping 29.♖c4 but costing himself a vital tempo. Black is not losing now, he's just not winning.

29.a5   **♖8c6**
30.♔e2   **♖d6**
31.♔e1

Now we see why the lost tempo is important. If White's pawn were still on a4, Black would be close to scoring with 31...♘b6! 32.♖xd6+ ♔xd6 33.a5 ♘d5, followed eventually by ...♔c5 and ...♘b4.

31...   **♘c7?**

A second miscalculation of a two-move variation. Botvinnik said he was in a rush to exchange rooks, overlooking that 31...e5 32.♖d3 ♘c7! reaches the same position as in the game but with an extra ...e6-e5 thrown in (33.♖xb3 loses the d2-bishop).

32.♖xd6+   **♔xd6**
33.♗c3

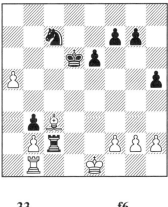

33...	f6
34.♖a1	♘a6?

Strike three, and this one is fatal. Black could draw with 34...♚c5! and 35.♖a3 ♚c4. White would have nothing better than repeating the position (36.♖a4+ ♚-moves 37.♖a3).

35.♖a3!

And this is the fourth two-move variation the world champion overlooked. He saw that 34.♖a1 threatens to ram the a-pawn but didn't realize that 35.♖a3, winning the b-pawn, was also threatened.

The game was over as soon as Black sealed his 41st move: **35...♚c7 36.♖xb3 ♘c5 37.♖b5 ♘a4 38.♗d4 e5 39.♚d1! ♖c4 40.♗e3 ♚c6 41.♖b8 ♚c7,** and Black **resigned** this adjourned position.

Notice that the cost of each little slip by Black was minor: He didn't lose rooks or pawns but only an extra tempo (31...♘c7?) or a chance for improved coordination of his pieces (28...♖bc8? and 33...f6?).

"Positional Players Don't Calculate"

From the last example you might conclude that positional players do nothing but calculate. Yet the image persists that strategists – such as

Reshevsky and Botvinnik – choose their moves abstractly, using only general principles, while the attackers are the ones who announce, "Mate in 27!"

But let's hear what a former world championship challenger has to say:

"Often a player who gravitates towards combinational solutions is automatically numbered among the calculating, logical brains," wrote David Bronstein. "In contrast," he added, "the one who is inclined towards positional play is said to possess an intuitive cast of mentality.

"Sometimes these characteristics are wrong by 180 percent, if only when one is talking about Capablanca or Tal."

By this Bronstein was suggesting that a positionally minded player could be a constant calculator – like José Capablanca. Or he could be a combinational player who relies to a great deal on intuition rather than long variations – like Mikhail Tal, another world champion. Of today's generation, we can speak of remarkable calculators as different in playing style as the "tactical" Magnus Carlsen and Hikaru Nakamura are from the "positional" Levon Aronian and Anish Giri.

IVANCHUK – HARIKRISHNA
FIDE World Championship 2004

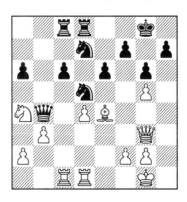

White to move

White has a positional edge because of his superior minor pieces and the weak black pawns. White can improve his chances with simple moves such as 1.♖c2. But he saw the benefits of forcing matters with **1.♗xd5!.**

Black had only two sensible replies and one of them, 1...exd5, would leave him with a chronic problem on c6. White would then have several ways of making progress, such as offering to go into an endgame (2.♕c3 or 2.♕d3/3.♕d2) or directing his major pieces at the weak pawns after 2.♘c5 ♘xc5 3.♖xc5.

He would not have to calculate any of these ideas when he first looked at 1.♗xd5. But he would need to look deeper into the position in case Black retook **1...cxd5,** as he did in the game. Since that eliminates the weak c-pawn, White would have to be sure he has a good follow-up.

He does. After **2.♖c7!** his advantage had grown considerably. His immediate idea is 3.♖dc1, which would threaten ♖xc8 and would leave him with dominating pieces after 3...♖xc7 4.♕xc7.

White was able to visualize a likely continuation, **2...♖xc7 3.♕xc7 ♕b8 4.♖c1,** and that's what was played. He could see that White would be close to a winning advantage after 4...♕xc7 5.♖xc7.

Instead, Black played **4...♕a8** but White's **5.♖c6** threatened ♖d6/ ♖xd7. The game quickly drew to a close: **5...♘f8 6.♘c5** (this wins the a-pawn in view of 6...a5 7.♖a6) **6...e5?! 7.♖f6! exd4 8.♕xf7+ ♔h8 9.♖xa6 ♕b8 10.♖a7! ♕e5 11.♘d3 1-0.**

In fact, a primary use of calculation is to tactically justify a move you really would like to play for positional reasons:

MUREY – VOLKE
Podolsk 1991

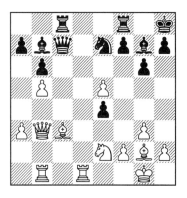

White to move

White has no particularly forcing idea. But ask yourself this question: "If there is one piece I'd like to reposition on an ideal square, which piece and which square would it be?"

Most players would probably say, "I'd like to move my bishop to d6 – but it's not legal to play 1.♗d6 here. Can I tactically justify 1.♗b4 and 2.♗d6?"

Through calculation, White can answer "Yes." After **1.♗b4!**, the e-pawn is taboo (1...♗xe5 2.♖bc1 ♕b8 3.♗xe7; or 1...♕xe5 2.♖d7 ♗d5 3.♕d1!).

So Black has to console himself with **1...♖ce8.** But after **2.♗d6! ♕d7 3.♖bc1,** White has transformed the slight positional edge in the diagram to a substantial advantage (3...♕g4 4.♘d4 ♗d5 5.♕b4!, or 3... ♖c8 4.♖xc8 ♖xc8 5.♕xf7).

"Calculation Means Finding Mates and Sacrifices"

Most calculation is concerned with minor aspects of the game: Can I win a pawn here? What are the risks of repositioning my knight? Can I afford to trade rooks? How favorable is the approaching endgame?

When we say it is essential to calculate major decisions well, we don't necessarily mean combinations. A major decision may be a primarily positional one.

SEIRAWAN – TAL
Candidates' Tournament
Montpellier 1985

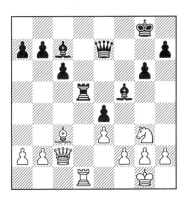

Black to move

Black's active pieces, particularly his c7-bishop and rook, provide compensation for his slightly loose pawn structure and inferior bishop on f5. With 1...♕d7 or 1...♕d6 and then 2.♖xd5 ♕xd5 he would have good chances. Instead, he decides to play for a draw:

1...   ♗xg3?

This is a major decision because the bishop is such a strong piece. Tal concluded that after 2.hxg3 ♖xd1+ 3.♕xd1 ♕d7! the invitation to an almost certainly drawn bishops-of-opposite-colors endgame could hardly be avoided, e.g. 4.♕e1 ♗g4 and 5...♕d1, or 4.♕b3+ ♕d5 5.♕xb7 ♕d1+ 6.♔h2 ♕h5+ with perpetual check.

But this is all based on a faulty assumption.

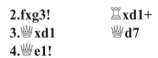

2.fxg3!   ♖xd1+
3.♕xd1   ♕d7
4.♕e1!

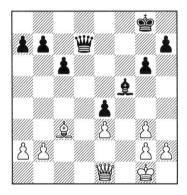

This retains queens (and winning chances) since 4...♗g4 is met by 5.h3. Black finds he must now play a bishops-of-opposite-colors endgame but with the deadly addition of queens. The presence of the white queen creates severe threats to Black on the dark squares around his king and on the queenside.

This required some subtle foresight. But Tal would have seen that Black was probably lost after 2.fxg3 if he had bothered to calculate its consequences. The rest of the game saw him pay for this elementary miscalculation: **4...♗e6 5.b3 c5 6.h3 b5?! 7.♕f1 b4 8.♗e5 ♕d8 9.♕b5 ♕c8 10.♔h2 ♗d8 11.♗d6 a6 12.♕a8 ♔f7 13.♗xc5 ♕c6 14.♕xb4 ♗e6 15.♗d4 h5 16.♕b8 ♔e7 17.♕e5 ♕d5 18.♕f6+ 1-0.**

Sometimes calculation means the simple visualization of a plan. Instead of "I go here and he goes there and then I'll think of something," it can be "I win by doing this, this, and that."

SHORT – TIMMAN
Tilburg 1991

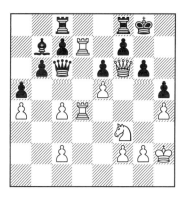

White to move

White's rooks are dominating and the black kingside is weak. But adding the one attacking piece that would lead to a fast mate actually is a boomerang (1.♘g5?? ♕xg2#).

1.♕g3!	♖ce8
2.♔f4!	

White had the rare opportunity in the diagram to calculate "without an opponent" – that is, without having to concern himself over Black's moves. He just had to visualize a winning idea: Put the king (!) on h6 and play ♕g7#.

In fact the game ended with:

2...	♗c8
3.♔g5!	1-0

As we'll see, the more forceful the moves involved, the easier it usually is to calculate a series of moves. Yet even when a master uses mating ideas he is often seeking no more than a positional edge.

POLUGAYEVSKY – WOJTKIEWICZ
Haninge 1990

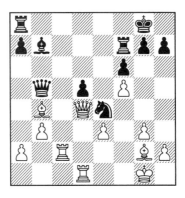

White to move

Tal once compared Lev Polugayevsky with another so-called "positional" master, Viktor Korchnoi: "Both move the pieces about feverishly, demonstrating a wide range of variations," he said. "These two are the most characteristic representatives of this class of calculators. To them, everything is very exact."

Here Polugayevsky holds a positional edge because of his rooks and excellent dark-squared bishop. But to realize an advantage he needed something concrete.

In chess, if you search you find. Polugayevsky found:

1.♗xe4	dxe4
2.♖c7!!	♖xc7
3.♕d8+	

A stunning idea, whose crucial point leads to 3...♖xd8 4.♖xd8+ ♔f7 5.♖f8#. But in its main line, which White had to consider in some detail, it leads only to a magnification of the positional plus that he held in the diagram.

3...	♕e8

4.♕xc7   ♗c6

The bishop is embarrassed (4...♗a6 5.♖d7).

5.♖d6   ♗b5
6.a4!

And White won after **6...♖c8 7.♕a5.**

The Joys of Calculating

Calculation is an enormously valuable tool because it can compensate for a lot of other deficiencies. It can, for example, make up for a player's poor winning technique.

A case in point:

BARCZA – TAL
Tallinn 1971

1.♘f3 g6 2.g3 ♗g7 3.♗g2 d6 4.d3 e5 5.e4 ♘c6 6.♘c3 ♘ge7 7.♗e3 0-0 8.♕d2 ♘d4 9.♘e2??

After this natural but tactically careless move, White is lost.

9...   ♗h3!

Since the attacked bishop may not move (10...♘xf3+!), and since castling loses the exchange to the same 10...♘xf3+, White is forced into:

10.♘fxd4   ♗xg2
11.♖g1   exd4!

Because this attacks the e3-bishop, Black now remains a piece ahead.

12.♘xd4   c5

13.♘b5   ♗f3

White only has a pawn for the piece, and the rest of the game score could have been omitted with the comment, "and Black won."

But what is remarkable is the way Black won. Instead of slowly exchanging off pieces and avoiding complications, Tal sought a knockout with his extra piece in the middlegame. This required a bit of enterprising calculation, particularly at move 18 below. But by making the effort, Tal ensured that the game would be resignable by move 23, not 43.

14.g4   d5!
15.♗xc5   ♖c8
16.♗a3   dxe4

Tal once cited the experience of another former world champion, Vassily Smyslov, in a difficult tournament, the 1967 Soviet Championship. Thanks to his general positional instincts and opening preparation, Smyslov had a clear edge in virtually every game by move 25. But by move 35 he was often lost, because he had to resolve the position by calculation, which was a problem for him.

Tal resolved his technical problems with:

17.dxe4   ♛b6!
18.♗xe7   ♛xb5!

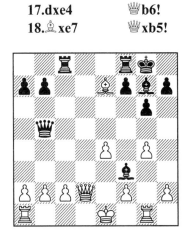

$$19.\text{♗xf8} \qquad \text{♛xb2!}$$

Black gives back much more material than he had gained. But he has calculated that, even though he is down a pawn and the exchange, his threats will be overwhelming.

$$20.\text{♗xg7} \qquad \text{♚xg7}$$
$$21.\text{♖c1} \qquad \text{♖d8!}$$

From here on the variations are short, like 22.♛xd8 ♛xc1+ and Black mates.

$$22.\text{♛e3} \qquad \text{♛xc2!}$$

And here both 23.♖xc2 ♖d1 and 23.♖g3 ♛d1+! 24.♖xd1 ♖xd1 are mates.

$$23.\text{♚f1} \qquad \text{♖d1+}$$
$$0\text{-}1$$

Understandable in view of 24.♖xd1 ♛xd1+ 25.♛e1 ♛d3+ and mates.

In this manner, Tal avoided having to play an endgame. But when you get into an ending, even a textbook one, calculation can be invaluable. It can be a substitute for "book knowledge" you never learned.

The subtle nature of endgame play often misleads improving players into believing that only memorizing a lot of similar positions – or having years of practical experience – will bring them mastery of basic endings.

POLUGAYEVSKY – KORCHNOI

Candidates' Match (6) 1977

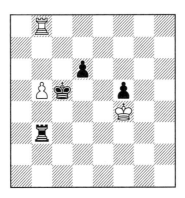

White to move

Here White makes a losing blunder just after resumption of an adjourned game. As it turned out, this virtually decided what might have been a close match leading to the world championship.

The moves White needed to find to achieve a draw were not difficult. They were based on the most elementary of endgame principles: 1.♔xf5! (eliminate as many of the enemy's pawns as possible) and then 1...♖xb5 2.♖a8! (keep the rook flexibly distant from the enemy king so as to maximize the potential for checks).

After 2.♖a8! the game should have been quickly drawn – 2...d5 3.♔e5 and 4.♖c8+, or 2...♔d4+ 3.♔f4 ♖b1 4.♖a4+! ♔d3 5.♖a3+ ♔c4 6.♔e3.

What happened in the game is that White followed other basic principles – overlooking a simple but decisive reply.

1.♖c8+??   ♔xb5
2.♔xf5

White has succeeded in eliminating one of the remaining black pawns and, in contrast to the drawing line cited above, has pushed the black king farther from the defense of his remaining pawn.

$$2... \qquad \text{\Rook}e3!$$

But he didn't visualize this stroke. It wasn't a matter of failing to evaluate this position correctly. As a grandmaster, Polugayevsky would know instantly that with the white king cut off from the e-file, Black can force the 400-year-old Lucena position, a simple win.

The rest of the game, although requiring many moves, took less than 20 minutes: **3.♔f4 ♖e1 4.♖d8 ♔c5 5.♖c8+ ♔d4 6.♔f3 d5 7.♔f2 ♖e5 8.♖a8 ♔c3 9.♖a3+ ♔b4 10.♖a1 d4 11.♖c1 d3 12.♖c8 d2 13.♖b8+ ♔c3 14.♖c8+ ♔d3 15.♖d8+ ♔c2 16.♖c8+ ♔d1 0-1** (in view of the familiar "bridge-building" technique).

The point here is that Black didn't have to calculate very long to win, and White didn't have to see far to draw. White simply didn't visualize two somewhat obvious moves ahead.

Learning to Visualize

In the last example, White thought one minute each over **1.♖c8+** and **2.♔xf5** and then lost because he failed to visualize **2...♖e3**. The power to consider positions that have yet to occur – and to recognize the possibilities in those positions – is essential to calculation.

Many newcomers to chess believe such visualization to be almost magical – so extraordinarily difficult that it's an ability you must be born with. Actually, it is a skill like any other chess skill.

In the pages that follow we'll consider the various components of good calculation: the selection of candidate moves, the role of force, the identification and evaluation of end positions, and so on. But first let's do a bit of practice with our innate powers to visualize. This is an exercise to show what you are already capable of visualizing, and what you can develop into.

Let's visualize our way through an entire game. Don't use a chess set for the following. We are going to play through a grandmaster game in our minds.

This may sound impossible. But, with practice, it is quite within the range of most of the people who take chess seriously – provided you take your time. This will be the longest exercise in this book and should take you at least half an hour.

CARLSEN – ANAND
Moscow 2013

1.d4 ♘f6 2.c4 e6 3.♘c3 ♗b4

This is how a standard opening, the Nimzo-Indian Defense, begins. Try to play through these three moves in your head. But take your time.

Don't try to see the entire board. *Nobody* does that.

If you go slowly, adding one move by White to what you've already been able to see, then add one move by Black, you should be able to walk through this 29-move game.

If the position isn't clear after 3...♗b4, close your eyes and ask yourself simple questions, beginning with: What does the center pawn structure look like? (Pawn structures are important in visualizing because they are the most enduring features of a position.)

Once you see in your mind the white pawns at d4 and c4 and the black one at e6, ask yourself which minor pieces have moved. It's only three so far and if you go slowly you should be able to "see" them.

Let's go on.

4.e3 0-0 5.♘ge2 d5

Don't try to do more than two or three moves at a time before you refresh your vision. At this point: Can you see the new pawn structure? Did you notice that all of Black's kingside pieces are developed?

6.a3 ♗e7

This is the first retreat. When you visualize the position, you may be able to see the black bishop at e7 – but also think there's one at b4. It isn't. One of the hardest parts of looking several moves into the future is that your mind is likely to retain the image of a piece still sitting on a square it has abandoned.

7.cxd5 ♘xd5 8.♗d2 ♘d7

Close your eyes and try to think where all four knights are before looking at the next diagram.

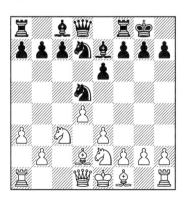

Were you right? If not, you might want to try again from move one.

9.g3 b6 10.♘xd5 exd5

Stop here. This is an important point because a major change in the pawn structure has taken place.

There aren't going to be other major changes until we're into the middlegame, so it's worth pausing to take stock: In your "mind's eye," see if you can visualize where each of the pawns is. Again, go slowly, one pawn at a time.

Did you remember that White's a-pawn had moved to a3? (That's easy to forget.) Did you see that the c-file is half-open? (The only pawn on it is the black one at c7). What about the e-file?

When you're ready to continue, try the next batch of moves.

11.♗g2 ♗b7 12.♗b4 ♘f6 13.0-0 ♖e8

We're on the verge of the middlegame now. Did you see how either player can trade bishops? (White can play ♗xe7 or Black can do ...♗xb4.)

14.♖c1 c6 15.♗xe7 ♖xe7

A second pair of pieces is gone. This is a good time to stop and do a count: Where are the pawns? Where are the major pieces? Start with White's queen, then his rooks. Then do Black's queen and follow with his rooks. Finally, try to visualize where the four remaining minor pieces are.

If you can't do it, take a good look at the last diagram and then imagine adding each of the seven moves played since then.

16.♖e1 ♕d6 17.♘f4 ♗c8 18.♕a4 ♖c7

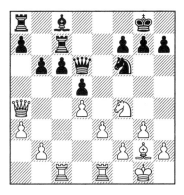

These moves may have come easier to you because the pawn structure didn't change; it's only the pieces that shifted around.

Try to visualize a chunk of the board – say, the right-hand corner. Can you see what White's castled position looks like? How about Black's?

If you can do that, try to see the left-hand corner. Then try to visualize the last corner, in the upper left.

19.f3 ♗e6 20.e4 dxe4 21.fxe4

The advance and trade of pawns has given White an advantage. Can you see White's threat? It's a pawn fork.

21...♕d7 22.d5

Big changes are coming from pieces and pawn trades. But before we get there, ask yourself where all of the pieces and pawns are. Did you realize there's one piece that hasn't moved yet?

22...cxd5 23.♕xd7 ♖xd7 24.♘xe6 fxe6

A major simplification has taken place. Half of the pieces have been captured, so this is a good time to try to see which ones remain. If necessary, ask yourself questions such as: Does Black have any bishops? Does White? What about knights? Then do the rooks.

The pawn structure has also become easier to see. Are there any open files?

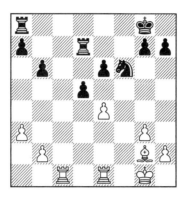

25.♗h3 ♚h8 26.e5 ♘g8

We're getting close to the finish now. You should be able to play out the rest of the moves mentally, even if you need to peek at the last diagram.

27.♗xe6 ♖dd8 28.♖c7 d4 29.♗d7 1-0

The game is over but you need to do one more review. How many pawns are left? Name the squares they're on. Then do the pieces.

This exercise should give you a good idea of how strong your visualization powers already are. If it proved too difficult, don't get discouraged. Practice with some shorter games, even with 10-move miniatures, until you can handle the longer ones.

Of course, in most situations you won't have to visualize more than three moves ahead. So let's turn our attention to what lies behind calculation: ideas that count.

Chapter 2

IDEAS

"The combination is born in the brain of a Chessplayer. Many thoughts see the light there – true and false, strong and weak, sound and unsound. They are born, jostle one another, and one of them, transformed into a move on the board, bears away the victory over its rivals."

–Emanuel Lasker

Before a player can begin his calculations he needs something to calculate. It will probably come from a tactical or strategic pattern, perhaps from a particularly fortunate configuration of his pieces or weak spot in his opponent's position. In short, an idea.

Ideas inspire calculation. Without them we'd have to think like computers, searching through dozens of moves and evaluating hundreds of irrelevant positions. The absence of an idea is the most common cause of oversights. When we miss a two-move combination, it's usually because we simply weren't aware of the *primary tactical idea* in the position. And usually this is because it didn't occur to us that there was one.

ALEKHINE – EUWE
World Championship (16) 1937

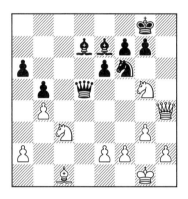

Black to move

Here, in a world championship game, we witness a remarkable double oversight by the two best players of the day. Black moved his attacked queen with:

1...   ♕**e5??**

If this position appeared in a magazine under the heading "White to play and win," most amateur tournament players would be able to find 2.♕h8+!. Certainly 99 out of 100 masters would find this elementary queen fork.

An amateur, however, might have some doubt about how good White's position is after 2.♕h8+ ♔xh8 3.♘xf7+ ♔h7 4.♘xe5. As we'll see in Chapter 5, it is the ability to properly evaluate a position at the end of a calculated sequence, rather than the ability to see 20 moves ahead, that most distinguishes the masters from the wannabes.

But here the amateur would surely conclude that the position after 4.♘xe5 is more favorable for White than the position in the diagram. (In fact it is close to a win.)

But there are no such magazine headings at the board while you're playing the game. So, without being aware that there was something important to find, Alexander Alekhine and Max Euwe both missed a primary tactical idea. Ideas are clues to the position and in this case, neither player had one.

2.♗b2??   ♝c6??
3.a3??

And the game drifted on to a 65-move draw.

Of course, Alekhine and Euwe had other things to think about. They were thinking about general principles such as: Maximize the mobility of the minor pieces, centralize the queen, set priorities for the endgame, and so on. They weren't in the market for an idea as simple as a two-move combination.

More embarrassing was the following – another series of double oversights in which neither side realizes how close White is to mate. It ends when Black virtually forces White to see the mating idea.

HORT – PORTISCH
Madrid 1973

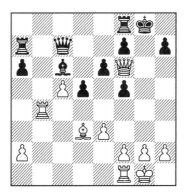

White to move

With plenty of time left on the grandmasters' clocks, there followed:

1.♕g5+?	♚h8
2.♕f6+	♚g8
3.♖fb1?	

Twice White has missed a forced checkmate (1.♖g4+! or, later, 3.♖g4+!).

3...	♝b5??

Black tried to plug the b-file and gain counterplay from 4.♗xb5 axb5 5.♖xb5 ♖xa2. Let's see, White asks himself, what else can I do with my rooks?

4.♖g4+!	fxg4
5.♕g5+!	♚h8
6.♕h6	1-0

Because mate can be stopped on f8 or h7, but not both.

The first task of the calculator, then, is to be aware of the possibility of tactical ideas in the position he holds. Combinations like this are the simplest of all sequences to calculate because they are forcing (two of the three key moves were checks) and their final positions are the most clear-cut to evaluate (it's mate). But the point to remember is that combinations are not invented, they are merely discovered.

Of course, not every position yields a combination. In most positions you can calculate only in the most general manner, usually only a move or two into the future. But because of the power of tactical ideas you must be able to recognize them quickly: pins, checks, double attacks, skewers, unprotected pieces, vulnerable back ranks, you name it.

Tactical ideas can arise suddenly:

LARSEN – BEDNARSKI
La Habana 1967

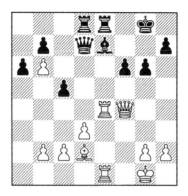

Black to move

Black faces some discomfort because of the doubled enemy rooks along the e-file. He would like to swap major pieces with a move such as 1...♗f8. But a bit of calculation tells him that after the final recapture (3...♕xe8) his f-pawn would be unprotected. Therefore, Black inserts a move which he believes will gain time (by attacking the e4-rook) and place the f-pawn on a safer square in preparation for the desirable 2...♗f8.

	1...	f5?

Most ideas are hard to verbalize, but easier to visualize. When White saw 1...f5, he may have been thinking, logically, "My rook is attacked, I must move it. Where can it go so that it attacks something?" But White's eyes are telling him something else: "Hmmm, aren't there an awful lot of vacant squares around his king, especially leading in along the long diagonals?"

Once the tactical idea is recognized ("Exploit those diagonals!"), the calculation process is streamlined. White looks for immediate methods of landing his queen on one of the key diagonals. He might start by considering 2.♖4e2, with a threat of 3.♕c4+ and 4.♗c3+. But this packs no punch since Black has a free hand to defend with 2...♗f6 and 3...♚g7!.

This exercise leads White to examine a method of stopping the 2...♗f6 defense, and he therefore turns his attention to 2.♖e6. But another look at the position shows him that 2.♖e6 ♗f8 3.♕c4 is resolved unsatisfactorily for him by 3...♖xe6 4.♖xe6 ♕f7!.

So there is no obvious way of cashing in on the diagonals. But White can't get over how porous Black's king position is. As an experienced player, he knows that positions like this often generate explosive sequences, and that such opportunities arise and disappear quickly. And this leads him to look for a more complicated (i.e., more forceful, riskier) sequence. And he finds it.

2.♗c3!!

It is natural to admire White's ability to work out a 15-move winning combination. It is all the more admirable because it leads not to a mate but to an endgame – a final position that must be correctly evaluated. *Yet for the experienced tournament player the counting out of variations, even 15-movers, is not as crucial to his success as finding the tactical ideas to begin with.*

2...   fxe4

Black can keep the white queen off the dark-square diagonal with 2...♗f8, but that permits 3.♖xe8 ♖xe8 4.♕c4+! – exploit those diagonals! – and 5.♖xe8.

3.♕e5   ♗f8

The bishop has to move to permit Black's queen to cover g7. Of no help is 3...♗f6 4.♕xf6 because 5.♕h8+ cannot be stopped.

| 4.♕h8+ | ♚f7 |
| 5.♖f1+ | ♕f5 |

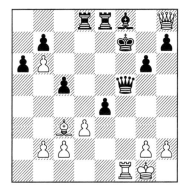

The alternative is 5...♔e6 6.♕e5#. Notice that Black has had virtually no choice so far (it didn't really matter where he moved his bishop at move 3). Thus White did not have to juggle several different positions in his head. If White saw as far as 5...♕f5, he knew he would win back his sacrificed material with interest. This may be a 15-move combination, but White had to see only the first four moves to feel confident about playing 2.♗c3!!.

The game continued 6.♖xf5+ gxf5 7.♕f6+ ♔g8 8.♕g5+ ♔f7 9.♕xf5+ (why not pick off another one before forcing the king out into the open again?) 9...♔g8 10.♕g5+ ♔f7 11.♕f6+ ♔g8 12.♕h8+ ♔f7 13.♕xh7+ ♔e6 14.♕xe4+ ♔d6 15.♕xb7, and White won directly.

Few combinations are provoked in the manner of the last two examples. More often an opportunity arises because a player notices some subtle idea, such as an overworked or unprotected piece well inside the enemy ranks:

TIMMAN – SIIORT
Candidates' Match (3) 1993

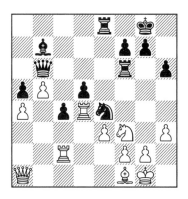

Black to move

White has just moved a rook from d1 to d4, when it was better to put the knight on that square.

Black's position is somewhat freer but there doesn't seem to be anything immediate that he can do about it. Yet if we ask simple questions we can sometimes break down a complex position into its elements. A beginner's question here would be: Which enemy pieces are unprotected?

Once Black realizes that the c2-rook is not covered, he can begin figuring out ways to attack it, such as:

1...   ♖xf3!
2.gxf3   ♛g6+

The queen is now lined up against the rook (3.♔h1 ♘g3+ 4.fxg3 ♛xc2 with advantage, or 3.♔h2 ♘g5! 4.♛d1 ♘xf3+ 5.♛xf3 ♛xc2). Black now has a draw, if that's what he wants. After **3.♗g2 ♘g5! 4.♖c1** he repeated the position (**4... ♘xf3+ 5.♔f1 ♘h2+ 6.♔g1 ♘f3+ 7.♔f1**) but then clarified matters and clinched victory soon after **7... ♘xd4.**

Sometimes you have to visualize the simplest situations of the board, mentally stripping away all but two or three key pieces, in order to "get it."

BIELCZYK – SŁABEK
Katowice 1992

1.e4 d5 2.exd5 ♘f6 3.d4 ♘xd5 4.c4 ♘b6 5.♘c3 e5 6.d5 c6 7.♘f3 ♗b4 8.♗e3 cxd5 9.c5! d4 10.♘xe5 dxc3 11.♕xd8+ ♔xd8 12.0-0-0+ ♔e7 13.cxb6 axb6 14.♗c4! cxb2+ 15.♔xb2 ♗a3+ 16.♔a1 f6

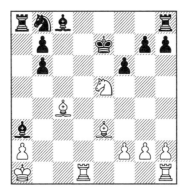

This looks like a complicated position. But it isn't. Strip away two pieces and the game is almost instantly over. Which pieces, you ask?

17.♘g6+!	**hxg6**
18.♗c5+!	

With these two pieces gone, White's h1-rook will all but deliver mate on e1. After **18...♗xc5 19.♖he1+,** White mates on d8 after 19...♔f8. The game actually ended with **19... ♗e6 20.♖xe6+** and **1-0** in view of 20...♔f7 21.♖e2+.

These last diagrams offer graphic examples of rather simple tactical ideas – open diagonals, an unprotected rook, a vulnerable king in the center of the board. But on the other extreme, the "idea" often is something amorphous and difficult to quantify. It may have to do with indefinable feelings about the position. Consider this early game by Garry Kasparov:

KASPAROV – LUTIKOV
Minsk 1978

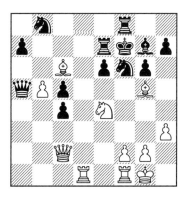

White to move

Black has managed to bring his king to relative safety and to connect most of his pieces through mutual lines of support. White should be able to regain the two pawns he sacrificed earlier, but the time it takes to do that may enable Black to make his position whole again.

Yet here Kasparov makes a revealing comment. While searching the position for clues, "I suddenly noticed something wrong with the development of Black's rooks."

It is hard to imagine a computer using a concept as vague as "something wrong." But it led Kasparov to find the correct move, **1.♗f4!**. That threatens the 2.♗d6 skewer and exploits the absence of safe squares along the seventh rank for Black's e7-rook.

True, 1.♗f4 does not win by force as 2.♗c3 did in the Larsen–Bednarski example a few pages ago. But after the resulting **1...♘xc6 2.bxc6 ♘e8 3.♖d7! ♖xd7 4.cxd7 ♘f6 5.♘d6+,** Black's position was perceptibly unraveling. Although he managed to keep the game going for another 20 moves, the situation was beyond redemption after **5...♔e7 6.♘xc4**

♕a6 7.♗d6+ ♔xd7 8.♗xf8 ♗xf8 9.♕d3+ ♔e7 10.♖d1 ♘d5 11.♕e4 ♔f7 12.♘e5+ ♔g8 13.♘d7 and so on.

As an exercise we'll offer this game:

FISCHER – CIOCÂLTEA
Varna 1962

1.e4 e5 2.♘f3 ♘c6 3.♗b5 a6 4.♗a4 d6 5.c3 ♗d7 6.d4 ♘ge7 7.♗b3 h6 8.♕e2 ♘g6 9.♕c4 ♕f6 10.d5 b5 11.♕e2 ♘a5 12.♗d1 ♗e7 13.g3 0-0 14.h4 ♖fc8?

White noticed something funny about this position. What is it? The solution is at the end of the chapter.

Sometimes your opponent's position suggests an idea to you even though at first it doesn't appear that you have the pieces to exploit it. One example, by Kasparov's predecessor as world champion, illustrates this.

KARPOV – YUSUPOV
Moscow 1983

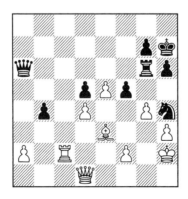

White to move

Black has active pieces and enemy weaknesses on the light squares as compensation for his pawn minus. But something occurs to White:

Black's knight has no moves. How do I go about exploiting that, he asks himself.

1.♔g3!

It requires nerves and good calculating ability to go piece-hunting this way. But here it is the fastest means of eliminating Black's counterplay.

The hard part of this was visualizing the game continuation: **1...fxg4 2.♔xh4 gxh3** (stopping the king from retreating the way it came) **3.f4 ♕e6 4.♕h5 ♕e7+ 5.♔xh3 ♕f7,** and now **6.♖h2!!** ended the threat of 6...♖g3+ and with it the game: **6...♕d7+ 7.f5 1-0.** But the easy part was coming up with the idea of ♔h2-g3xh4.

Sometimes ideas occur to you not because of obvious enemy weakness but because of the preponderance of your own firepower. If you ask yourself to find the weakest point in Black's armor in the next diagram, it is unlikely that you'll think first of f6 or g7. They seem very secure.

KHALIFMAN – SEIRAWAN
Wijk aan Zee 1991

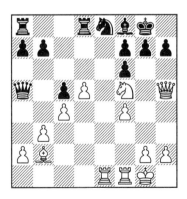

White to move

Perhaps, you wonder, you should take aim at a more vulnerable point like f7, with 1.♘e7+ ♗xe7 2.♖xe7.

But the most important feature in this position is simply that White has five excellent pieces available for attack. Even against an apparently solid kingside like Black's, there are possibilities of a tactical breakthrough.

> **1.♖xe8!**   **♖xe8**
> **2.♘h6+!**

Not particularly hard to find (2...♔h8 3.♕xf7 gxh6 4.♗xf6+, or 3... ♗e7 4.♕g8+! ♖xg8 5.♘f7#). But most players would not have looked for such a combination if the idea hadn't occurred to them that White has so many attackers.

> **2...**   **gxh6**
> **3.♕g4+**   **1-0**

While we are focusing in these first pages on the creation of forcing lines that give us an advantage, we also must be aware of the flip side – anticipating your opponent's ideas and sequences. We'll call this defensive calculation.

This is a more difficult skill than you might think. Just because you're a great attacking player doesn't mean you won't overlook the simplest of tactics when the game turns against you.

TAL – PETROSIAN
Curaçao 1962

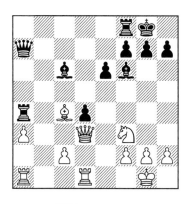

White to move

Here, Mikhail Tal, then the world's foremost calculator, was trying to defend his weak queenside and to reduce the scope of the terrible enemy bishops. He reasoned that the best way to protect the queenside pawns as well as to meet the possibility of 1...♗xf3 2.♕xf3 d3, attacking his a1-rook, was with:

1.♖a2??

Certainly if Tal had been sitting on the other side of the board he would have instantly spotted what's wrong with this move. But he wasn't.

1...   ♖xc4!

And White **resigned** in view of 2.♕xc4 ♗d5, skewering queen and rook. Being able to anticipate enemy tactics like this is the hallmark of a great positional player.

Master vs. Novice

Throughout this book we will investigate why masters calculate better than novices. Most people who don't play chess – and many who do – believe the greatest difference lies in how far ahead a player can see. "The master can see ten moves ahead, the amateur maybe only two," is a common attitude.

But a noted study by Adrianus de Groot, a Dutch psychologist and chess master, found that a key element is the master's ability to recognize patterns of pieces. A master can quickly memorize the placement of pieces in a particular position, breaking down the board into four or five chunks. Each chunk will have features that he remembers from other games and other positions. (We're talking about "normal" positions here. Masters show no superiority whatsoever in memorizing bizarre, problem-like positions. Such positions have no rational order, no "meaning" to them.)

Many familiar chunks, each having as few as five to as many as 16 squares, can be said to be "tactically neutral." Nothing much is happening in them. A typical example is a normal fianchetto king position: king at g1, bishop at g2, knight at f3, and pawns at h2, g3, and f2.

But many chunks do have tactical ideas inherent in them, ideas that masters recognize much faster than amateurs. This is particularly true of weaknesses in an opponent's camp.

PÄHTZ – FERNANDES
Albena 1989

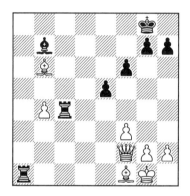

White to move

An amateur might first note the balance of material on the board or whether one player is in check. A master, however, might be drawn to other features, particularly the diagonal leading to Black's king. As White, he immediately begins thinking of getting a checking piece – a bishop or queen – somewhere between a2 and e6. A pity, he thinks, that my bishop is pinned.

An amateur might miss that idea entirely. Or he might give up on exploiting it after a brief search of ways to unpin the bishop. But the master will be so struck by that long light-squared diagonal he will probably search and search until he finds the winning move. It's **1.♕a2!!** and once you spot it, the position seems easy.

According to De Groot and others, masters assimilate many more chunks than non-masters; some claim that masters have 50,000-plus patterns in their heads.

How can you build up your storage of chunks? One obvious method is to play over many tactical games. David Bronstein, among other grandmasters, has suggested that most combinations are inspired by previous games that the calculator recalls. Some tactical themes, made famous by ancient brilliancies, are so familiar to modern masters that even a spectacular example like the following can be reduced to a matter of routine.

KUZMIN – SVESHNIKOV
USSR Championship 1973

1.e4 c5 2.♘f3 e6 3.d4 cxd4 4.♘xd4 ♘c6 5.♘c3 a6 6.♗e2 ♕c7 7.0-0 ♘f6 8.♗e3 ♗b4 9.♘xc6 bxc6 10.♘a4 0-0 11.c4 ♗d6 12.f4 ♘xe4 13.c5 ♗e7 14.♗d3 ♘f6 15.♗d4 ♘d5?

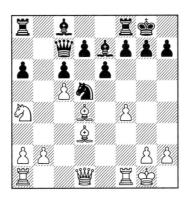

A typical modern gambit has given White excellent piece activity and Black some obvious weaknesses. That in itself suggests a general notion: White should attack the enemy king position. And Black's last move, aimed at stopping ♘b6, should be a bright green light to White. It removes the only piece directly committed to the defense of Black's king.

From that general notion comes a specific tactical idea, the double-bishop sacrifice.

| 16.♘b6! | ♘xb6? |
| 17.♗xh7+ | ♔xh7 |

18.♕h5+	♔g8
19.♗xg7!	♔xg7

Black's kingside has lost virtually all natural protection and the game ended immediately: **20.♕g4+ ♔h7 21.♖f3 ♗xc5+ 22.♔h1 1-0.**

If this is the first time you've seen such a combination, five forcing and sparkling moves long, it seems a work of genius. Actually it is merely a matter of good calculating technique. Some themes are so well worn they may eventually be catalogued by numbers and letters like openings. This is one such theme, made famous by the following game.

LASKER – BAUER
Amsterdam 1889

1.f4 d5 2.e3 ♘f6 3.b3 e6 4.♗b2 ♗e7 5.♗d3 b6 6.♘f3 ♗b7 7.♘c3 ♘bd7 8.0-0 0-0 9.♘e2 c5 10.♘g3 ♕c7 11.♘e5 ♘xe5 12.♗xe5 ♕c6 13.♕e2 a6 14.♘h5 ♘xh5

And now the same basic idea – **15.♗xh7+! ♔xh7 16.♕xh5+ ♔g8 17.♗xg7! ♔xg7** – clears away the protective pawns for the major pieces: **18.♕g4+ ♔h7 19.♖f3 e5 20.♖h3+ ♕h6 21.♖xh6+ ♔xh6 22.♕d7!.**

As we can see, the 1889 game was even more sophisticated than its 1973 imitator. In the modern game Black had no method of stopping mate. In 1889 Black did, and White had to foresee this final move of the combination (22.♕d7), winning more material, before he went into the sacrificial line. The rest is a mop-up: **22...♗f6 23.♕xb7 ♔g7 24.♖f1 ♖ab8 25.♕d7 ♖fd8 26.♕g4+ ♔f8 27.fxe5 ♗g7 28.e6 ♖b7 29.♕g6 f6 30.♖xf6+ ♗xf6 31.♕xf6+,** and White won.

In fact, when Siegbert Tarrasch managed to play yet another version of the two-bishop sacrifice at St. Petersburg 1914, he failed to win the first brilliancy prize because the judges believed he was merely reworking the by-then familiar idea of Lasker–Bauer. And the moves of Kuzmin–Sveshnikov were repeated exactly in another game, Barsegian–Garafutdinov, Tashkent 1989, until the very end when Black played 21... ♗xc5+ 22.♔h1 ♕xf4 23.♖xf4 f5 24.♕g5 before resigning.

As Tal once put it, to win a game you don't have to invent the bicycle. Great players do have great imaginations and that helps them play great combinations. But you are not required to invent anything to be able to calculate well. What you do need to do is recognize.

You should, for example, be able to recognize a more veiled and complex version of a single idea in the next three games, separated from one another by more than 75 years.

BIRD – MORPHY
London 1858

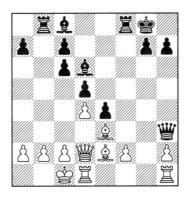

Black to move

Black has an extra pawn, and it appears that all the action is on the open kingside. But White is actually more vulnerable on the other side of the board, where he has fewer defenders.

BOGOLJUBOW – MIESES
Baden-Baden 1925

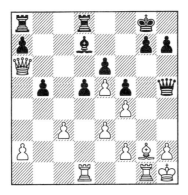

White to move

The pawn structure seems to deny the possibility of a sharp combination. And how can White's queen, far away on a6, have anything to do with the rest of his pieces?

LILIENTHAL – KAN
Moscow 1935

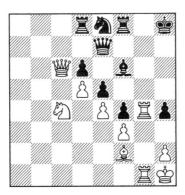

White to move

One more white piece must be added to the kingside to break through. Which one?

The three positions seem to have nothing in common. But a careful study will reveal a similar idea: the offer of one or two pieces and the sweep of the queen laterally along the sixth rank and into the camp of the enemy king.

In the first example, Paul Morphy accomplished this with **1...♖xf2! 2.♗xf2 ♕a3!.** The queen threatens mate, and since taking it allows mate in one (3.bxa3 ♗xa3#), Black was able to capture next move on b2 or a2 with a powerful attack that eventually won.

In the second example, White forced a favorable liquidation with **1.♗xd5! exd5 2.♖xg7+! ♔xg7 3.♕f6+ ♔g8 4.♖g1+.** After **4...♕g4 5.♖xg4+ fxg4 6.f5!** and **7.e6,** White emerged with a winning endgame.

And in the final example, the first step, **1.♗xh4!,** set the table for the second: **1...♗xh4 2.♘xe5!,** with a further threat of 3.♘g6+. In this instance, the queen-sweep is confined to a footnote (if 2...dxe5, then 3.♕h6+ and mate next), but it is still essential to the sequence.

Once you recognize such an idea it is your job to figure out whether, in fact, it works in the particular situation at hand. Calculating is not just a matter of making moves that have been played before in similar positions.

RÉTI – BOGOLJUBOW
New York 1924

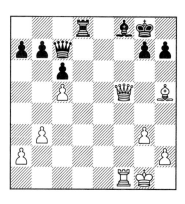

White to move

This position, from a brilliancy-prize game, is familiar to every master. White wants to exploit the vulnerability of the enemy's back rank, but only **1.♗f7+ ♚h8 2.♗e8!!** does it.

There is a danger of being carried away by ideas. Five years after the Réti game, one of the Czech master's rivals saw an opportunity to win another brilliancy prize with a Réti-like finish.

SÄMISCH – VIDMAR
Karlsbad 1929

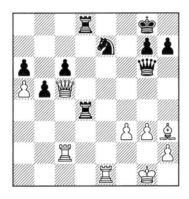

White to move

White can win simply and effortlessly with 1.♖xe7, and if 1...♖d1+, then 2.♗f1. But he saw the chance for immortality and played:

1.♕xe7??	**♕xc2**
2.♗e6+	**♔h8**
3.♗d5	

Very nice. By cutting the communication between the enemy rooks with that Réti-like bishop move, White threatens a back-rank mate (4.♕e8+) as well as 4.♕xd8+.

3...	**h5??**
4.♕xd8+	

And White was winning. But he shouldn't have been. If Black had seen 3...♖g8!, he might have turned the tables. Then 4.♗xg8 ♖d2! threatens mate in three beginning with 5...♖g2+ and forces 5.♕h4 ♕c5+ 6.♔h1 ♔xg8! when Black is simply a pawn ahead.

There is a further irony to this ill-fated brilliancy. After **4.♕xd8+ ♔h7,** White could have won with either of the two checks on g8. But instead he played the attractive **5.♗e4+??** and had to agree to a draw after **5...♕xe4!.** A classic example of bad calculation by both players.

Looking for the Weakness

A noted authority on composed endgames, C.M. Bent, once explained that studies are created in two ways, one "warm and spontaneous," the other "cold and efficient." The first is a matter of random exploration: A composer juggles the pieces, adding and subtracting them on a board, until something occurs to him. In the latter method, which he called the scientific, the composer begins with an idea, often even away from a board.

Competitive players don't have the luxury of random exploration. And ideas don't often suggest themselves as in Bent's "scientific" approach. But like a scientist, the player can ask the right questions to make inspiration easier.

SHORT – KARPOV
Candidates' Match (10) 1992

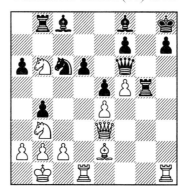

Black to move

To prevent ♘d5, Black played:

1... ♘e7

Improving players know enough to ask themselves such questions as, "What does he threaten now?" and, "What did he protect with his last move?" But they don't always ask, "What did he just leave *unprotected?*" You'll be surprised how often that question gives you an idea.

Here no ideas readily suggest themselves. But there is something a bit confused and uncoordinated about Black's position. What is it?

2.♘xc8? ♖xc8
3.♗xa6 ♖d8

And life went on. But had White spotted the problem with Black's major pieces he would surely have found the simple 2.♗xa6!, which would have won quickly (2...♗xa6 3.♘d7).

Sometimes a weakness is well concealed. For example, would you detect the vulnerability of f8 in the following diagram?

LEE – SAKHAROV
World Junior Championship 1963

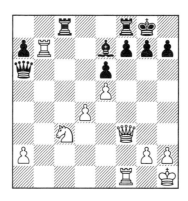

White to move

51

White's position looks as fragile as Black's because his intended 1.♖xe7 is met by 1...♖xc3, and if 2.♕xc3?? he's mated on f1. But a good calculator learns not to give up too early on a move he wants to play. As the Hungarian grandmaster Zoltán Ribli said, usually the first move you look at turns out to be the best.

> **1.♖xe7**   ♖xc3
> **2.♕xf7+!**

And Black was mated on the last rank, specifically on f8 (2...♖xf7 3.♖e8+).

Patterns

As you play over master games you will notice patterns, both tactical and strategic. A strategic pattern might be a favorable pawn structure or a thematic knight maneuver. A typical tactical pattern would be a formula for checkmate.

For example: a white bishop on c4 and rook on h1 facing a black king on h8 and pawn on g7.

The basic elements here are the bishop's control of the g8-square, cutting off the king's escape, and the check by the rook along the h-file. There are minor variations on this theme. For example, the checking piece can be a queen, not a rook; and Black can be denied g8 because of a pawn (on f7) or a knight (on e7 or f6) instead of a bishop along the diagonal.

Once you become acquainted with this mate pattern you will find it easier to recognize when it's hidden in a position.

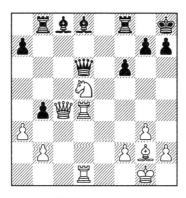

White to move

We can find the winning combination here in a variety of ways. We may recall similar past combinations. Or we could reason this way: Where is Black most vulnerable? Along the d-file, especially on d8, where there are latent back-rank weaknesses (1.♘-moves ♕c7 2.♖xd8! ♖xd8 3.♕xc7; or 1...♕e6 2.♖xd8! ♕xc4 3.♖xf8+).

But there is also the glimmer of a weakness at h7, which has no defenders except the king, yet can be attacked by rooks, a queen, and a bishop.

Finally, however, there is the mating pattern we mentioned earlier. If we are familiar with such patterns, we should be able to find some way of reaching one of them. And then we find:

1.♘f4!　　　　**1-0**

Because 1...♕e7 will allow 2.♘g6+! hxg6 3.♖h4#.

Once you recognize the basic elements of such a pattern, the addition of several irrelevant and distracting factors should not prevent you from identifying the winning idea. You should, for example, be able to see the same pattern in the following. The solution is at the end of the chapter.

KAISZAURI – SZNAPIK
Poland 1970

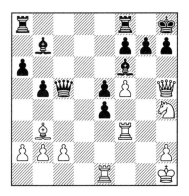

White to move

There are several basic mating patterns to be learned, including such elementary devices as Philidor's Legacy (the familiar combination that leads to a smothered mate) and back-rank mates with rooks and queens. Playing over master games is the easiest way to find and recognize them.

Hints

Besides mating patterns a position will contain other hints. They include: (1) vulnerable (unprotected or otherwise exploitable) pieces, (2) "stretched" pieces, and (3) invasion squares.

1) Vulnerable Pieces

Most calculated sequences involve, at least in part, the exploitation of hanging pieces. The more enemy pieces that are unprotected, the greater the chances that you can calculate something favorable.

Even in the early stages of a game, when few pieces venture beyond the fourth rank, those that do run a risk.

PORTISCH – KARPOV
Moscow 1977

1.♘f3 ♘f6 2.g3 b6 3.♗g2 ♗b7 4.0-0 e6 5.d3 d5 6.♘bd2 ♘bd7 7.♖e1 ♗c5 8.c4 0-0 9.cxd5 exd5 10.♘b3 ♗b4 11.♗d2 a5 12.♘bd4 ♖e8 13.♖c1 c5 14.♘f5 ♘f8 15.d4 ♘e4

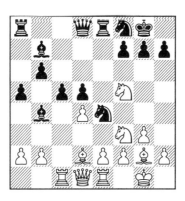

16.dxc5?

White assumes Black will now recapture on c5 to maintain material equality. He also assumes Black will not exchange off his well-placed knight on e4.

We'll explore the role of faulty assumption in Chapter 7. Here the main reason Black forces a win is that White has one piece hanging at f5 and another that will soon be unprotected.

| 16... | ♘xd2! |
| 17.♘xd2 | ♕g5! |

Even if White could safely retreat his knight to e3 he would stand poorly from a positional point of view. But it's worse for him from a tactical viewpoint since 18.♘e3 allows 18...♖xe3! 19.fxe3 ♕xe3+ and 20...♗xd2 with a substantial material edge.

The game actually continued **18.♘d6 ♗xd2 19.♘xb7 ♗xc1** and White soon resigned.

Pieces need not be entirely unprotected to be exploitable – just vulnerable, perhaps simply placed on high-risk squares.

KORCHNOI – BALASHOV
Moscow 1971

1.d4 ♘f6 2.c4 g6 3.♘c3 ♗g7 4.e4 d6 5.f3 e5 6.♘ge2 c6 7.♗g5 ♕a5 8.♕d2 ♘bd7 9.d5 cxd5 10.cxd5 h6 11.♗e3 a6 12.♘g3 h5 13.♗d3 ♘h7 14.0-0 0-0 15.a4 ♘c5?

The first thing White notices after Black's last move may depend on how optimistic or aggressive he is. A cautious player will see the knight threatening 16...♘b3, forking major pieces. He'll then notice that if he safeguards b3 with 16.♗c2 or 16.♖a3, Black can take greater control of queenside squares with 16...♕b4.

But after he examines those positions for a bit, an idea occurs to him: The black queen could get itself trapped after, say, 16.♗c2 ♕b4 and now 17.a5. And once he gets that idea he tries to find something more forceful than 16.♗c2.

On the other hand, a more aggressive player will immediately focus not on the ...♘b3 knight fork, but on the other fork in the position, 16.b4. That gives him the idea, and all he has to work out is a way of handling 16...♕xb4.

Both players may find the winning sequences but they'll come about it in a different way. "Mr. Cautious" works on protecting against and then exploiting the queen. "Mr. Aggressive" focuses first on the b4-fork.

| **16.b4!** | **♕xb4** |
| **17.a5!** | |

Now 18.♖fb1, trapping the queen, is threatened. Black can interpolate 17...♘xd3, but after 18.♕xd3 the black queen still has no escape route. And the fork 17...♘b3 no longer works because of 18.♕b2, followed by winning the pinned knight (19.♖a4).

In the game, Black actually tried **17...♗h6?!** but resigned soon after **18.♗xh6** because of **18...♕d4+ 19.♔h1 ♕xd3 20.♕xd3** and **21.♗xf8.**

Often a strong player will walk straight into his opponent's crushing combination. "Didn't you see that coming?" he'll be asked afterwards. And he'll reply, "No, I saw his other threat but not the one he played."

This is what happens when we confuse variations with ideas. We see how an opponent can exploit a particular feature of the position, a pin or a double attack. But instead of countering the idea by getting out of the pin or protecting a potentially attacked piece, we convince ourselves that all we have to do is deal with one specific *variation.*

Sometimes that is sufficient. Other times it's not:

LJUBOJEVIĆ – STEIN
Las Palmas 1973

1.b3 e5 2.♗b2 d6 3.e3 ♘f6 4.c4 g6 5.d4 ♗g7 6.♘f3 exd4 7.♕xd4 0-0 8.♘c3 ♘bd7 9.♗e2 ♘c5

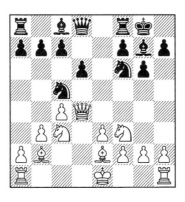

The idea Black is trying to work with is the vulnerability of the white queen and, behind it, the c3-knight. The queen stands on a square that can be threatened by the fianchettoed bishop after any move of Black's f6-knight. After his last move, Black has the specific threat of 10...♘fe4, and after the queen escapes to d1 or d5, White loses the knight.

10.♖d1?

White, an excellent calculator, disdained the precautionary 10.♕d2 in favor of the text, which allows him to meet the most dangerous-looking reply with a fine queen sacrifice (10...♘fe4 11.♕xg7+! ♔xg7 12.♘xe4+ f6 13.♘xc5, and if 13...dxc5?, then 14.♖xd8).

10... ♘g4!

This wins because the queen has no safe square. After 11.♕f4 or 11.♕d5, it is too far away from the knight (11.♕f4 f5! and 12...♘e4!, or 11.♕d5 c6 12.♕xd6 ♕xd6 13.♖xd6 ♗xc3+ 14.♗xc3 ♘e4).

11.♕d2 ♘xf2!

And White is lost. The exploitation of the c3-knight is realized in the key variation 12.♔xf2 ♗xc3! and 13...♘e4+. The game actually continued **12.0-0(!) ♘xd1** and White found a convenient spot in the middlegame to resign.

2) "Stretched" Pieces

Related to unprotected pieces are ones we can call "stretched." These are pieces that are being overused – they are performing more functions than they are capable of. Knowing how to recognize such pieces sometimes requires a fine tactical nose.

SPEELMAN – PLASKETT
London 1986

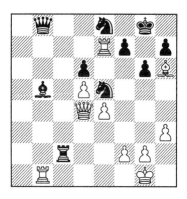

White to move

Black has two pieces for a rook and pawn and seems to be doing OK. The first tactical element you might notice here is the pin along the b-file, but there doesn't seem to be a way to exploit it. The second thing you'll probably see is that there's only one unprotected black piece. Can you exploit that situation? (Yes, with 1.♕a4.)

But there's something more subtle going on here. Black's pieces seem to be mutually protected but they are actually overworked. And with that in mind you can find the strongest continuation:

1.♖xb5!	**♕xb5**
2.♕b6!	**1-0**

The queen cannot both protect itself and prevent 3.♖xe8#. Its abilities were simply stretched too far.

Even when enemy pieces give the appearance of close coordination, they are often held together by light tethers:

TARJAN – BYRNE
U.S. Championship 1981

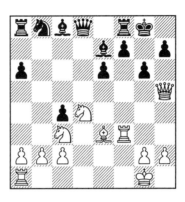

White to move

Black has just defended against the possibility of ♖h3 by attacking the queen (...g7-g6!). After 1.♕h6 e5, Black beats back the attack.

But with the centralizing 1.♕e5!, preparing ♗h6 and in some cases ♕e4, White maintains his initiative. He preferred:

1.♖g3?

This natural move has the drawbacks of (a) lacking force and (b) denying White the ♖h3 resource because the rook is needed on g3 to pin the g-pawn. This last role of the rook also reveals how fragile White's attacking force is.

1...   ♗d6

Now 2.♖g4 allows a strong 2...e5.

2.♖g5   ♗f4!

Devastating. White can't take (3.♗xf4 ♕xd4+ and 4...♕xf4), so he has to beat a hasty and expensive retreat. He got nothing for his lost rook after **3.♕f3 ♗xg5 4.♗xg5 ♕xd4+ 5.♔h1 ♖a7.**

A more elaborate example of stretched pieces:

PORTISCH – GHEORGHIU
Siegen 1970

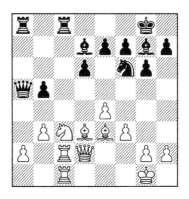

White to move

White has exchanged pawns on b5 and is looking at the one obvious target in the position, the enemy b-pawn. At first it appears more than adequately defended. In fact, all of Black's pieces protect one another.

But White notices how fragile that protection is:

1.♘xb5!   ♖xc2

On 1...♕xd2 Black trades off a defender of b5, allowing White to keep his extra pawn with 2.♗xd2. And 1...♗xb5 2.♕xa5! costs Black a rook.

2.♖xc2   ♗xb5

Now it appears that Black's pieces will be stretched to the limit by 3.♕xa5 ♖xa5 4.♗d2, e.g. 4...♗xd3 5.♗c8+ and 6.♗xa5. However,

Black improves his chances in this line with 4...♖xa2! 5.♖xa2 ♗xd3, with some compensation for the exchange.

3.♖c8+!

This breaks the connection of the stretched pieces. On 3...♗f8 there follows 4.♖xa8 ♕xd2 (or 4...♕xa8 5.♗xb5 with an extra pawn and those great queenside passed pawns) 5.♗xd2 ♗xd3 6.♗h6 ♘d7, and Black is so tied up that 7.a4! followed by the advance of the a- and b-pawns will win.

3...   ♖xc8

Black recognizes that on 3...♗e8 4.♕xa5 ♖xa5 5.a4!, the immediate threat of 6.♗b6 trapping the rook, as well as the long-term threat to promote a queenside pawn, will win.

4.♕xa5   ♗xd3
5.b4

And even though Black does not stand badly from a material point of view, he has poor chances because his pieces lack coordination. He lost after **5...♘d7 6.b5 d5 7.b6 d4 8.b7 ♖b8 9.♗f4 e5 10.♕c7.**

3) Invasion Squares
Often an unoccupied square is more important than any square with a piece on it. Noticing such a vulnerable point is the hard part.

RHODES – FORMANEK
Whitby 1969

1.c4 e5 2.♘c3 d6 3.g3 ♗e7 4.♗g2 ♘c6 5.e3 f5 6.♘ge2 ♘f6 7.0-0 0-0 8.d3 ♕e8 9.♖b1 g5 10.f4 gxf4 11.gxf4 ♔h8 12.♔h1 ♖g8 13.♘d5 ♕g6 14.♖g1?

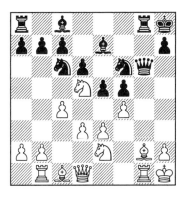

Black's major pieces are massed against g2, and White felt compelled to defend with ♔h1 and ♖g1. But this creates a new danger because of a square that has become newly vulnerable and very harmful to White: f2.

14...	♘g4!
15.♕e1	

White must stop the smothered mate ...♘f2. Black now sees that another idea in the position, 15...♘xh2 16.♔xh2 ♕h5+, is not convincing after 17.♗h3. So he returns to the ...♘f2 idea. Is there some way, he wonders, of drawing the queen away from the defense of f2?

15...	♗h4!!
16.♘g3	

The brilliant point of Black's last move is 16.♕xh4 ♕h5! and then either 17.♕xh5 or 17.♕e1 allows immediate mate (on f2 or h2). And the apparent protection of both squares by 17.♕g3 allows 17...♕xh2+! 18.♕xh2 ♘f2#.

16...	♘xh2!
0-1	

The position is quite hopeless after 17...♗xg3 and a check on the h-file.

A more difficult case of the vulnerable square is the following. Black appears to be on the offensive – and also the defensive – on the king's wing.

MORTENSEN – KARLSSON
Esbjerg 1988

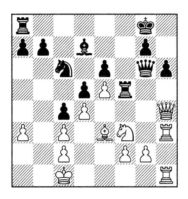

Black to move

Black would like to snap off the g-pawn, but 1...♕xg2?? 2.♖g3 costs him the queen. Moreover, he has to do something about White's threat of 2.♖g3 ♕-moves 3.♕xh6.

But there is another way of looking at the position, and that is in terms of White's weaknesses. Where, Black asks, is White vulnerable? The g2-square is protected tactically, and he would have to overcome major transportation problems to get his pieces to a3. But there is one square that is not immediately attacked yet can be threatened by three different pieces very quickly. Take another look at the diagram and see if you can guess which one.

Time's up. The answer is revealed by Black's crushing sequence:

1...   ♖xf3!!

This does two things. It eliminates the only piece that can come to the aid of the target square – c2 – and it opens the queen's diagonal leading

to it. Regardless of how White captures on f3, Black follows with 2...
♘b4! 3.axb4 ♗a4 and wins (4.♔d1 ♕xc2+ 5.♔e1 ♕d1#; or 4.♔b2
♕xc2+ 5.♔a1 ♗b3 and 6...♕a2#).

Ideas, as we've seen, are the building blocks of calculation. You simply can't start to analyze variations without them. In the pages that follow we move on from the inspirational side of calculation to the mechanical.

(Solutions: Fischer–Ciocâltea: Black's queen has no moves and can be trapped by 15.♗g5! hxg5 16.hxg5. Kaiszauri–Sznapik: 1.♘g6+! and 2.♕xh7+! followed by 3.♖h3+.)

Chapter 3

TREES
AND HOW TO BUILD THEM

"Often at the chessboard we fail through simple ignorance rather than a lack of ideas, and on the verge of executing a magnificent combination we sit perplexed, at a loss how to realize it. Inexperience makes the most fertile imagination powerless."

–Eugene Znosko-Borowsky

Once you've identified the primary ideas in a position, your task is to work out the details of exploitation. Ultimately, these details will result in a calculated sequence, a series of moves that lead to a position about which you can form a judgment.

This is as true for a 10-move combination that results in mate as it is for two-move sequences of semi-forcing moves that just slightly improve your position. You are working with ideas in both.

Even many beginners will be able to spot the idea in the following...

White to move

...and also the two-move combination that takes advantage of it: **1.♖e8+ ♖xe8 2.♖xe8#.** The back-rank mating scenario is one of the oldest and most primitive in chess, and also one of the most common.

But consider the following:

KR. GEORGIEV – GULKO
Saint John 1988

Black to move

Here again the idea is not greatly disguised: White's back rank is vulnerable. The immediate 1...♖d1+ works in one variation (2.♘xd1?? e1♕+) but not in another (2.♖xd1 exd1♕+ 3.♘xd1 ♕b1 4.♕d4).

So Black must work with the basic idea a bit.

1...	♛**c2!**
2.♛**b3**	

White's reply is forced since 2...♖d1+ was threatened, and eliminating the pregnant pawn with 2.♛xe2 costs him a knight. After 2.♛b3 Black can force the win of that knight anyway with 2...♛d2, preparing to promote the e-pawn. Then, following 3.♘xe2 ♛xe2 4.h3, he should eventually be able to make his slight material edge count.

But a bit of inspiration will reveal a better use of the idea, a little combination, no more than three moves long, that is as decisive and pretty as it is hard to see.

2...	♖**d1+!**
3.♖**xd1**	

Naturally not 3.♘xd1 e1♛#. But after 3...exd1♛+ 4.♘xd1, where is the mate?

3...	♛**xc3!!**
0-1	

The best White can do to meet the threats of 4...e1♛+ and of 4...♛xb3 followed by 5...exd1♛+ is the humble, and quite hopeless, 4.♛b1 exd1♛+ 5.♛xd1 ♛xb4.

Aron Nimzowitsch made a distinction in his classic text, *My System*, between two means of executing a middlegame or endgame plan. One he called the "evolutionary" – the slow buildup. The other he called the "revolutionary" – the explosive, tactical method.

This distinction applies as well to calculated sequences:

CAVELLOS – MOHRING
Tel Aviv 1964

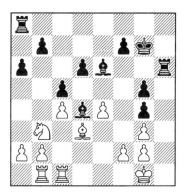

Black to move

Clearly, Black is on the attack and his primary route of invasion will be along the vulnerable h-file. The evolutionary means of exploiting this is 1...♖ah8, threatening mate in one.

That would force 2.♔f1, after which 2...♖h1+ 3.♔e2 ♖xc1 4.♘xc1 is the most natural sequence (not 4.♖xc1 ♗xb2), and Black is left with some means of improving his position but no obvious method of making major progress (4...b5 5.b3).

But before dropping the idea of h-file attack, Black should consider the revolutionary method. If he does he will find:

1...	♖h1+!
2.♔xh1	♗xf2

And White **resigned** in the face of 3...♖h8#. The point here is not to assume that there is one and only one application of an idea. There may be two, three, or several.

A Family of Ideas

When we speak of a tactical idea, we may mean one specific combinational idea (♕h8+/♘xf7+ in Alekhine–Euwe, Chapter 2) or a general concept (White's first rank in the Georgiev–Gulko example). It can also be a family of ideas bound together by the common use of certain pieces, such as Black's knights and queen in the following illustration.

ANDRUET – SPASSKY
Coblenz 1988

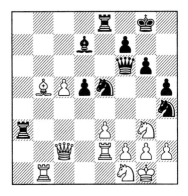

Black to move

Black's attention is directed to the kingside, where he has more space as well as four potential attacking pieces. The experienced player develops a sense of where the tactics apply; here a master will smell something happening on f3 or g2.

How does he get the black queen to one of those squares? He might examine 1...♘ef3+ (2.gxf3 ♕xf3 and 3...♕g2#) until he fails to find a follow-up to 2.♔h1!.

Then he may turn his attention to 1...♘xg2 (2.♔xg2 ♕f3+ and 3...♗h3). But he will probably reject that once he sees 2.♗xd7!.

The vulnerability of f3 is so sharply defined to the master's eye that he doesn't stop there. Boris Spassky didn't. He played:

1...   ♕**f3!!**
0-1

It's a forced mate: 2.gxf3 ♘exf3+ 3.♔h1 ♗h3 and 4...♗g2#. Though it may seem difficult, almost anyone who works hard enough with an idea can find moves like 1...♕f3.

As we've seen, there is often more than one idea at work in a position. Choosing between two or three ideas is taxing. But sometimes, as in the following example, you can use two ideas together.

JONES – DUEBALL
Nice 1974

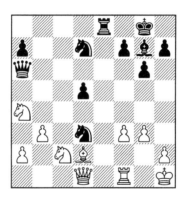

Black to move

Black sees that if the white rook weren't where it is, ...♘f2+ would fork king and queen. He also notices that if White's queen were not on the first rank, there would be a masked threat of ...♕xf1#.

Neither idea in itself is enough. But mixed together...

1...   ♖**e1!!**

This wins the queen because of 2.♖xe1 ♘f2+ (idea no. 1), while on 2.♗xe1 or 2.♘xe1 the reply 2...♘b2! threatens both ...♘xd1 and ...♕xf1 (idea no. 2).

Actually, it's quite a simple combination. But looking back at the diagram, it would seem that the one square White has sufficiently protected, the one he doesn't have to worry about is: e1!

BUKIĆ – ROMANISHIN
Moscow 1977

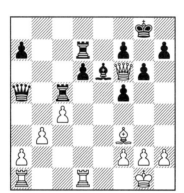

White to move

In this example, we have two more ideas melding. One is the pawn fork at b4. White can threaten it, say by way of 1.a3, but it is easily parried (1...♖c8; 1...♕d8; 1...♕c7).

The other idea is a back-rank mate. White begins to put one and one together and sees 1.b4 ♕xb4 2.♖ab1. But Black can then capture on c4 so that 3.♖b8+ allows 3...♖c8.

At this point White can do one of two things: He can either give up on trying to make 1.b4 work and turn his attention to other moves, or he can look for a forcing continuation.

1.b4!   ♕xb4
2.♖db1

2.♖ad1 also wins.

2..	**♕xc4**
3.♗e2!	**1-0**

White correctly kept looking and realized how stretched Black's pieces were after 2...♕xc4. Black must move his attacked queen after 3.♗e2 and must also avoid ♖b8+. There could have followed 3...♕c2 4.♗d3! ♕c3 (the only move) 5.♖b8+ ♖c8 6.♕xc3!.

Often, when we miscalculate we overlook a single idea. That idea, perhaps a key move, may recur in several different lines:

PSAKHIS – J. POLGÁR
Amsterdam 1989

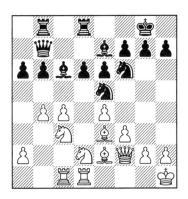

Black to move

After lengthy maneuvering, Black believes it is time for the liberating break in the center. What she overlooks is not apparent for four moves.

1...	**d5?**
2.cxd5	**exd5**
3.♗f4!	

This pins the knight and forces Black's reply. It won't be 3...♘fd7 because of 4.exd5 ♗xd5 5.♕g3!.

3...	**♗d6**
4.exd5	**♗xd5**

Black would have preferred 4...♘xd5 5.♘xd5 ♗xd5. But then comes 6.♘e4 ♗xe4 7.♖xd6!! – the idea she overlooked. Then Black loses a piece in all variations (7...♖xd6 8.♗xe5 ♖bd8 9.♗xd6 ♖xd6 10.fxe4).

5.♘de4!	**♗xe4**

And here the same idea works against Black: 5...♘xe4 6.fxe4 ♗xe4 7.♖xd6!!.

6.♖xd6!

And once more. Here at least Black could complicate matters with **6...♘d3!**, after which **7.♗xd3 ♗xd3 8.♖d1? ♖xd6 9.♗xd6 ♖d8 10.♖xd3 ♕c6** got a bit sticky (8.♕d4! would have won outright).

Candidate Moves

After you've had some experience calculating, or just playing chess, you develop a sense of what moves are likely to be best in a particular position. In one position you might recognize quickly that a single move absolutely looks correct, but in another there may be several "candidates." Each candidate move may involve its own tactical or strategic idea, or they may share a common idea.

The task of the calculator is to identify the candidates and determine which is best. Here is a position with considerable choice:

KHALIFMAN – P. NIKOLIĆ
Moscow 1990

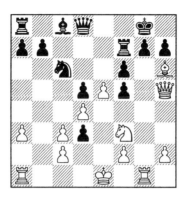

White to move

Black has just captured an enemy bishop (...cxd3). Because of the half-open g-file and the four white pieces attacking a king position defended by only a rook, White has reason to be optimistic. Some kind of tactical assault on g7 is likely to work, if not now (i.e., 1.♗xg7), then perhaps in a move or two. What are the candidate moves here?

First, there are the two most violent moves, 1.♗xg7 and 1.♕xf7+. Because they are the most forcing, they are probably the easiest to calculate.

Second, there is the attempt to create a new threat, 1.♘h4, which intends 2.♘xf5 and then a capture on g7.

Third, there are the moves that bring up reinforcements, i.e., 1.0-0-0 or 1.♔d2, followed by the entrance of the other rook.

Finally, there is the least forcing move, 1.cxd3.

That makes a total of six candidates, a large number. But we can whittle them down quickly: As a practical rule of thumb, we start with the most *forceful*. We can always play 1.cxd3 if we find that the other five are faulty. But if we discover that 1.♕xf7+ wins outright, there is no need to calculate the others.

Actually, White can eventually win with 1.♔d2!, or with 1.♗xg7 ♖xg7 2.♔d2 (followed by 3.♕h6, 3.exf6, or 3.♖xg7+).

After some thought, White settled on **1.♔d2** and won quickly: **1... ♗e6 2.♗xg7 ♖xg7 3.♖xg7+ ♔xg7 4.♖g1+ 1-0** (4...♔h8 5.♘h4 and 6.♘g6+; or 4...♔f8 5.♕xh7 ♔e8 6.♖g7).

Being able to recognize candidate moves is an essential, timesaving skill. The principal difference between human players and many computers is that those machines cannot identify candidate moves and as a result cannot budget their time. They might consider all 35 legal moves in a position rather than the only two that make sense. Humans can budget their time, if they develop good instincts and intuition. These are qualities that may seem innate but can be trained.

Some young players consider too many moves in a position, and others not enough. Alexander Kotov, a Soviet-era player who taught a generation how to calculate, recalled how he tried to improve when he was a young master. Kotov discovered that he wasn't examining enough candidates, looking at only one or two "natural" moves when there were three or four.

Kotov provided unintended documentation of this in a series of lectures on the theme "How to Become a Grandmaster" (later issued as the book *Think Like a Grandmaster).* Kotov's very first example was:

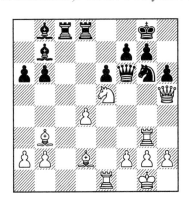

White to move

According to Kotov, in this amateur game White decided he should sacrifice and began to consider three candidate moves: 1.♗xh6, 1.♘xg6, and 1.♘g4 (intending 2.♘xh6+). But his "faulty unsystematic thinking" undid him, Kotov said, because he considered 1.♘xg6, then gave up after a few moves of analysis and turned to 1.♗xh6, which he also gave up on. Then he analyzed 1.♘g4, found problems with it, and went back to 1.♗xh6 and 1.♘xg6 again.

In the end, White, thoroughly confused, ended up playing something completely different (1.♗c3?), which got him quickly crushed (1... ♘f4!).

It's a nice, instructive story, but there's a question that goes unanswered: Why, if White was looking to sac a piece, didn't he consider one of the most natural moves in the position?

After 1.♘xf7, it's easy to see that if the knight is taken, 2.♗xe6 wins. So the real calculation involves 1...♗xg3 and then 2.hxg3 or 2.♘xh6+ ♔f8 (not 2...gxh6 3.♗xe6+ ♔f8 4.♗xh6+) 3.hxg3. This appears to be at least as promising as the line endorsed by Kotov (1.♘g4 ♕h4 2.♘xh6+ ♔f8 3.♕xh4; however, 1.♘g4 ♕xd4! is unclear).

And why didn't Kotov mention it at all? Probably because candidate moves are a lot more personal than anyone likes to admit – and Kotov may have missed 1.♘xf7 himself. What Magnus Carlsen considers "natural" may be something that would never occur to Viswanathan Anand or Gata Kamsky. But for each of the remaining diagrams in this book you should try to pick out the move that seems most natural to you and then find at least one other candidate.

When we calculate the ramifications of a particular move we'd like to play, we look for our opponent's candidate moves. This is another form of defensive calculation.

BISGUIER – FUDERER
Göteborg 1955

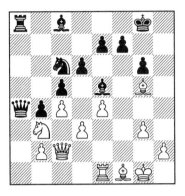

White to move

White understands that 1...♘d4!, winning a piece, is threatened. He has passive defenses such as 1.♔g2 or 1.♖e2. But he also notices that 1.♖a1 wins material. Should he pass, or grab?

White chose:

1.♖a1??

He mistakenly stopped looking for Black's candidate moves after calculating 1...♕xa1? (2.♘xa1 ♖xa1 3.♔g2).

1...   ♕xb3!
0-1

This, too, surrenders the queen, but what a difference: 2.♕xb3 ♖xa1 with two devastating threats (3...♗h3 and 4...♖xf1#; and 3...♘d4, trapping the queen).

In more difficult positions, you may be required to find enemy candidates several moves into the future. Kotov himself cited the following example in a magazine article.

EINGORN – MALANIUK
Baku 1979

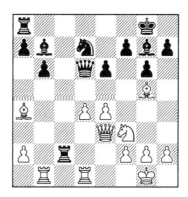

Black to move

Can Black's attacked rook take on a2? Black decided it can because he had calculated **1...♖xa2 2.e5** as the most dangerous candidate move that White has in reply (2...♕c7 3.♖dc1 and the queen has no good retreat). But he saw that **2...♕d5 3.♗b3 ♕a5! 4.♗xa2 ♕xa2** gives Black excellent compensation for the exchange and pawn.

Yet, as Kotov pointed out, Black failed to look for candidate moves throughout the sequence. At the fourth move White need not take the rook. "If [Black] had added one candidate move, 4.d5!, he would have understood without difficulty that his position immediately becomes hopeless."

In fact, White did play **4.d5!** – the second most forceful move in the position and one Black should not have missed. Black resigned not long after **4...♗xd5 5.♗xd5 exd5 6.e6!** and then 6...♘f6 7.exf7+ ♔xf7 8.♖bc1 and 9.♖c7+.

In Chapter 6 we'll explore the matter of choosing between equally appealing candidates. But, before you can make an educated choice, you have to know that there is a choice.

SPEELMAN – LEVITT
London 1992

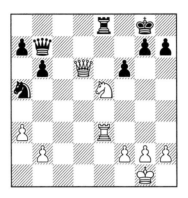

White to move

In this example, White instinctively looks for a way to meet Black's last move (...f7-f6) with a knight move. It doesn't take long for most players examining this position to see 1.♘d7, based on the idea that 2.♖xe8+ is threatened and that 1...♖xe3?? allows mate on f8.

But before he examines that move further, it should occur to White that there's another candidate with the same idea:

1.♘g6!

Once he understands that a choice is available, White can weigh the two and see that 1.♘d7 ♛c8! is not clear but that 1.♘g6 ♛a8 2.♖xe8+ ♛xe8 3.♛d5+! ♛f7 4.♛d8+ is. In fact, there is a second successful defense to 1.♘d7 that fails against 1.♘g6, and that is 1...♔f7 (which loses in the variation 1.♘g6 ♔f7 2.♘h8+! ♖xh8 3.♛e6+ and mates).

In the game White correctly chose 1.♘g6 and the game ended with **1...♖a8 2.♘e7+ ♔h8 3.♛e6!** and **1-0** in view of 4.♘g6+ hxg6 5.♖h3# (or 4.♛g8+! ♖xg8 5.♘g6+, etc.).

It's tempting to consider all the forcing moves in a position as candidates. But we should remember that less forceful moves may have other benefits that mandate their consideration.

In the following position, there's obviously only one really forcing move, 1.exf6:

KENGIS – ANASTASIAN
Frunze 1989

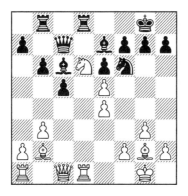

White to move

But he should also consider alternatives, such as 1.♕f4.

In the game, White rejected 1.exf6 ♗xd6 and then 2.♖xd6 ♕xd6 3.e5 because of 3...♕d2! 4.♗xc6 ♕xc1+ 5.♖xc1 ♖d2 6.♖b1 b5. He eventually chose 1.♕f4! since Black's knight cannot move (2.♕xf7+) and therefore White will be able to play 2.exf6 with almost a free move thrown in.

The game went **1.♕f4! ♗f8 2.exf6 ♗xd6 3.♖xd6 ♕xd6 4.e5 ♕d2 5.♗xc6,** and White won (5...♕xb2 6.♕g5).

The result of this identification and evaluation of candidate moves is that construct we call the Tree of Analysis.

The Tree of Analysis

So far we've talked a lot about calculating a sequence without considering its "shape." A calculated sequence resembles a tree; branches represent the sub-variations, and the trunk represents the sequence's main line. Trees come in various shapes and sizes – some tall and thin, some short and fat, and some very difficult ones that are tall and fat.

The simplest trees to calculate are, not surprisingly, the short, thin ones:

KRASENKOW – SVESHNIKOV
Moscow 1992

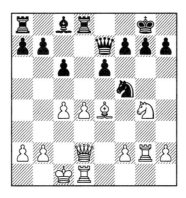

White to move

Here White began a winning combination with **1.♗xf5!.** Black, with no forcing alternatives, naturally responded 1...exf5. After **2.♘h6+** he had a choice of two king moves, but in either case White replies 3.♖xg7!. Again, Black's hand is relatively forced since 2...♔f8 3.♖xg7! ♕f6 4.♖xf7+ loses the queen and 3...♗e6 4.♖g8 is mate. Therefore he played **2...♔h8 3.♖xg7! ♔xg7 4.♖g1+ ♔h8,** and after **5.♕e2!** he resigned (5...♕xe2 6.♘xf7#; 5...♗e6 6.♘xf7+ and 7.♕e5+).

The resulting tree looks something like this:

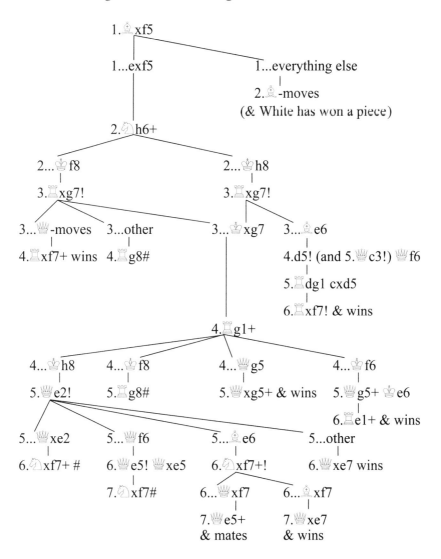

The branches look more impressive in size than they really are. Note how normally each variation branches off into two or more sub-variations. But at one point, Black's third move, two sub-variations merge to form the main line, 3...♔xg7.

Now let's recall Bent Larsen's rook sacrifice from the last chapter.

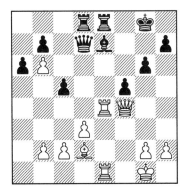

Here we get quite a different tree. Though there are a lot of branches at the top, all but one end after a few moves because of simple refutations by White. That leaves one long main line:

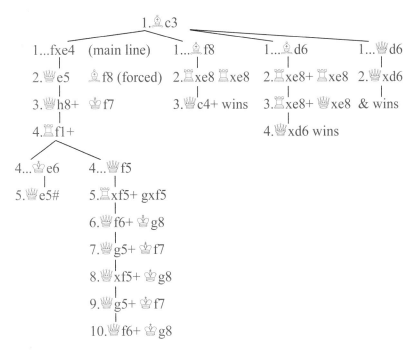

And so on until 15.♕xb7.

What aids our analysis of such long variations is the certainty of our conclusions. We don't have to calculate much into the side variations (1...♗f8; 1...♗d6, and 1...♛d6) because we find a forced win of decisive material after three or four moves.

The end positions, as we'll call them, of those lines are clear. Similarly, the 4...♔e6 branch leads immediately to mate. No doubt about evaluating that end position.

As mentioned earlier, the length of a calculation tree is not as significant as the breadth of the variations. But there is another factor: The hardest move to find in the last example was at the very top of the tree. No difficult moves are required of White past the second move.

Trees have, in fact, three dimensions. We have considered length and breadth. But there is a third one that is not easily represented visually: difficulty.

Sometimes the hardest moves to find appear on the shortest branches.

H. ÓLAFSSON – LEVITT
Reykjavík 1990

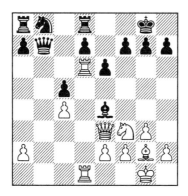

White to move

85

The ideas to work with here include: (a) Black's unprotected rook, (b) Black's potentially vulnerable first rank, and (c) the lincup of pieces on the g2-a8 diagonal.

White came up with this way of using the various elements: **1.♖xe6!** and then **1...fxe6 2.♘g5!.** In this tree, the longest branches consist of 2...♘c6 3.♕xe4 g6 4.♕h4 h5 5.♘e4 "with a strong attack," or 2...h6! 3.♘xe4 ♘c6 4.♘xc5 ♕c7 5.♘xd7! ♖ac8! 6.♕xe6+ ♔h8 7.♗e4, etc.

But White need not calculate that far, and in fact can stop examining these trees after the third move. The hardest aspect of this calculation, in fact, is finding the answer to 2...♗xg2. It is the spectacular 3.♕xe6+!, which leads to mate in all lines (3...dxe6 4.♖xd8#; 3...♔h8 4.♘f7+).

(Incidentally, you should be able to figure out what is wrong with the similar move order 1.♘g5 and then 1...♗xg2 2.♖xe6. This transposes into the above example after 2...fxe6. So why didn't White play it? The answer is at the end of this chapter.)

A similar example from one of Bobby Fischer's earliest successes:

FISCHER – SHERWIN
U.S. Championship 1957-58

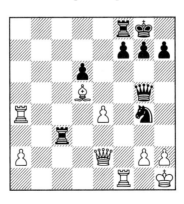

White to move

This tree is fairly short, only three moves long. But there are more branches and, perhaps most significantly, the most difficult move to see comes at the second level.

The first idea that probably occurred to White in the diagram was 1.♗xf7+ and if 1...♖xf7? then 2.♖a8+ and mates. But after 1...♔h8 White faces a number of pins and other tactical problems.

1.♖xf7!

Now there are three branches. The simplest and shortest runs 1...♖xf7 2.♖a8+ and mates. The longest and most complex begins with 1...h5! and runs into a variety of sub-branches after 2.♖xf8+ ♔xf8 3.♕f1+. But 2.♖c4 ♖xc4 3.♖xf8+ ♔xf8 4.♗xc4 keeps a small edge

But clearly 1...h5, while it may be the best move, is not the most dangerous. The key variation begins with:

1...   ♖c1+

What won this game for White was his realization that there were two branches here: the obvious 2.♖f1+, which gets White into severe difficulties after 2...♔h8, and...

2.♕f1!!

A difficult move to find even though 2...♖xf1+ 3.♖xf1+ results in a fairly short tree. There would be a branch for 3...♔h8 4.♖xf8#; another for 3...♖f7 4.♖a8+ ♕d8 5.♖xd8#; and a third that begins with 3...♕xd5!? and offers two sub-branches: 4.exd5?? ♖xf1#, which wins for Black; and 4.♖xf8+! ♔xf8 5.exd5, which wins for White.

In the actual game, Black played the desperate **2...h5** and saw that, after 3.♕xc1! ♕xc1+ 4.♖f1+ and 5.♖xc1, he would be lost. So he went off onto another limb with (2...h5) **3.♕xc1 ♕h4** and resigned soon after **4.♖xf8+.**

Chapter 3

How Chessplayers Really Think

"When all hopeful attempts at solving the problem by traditional methods have been exhausted, thought runs around in circles... like rats in a cage."

–Arthur Koestler

Kotov, in *Think Like a Grandmaster,* argued that a player must approach the tree carefully. He must examine each branch once and only once. To jump from one to another is "an unforgivable waste of time," something that no grandmaster would countenance, he claimed.

In reality, grandmasters think no more systematically than amateurs. They sometimes jump from branch to branch and back again. Or they calculate only a few moves deep into what should be a very large tree. As Mikhail Tal once put it, "To calculate sometimes all of the so-called 'tree of variations' is not simply difficult but impossible."

Tal spoke instead of a "zone of certainty" that allows a trained calculator to stop his calculation after a relatively brief testing of the various branches. There are many masters who follow Tal's example, calculating what end positions they can see and then evaluating other branches on instinct.

In the late 1970s, the English master Simon Webb conducted a series of experiments, the results of which appeared in the magazine *Chess.* Webb gave players of different playing strengths a position to look at and had them describe how they'd go about choosing a move. None of the positions were forced wins.

His results were surprising for followers of Kotov. For example, the grandmaster in the test group jumped around from one idea to another and then back again. In another case, the two strongest players tested spent 10 minutes failing even to consider what was clearly the best candidate, and then selected moves they had considered for less than a minute.

What really distinguished the better players, Webb found, was that they could come to accurate conclusions faster, thought in terms of concrete variations, and were therefore more efficient calculators.

There is no perfect calculating method for all players, Kotov notwithstanding. We all think differently. In reality there is a strong element of serendipity in chess. When we look at one idea, we sometimes come up with another.

A. RODRÍGUEZ – MILES
Palma de Mallorca 1989

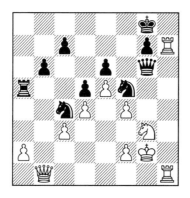

Black to move

Black studied the position in some detail, working down a tree that began with 1...♘ce3+ 2.♔g1 (not 2.fxe3 ♕xg3+). He looked at one branch that had 2...♕g4 as its key but gave up after he found that 3.♖h8+ ♔f7 4.♖c8! sets up a strong checking threat (although Black can hold the balance with 4...♕f3!? 5.♖xc7+ ♔g8 6.♖c8+ ♔f7 7.♖h2 ♖xa2). He turned to another branch that began 2...♘h4 with the idea of 3.♕xg6 ♘f3#. But he had to give up on it after he saw 3.♖h8+! and then 3...♔f7 4.♕xg6+ or 3...♔xh8 4.♖xh4+.

He examined other lines as well, and the main benefit of all this analysis was to tell him that Black's main problem was his king position. "If only it were somewhere safer," he thought. Therefore:

1... ♙f7!!

This idea would not have occurred to Black if he hadn't worked on a different tree. Now, for example, 2.♜h8 ♔e7! 3.♜c8 allows one of the clever ideas of the first tree: 3...♘ce3+ 4.♔g1 ♘h4! 5.♛xg6 ♘f3#. What neither player saw was that the unlikely 3.♔h2! is strong. Instead, White played:

2.♜7h5??	♘ce3+
3.♔g1	♛g4!
4.♜1h2?!	♘xg3
5.fxg3	♛xg3+

And White resigned after several more moves.

In the real world, players get ideas from one branch that they suddenly realize belong in another.

W. WATSON – GUTMAN
Brussels 1986

1.♘c3 c5 2.e4 d6 3.f4 a6 4.♘f3 e6 5.d4 cxd4 6.♘xd4 ♘f6 7.♗e2 ♛c7 8.♗e3 b5 9.♗f3 ♗b7 10.e5 dxe5 11.♗xb7 ♛xb7 12.fxe5 ♘d7 13.0-0

At this point, while waiting for Black's reply, White analyzed 13...b4 and came up with the inspired attacking device 14.♛h5 g6 15.♛h3!, with the idea of meeting 15...bxc3 with 16.♜xf7!.

Black did not play 13...b4 but chose instead **13...♘xe5.** White's compensation for the pawn was not clear until he found **14.♛h5 ♘g6 15.♛h3!!.** He admitted afterward that it would have escaped him if he hadn't seen the queen maneuver to h3 in the previous variation. On h3 the queen supports sacrifices on e6 (e.g., 15...♘c6 16.♘xe6 fxe6 17.♛xe6+) and f7.

In fact, the game went **15...♗e7 16.♖xf7!** and White had a winning attack, because 16...♔xf7 17.♕xe6+ ♔e8 18.♘f5 ♕d7 19.♘xg7+ ♔d8 20.♖d1 wins.

Finally, a revealing look inside an elite player's mind was provided by the winner of the following in his annotations of a brilliant win.

NEZHMETDINOV – CHERNIKOV
Rostov-on-Don 1962

1.e4 c5 2.♘f3 ♘c6 3.d4 cxd4 4.♘xd4 g6 5.♘c3 ♗g7 6.♗e3 ♘f6 7.♗c4 0-0 8.♗b3 ♘g4 9.♕xg4 ♘xd4 10.0-0 ♕a5 11.♕h4 ♗f6

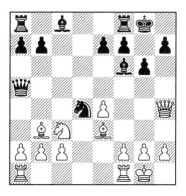

White noticed that his attacked queen can't go to g3 or f4 because then 12...♕xc3! and 13...♘e2+ regains the queen in a favorable ending. But there were three other candidate moves.

First he saw that 12.♕h6 allows Black to repeat moves with 12...♗g7 13.♕h4 ♗f6. He also saw that 12.♕g4 or 12.♕h3 allows 12...d5. He considered these lines before evaluating 12.♕g4 d5 13.♕d1! as slightly favorable to White.

Then he spotted the remarkable sacrifice 12.♕xf6!? exf6 13.♗xd4. Only two pieces for the queen – but they're terrific pieces after White gets to play ♘d5.

He wondered what would happen if Black inserts 12...♘xb3. He saw that 13.axb3! was playable – 13...♕xa1 14.♕xe7! and White has 15.♗h6 and 16.♘d5 coming up.

Then he found another way for Black to improve at move 12, with 12...♘e2+! 13.♘xe2 exf6, after which it will take White an extra tempo to bring the knight to d5.

So he went back to 12.♕g4 and kept coming to the conclusion that his chances were nice but "can you really win with it?" Finally, after a thorough review of 12.♕xf6 ♘e2+ 13.♘xe2 exf6 14.♘c3, he concluded that there was little Black could do to prevent him from continuing ♗d4, ♘d5, ♖ad1-d3-f3 with a winning position.

Finally, after much soul-searching and back-and-forth analysis he settled on the sacrifice and won a remarkably fine game: **12.♕xf6!! ♘e2+ 13.♘xe2 exf6 14.♘e3 ♖e8 15.♘d5 ♖e6 16.♗d4 ♔g7 17.♖ad1 d6 18.♖d3 ♗d7 19.♖f3 ♗b5 20.♗c3 ♕d8 21.♘xf6 ♗e2 22.♘xh7+! ♔g8 23.♖h3 ♖e5 24.f4 ♗xf1 25.♔xf1 ♖c8 26.♗d4! b5 27.♘g5 ♖c7 28.♗xf7+! ♖xf7 29.♖h8+!** and White won.

Moral: Find the method of calculating variations that you are most comfortable with.

(Answer to Ólafsson–Levitt: 1.♘g5 ♗xg2 2.♖xe6 allows Black to answer the threat of 3.♖e8+ with 2...♘a6 or 2...♘c6. White should play the more forceful idea, ♘g5, after the less forceful ♖xe6 – as we'll see in the next chapter.)

Chapter 4

FORCE

"Force and fraud are in war the two cardinal virtues."

—*Thomas Hobbes*

If ideas provide the spark for a calculated sequence, forcing moves are the fuel that keeps it running. Moves that capture enemy pieces, check the king or, to a lesser degree, threaten such captures and checks, provide the dynamic element to a sequence.

GRÓSZPÉTER – RADULOV
Biel 1989

1.d4 d6 2.e4 ♘f6 3.♘c3 c6 4.♘f3 ♕a5 5.e5 ♘e4 6.exd6 ♘xc3 7.bxc3 exd6 8.♗d3 ♗e7 9.0-0 0-0 10.♖e1 ♗e6 11.♖b1 b6 12.c4 ♕h5 13.d5! cxd5 14.cxd5 ♕xd5 15.♖b5 ♕b7 16.♘g5 ♗xg5 17.♖xg5 ♘c6

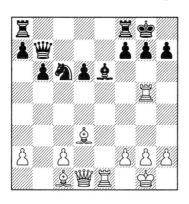

Here White begins a combination that lasts eight moves in its longest tree limb. Not only is it lengthy but it requires definite risks, the sacrifices of a rook and a bishop. A mistake in calculation would be irreparable.

But don't let this scare you. It is actually a fairly routine combination and one that, with training, you should be able to visualize accurately to its end. Let's go one step at a time:

18.♗xh7+!　♔xh7

Black has no real choice. On 18...♔h8 19.♕h5, a discovered check by the bishop next move must lead to mate.

19.♕h5+　♔g8

The only legal move.

20.♖xg7+!　♔xg7

Again, obviously forced.

21.♗h6+　♔h7

Black finally has a choice, albeit a slim one: On 21...♔g8, White mates in two with 22.♕g5+ and 23.♕g7#.

22.♗g5+　1-0

If he had continued, Black would have had a choice between 22...♔g8, which allows 23.♗f6 and 24.♕h8#, or 22...♔g7, which lengthens the game by one move because of 23.♕h6+! ♔g8 24.♗f6 and mate on h8 next move.

That's eight moves in all. But consider what a straight and narrow course the analysis took. At only three points did Black have any choice of replies. And none of those side variations extended more than two moves. This is a tree of analysis with a long stem but very few branches, and they are quite short.

Such trees are not found in remote forests. Garry Kasparov cited one in the notes to his game with Tigran Petrosian at Moscow 1982. The future world champion pointed out a better move for himself at one point, which in one key line called for a temporary queen-and-rook sacrifice. In another, a rook sacrifice was needed. And its main line demanded the offer of two pawns.

That last, main variation was *17 moves long.* But Kasparov went on to tell the reader that he shouldn't be surprised by that length. The forcing nature of the moves, almost all of them captures, checks, or mate threats, made the variation easier to digest.

On the other hand, much of the thinking you do during a game will involve very short trees. You won't be able to calculate more than perhaps two or three moves into the future, because there are few forcing moves in the position. This kind of calculation – the non-combinative kind – places a greater emphasis on evaluation.

IVANCHUK – BAREEV
Linares 1993

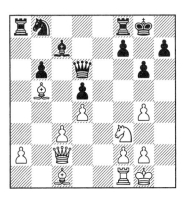

White to move

In this relatively quiet position, White saw nothing forcing and found instead a prophylactic, and very strong, move.

1.g3!

It is virtually impossible to calculate far in this position. But White was chiefly interested in the one line that could be examined in depth: He reasoned that if he held any advantage it lay in Black's inability to complete his development. After 1.g3, Black cannot bring his knight out to d7 because of 2.♗f4, after which the sacrificial 2...♕f6 3.♗xd7 ♗xf4 4.gxf4 ♕xf4 5.♘e5 is unsound.

That was all White really needed to see. Black has various other moves after 1.g3, but none that trouble the position. After 1...♘c6, for example, White continues to improve his position, such as with 2.♔g2 and 3.♖h1. He correctly saw that taking away Black's only good developing plan would leave White with a clear edge.

1...	**♖a7**
2.♖e1	**♘d7?**

After this mistake the game was virtually decided.

3.g5!	**♖d8**
4.a4	**♘b8**

Or 4...♘f8 5.♕b3 and White brings the bishop decisively to f4 or a3.

5.♘h2!

And the knight went to f6 with crushing effect: **5...♕f8 6.♘g4 ♗d6 7.♔g2 ♔h8 8.♖h1 ♕g7 9.♘f6 h5 10.♕d1!,** and the threat of ♖xh5+ led Black to resign.

To give a more elementary example, suppose you begin a game with 1.d4 and your opponent answers 1...d5. One idea may occur to you: Black has weakened his defense of c7 because a white bishop on f4 or g3 cannot be blocked by ...d7-d6.

Therefore, you might be inspired to develop this idea by way of ♗f4 and ♘c3-b5. But can you seriously calculate anything concrete after just 1.d4 d5 2.♘c3, with the idea of 3.♗f4 and 4.♘b5?

No, you are at least three moves away from threatening to capture on c7. We can say the position is just not forcing enough to generate specific calculated lines. All we can do is visualize a general course of events, say 2...♘f6 3.♗f4 c6 4.e3, and evaluate this as best you can, either as equal or slightly better for White.

Players must be able to perform both kinds of calculation, the concrete forceful kind and the generalized kind. And in fact they often perform both during the course of a game. But the element of force must remain close to your attention because the consequences of missing a forceful move of your own or a forceful reply by the opponent are so severe.

Let the Force...

The difference between forcing and non-forcing moves has been illustrated by some remarkable examples of grandmaster play:

HÜBNER – PETROSIAN
Biel 1976

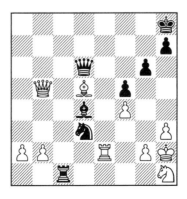

White to move

The winner of this game would almost certainly advance to the world championship elimination matches, and the loser would not. White had five minutes left to play four moves and reach the time control. He also had two healthy extra pawns. But more important, he had a mating attack.

White's search for candidate moves is relatively easy since he has only a few forcing moves (the two checks at e8 and the semi-forcing capture on d3). It is not particularly difficult to see that 1.♕e8+! is the best of the group. In fact, the only difficult task in selecting that move is to realize that after 1...♔g7 2.♖e7+ ♔h6 White can play 3.♕f8+ because the rook on e7 shields f8 from the black queen. After 3.♕f8+ ♔h5 4.♖xh7 it is mate.

Aside from the minor visualization problem concerning f8, this is the kind of combination most amateurs can find. Black's only alternative moves are 1...♕f8?? (which allows mate in one) and 2...♕xe7, giving up his queen. In the diagram White has essentially a *forced mate in four.*

But White didn't find it. Reluctant to move his queen away from the defense of his bishop, and seeing the threat of 1...♗g1+ 2.♔g3 ♕xf4#, he played:

1.g3?

And a desperate Black responded:

1...   ♘xf4!

This renews the threat of 2...♗g1+, only now it would be both check and mate. And the removal of the f4-pawn means Black's king has a flight square at g5.

Having missed a win when a forcing one was available, White misses a second one with 2.gxf4! ♕xf4+ 3.♘g3. Worse, he plays forcing moves that lead to disaster:

$$2.\text{♕}e8+ \qquad \text{♔}g7$$
$$3.\text{♖}e7+??$$

3.gxf4! is still possible.

$$3... \qquad \text{♔}h6$$
$$4.\text{♘}f2$$

A feeble attempt, but White is now lost.

$$4... \qquad \text{♗}xf2$$
$$5.\text{♖}xh7+ \qquad \text{♔}g5!$$

White **resigned** and his opponent took his place in the candidates' matches.

The same principle of force applies to defensive calculation – that is, anticipating your opponent's tactics.

SHAMKOVICH – ESPIG
Dubna 1973

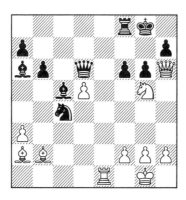

Black to move

White has just played 1.♘g5!. With mate looming on h7 and 1...fxg5 answerable by 2.♕g7#, Black appears to have nothing better than

1...♕d7. Then 2.♖e6! would be quite strong (2...fxg5? 3.♖xg6+ hxg6 4.♕xg6+ mates). But Black found a better try:

> **1...**   **♗xf2+!**
> **2.♔xf2??**

White is still winning after 2.♔h1! ♕d7 3.♖e6, the same winning plan mentioned above. The only significant difference is that here Black could complicate matters with 3...♗e3! (4.♖xe3 fxg5!), and White would have to come up with the stunning 4.h4! in order to score the point.

> **2...**   **fxg5+**

White simply overlooked that this piece could be captured with the most forceful of all moves, a check.

> **3.♔g1**   **♘xb2**

And having lost two of his attacking pieces almost instantly, White played **4.♕xg5** and **resigned** after **4...♘d3.**

During actual games, every time it's your turn to move begin your search for candidate moves by examining the most forceful moves available. And when considering any tree limb, make sure there are no enemy moves of any useful force in the end position. If there are, it ain't the end.

Force vs. Speed, Force vs. Force

As we've noted, people calculate differently from computers. One of the major differences is that humans tend to rely on the forcefulness of their moves, while machines concentrate on the fewest moves necessary to reach a conclusion.

In general, the most forceful line of play is usually the fastest way to reach a favorable conclusion. But not necessarily:

SVESHNIKOV – I. IVANOV
Minsk 1976

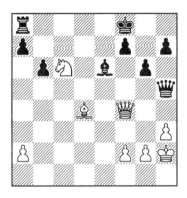

White to move

White found the most obvious idea in the position, the checks beginning with **1.♕d6+**. After he realized that **1...♔g8 2.♘e7+ ♔f8** sets up the opportunity for discovered checks and double checks, it wasn't hard to spot a second idea in the position, the smothered mate: **3.♘xg6+ ♔g8 4.♕f8+! ♖xf8 5.♘e7#.**

This is the easiest method for most humans to calculate *because it is the most forceful.* But if you give the diagram position to a competent chess computer, it will find 1.♕f6!, after which mate on g7, e7, or h8 can be delayed for only one move by a spite check. Thus, the "quiet" 1.♕f6 is two moves faster than the check on d6. Yet nine out of ten human players will tell you 1.♕d6+ is the easier to calculate.

On the other hand, there are bound to be times when long forcing variations are more difficult than simpler, short ones. Early in the twentieth century Emanuel Lasker pointed out this case:

LAWRENCE – FOX
Anglo-American Cable Match 1911

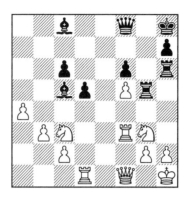

Black to move

Here Black began to examine the ideas ...♖xh2+ and ...♖xg3. After considerable thought he worked out a combination that began with the diversionary **1...♗a6** to draw the white queen away from the kingside. After **2.♕xa6 ♖xh2+! 3.♔xh2 ♕h6+,** Black continued with 23 consecutive checks, the final one delivering mate.

What amused Lasker was that even though the combination is sound (it won a gold medal), Black could have won much faster with the less forcing **1...♕d6!.** Then **2...♖xh2+ 3.♔xh2 ♖h5#** is the main threat and White has no adequate defense (e.g., **2.♖f4 ♗e3**).

Nevertheless, in the jungle of tournament tactics, it is often the forceful who survive. The failure to recognize the force of your own moves can be fatal. In a sense, it is suicidal.

MILEIKA – ROSENFELD

Tallinn 1966

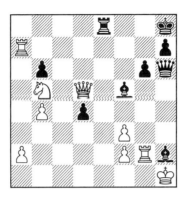

White to move

White appreciated the danger he was in. Black threatens a mate in two by way of 1...♖e1+ or via the discovered check 1...♗-somewhere. White would like to play his own fairly forceful defense 1.♖xh2, attacking the black queen. But Black's force is then greater than White's as he responds 1...♖e1+ 2.♔g2 ♕g5+ and mates. And the other obvious move of force, 1.♕xd4+, is met by the counterforce 1...♗e5+! So...

1.White resigns??

A blunder. White could have won if he had looked for another forceful idea: 1.♖xh7+!. After 1...♔xh7 2.♕f7+, White eliminates the rook or bishop *with check* next move and wins.

The move to worry about is 1...♕xh7, but then 2.♖xh2 is strong, e.g. 2...♖e1+ 3.♔g2 and Black is out of ammunition.

Black's best is 2...♗h3!, when 3.♕xd4+ begins a neat defensive maneuver to get the queen to the third rank with checks: 3...♔g8 4.♕c4+ ♔h8 (4...♔f8! 5.♕c3 g5 is unclear) 5.♕c3+ ♔g8 6.f4! ♕b7+ (else 7.♖xh3) 7.♔g1 ♖c8! 8.♕e3! ♗f5 9.♘d6 and White is winning, not losing.

In its simplest form, therefore, calculation becomes a matter of weighing the force of one move against that of another. For cxample, a check is more forceful than a threat to capture something. An attack on a queen is more forceful than a threat to a knight. And so on.

Often, when a player misevaluates a forcing situation, it is because it never occurs to him that there is a reply to his last move that is at least as forceful.

BRONSTEIN – BAREEV
Rome 1990

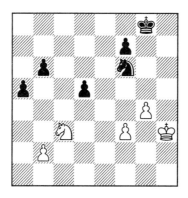

White to move

This is the beginning of the endgame, inasmuch as White has just forced an exchange of queens on f6. A draw is likely. Black is a pawn ahead but against the faster white king he cannot maintain any winning chances (1.♔g3 ♔g7 2.♔f4 and 3.♔e5, or 1...d4 2.♘b5 d3 3.♔f2 and 4.♔e3).

1.g5??

This is a gross oversight, overlooking the compelling nature of Black's reply. White incorrectly assumed that, with so little material on the board, there could be nothing as forcing as the threat of 2.gxf6.

1...	d4!
2.♘b5	d3

Only now does White realize that, after 3.gxf6 d2 4.♘c3 (forced) b5!, Black wins with 5...b4 6.♘d1 a4 and the advance of the a-pawn. In fact, White played **3.♔g3 d2** and **0-1** in view of 4.♘c3 ♘d5! 5.♘d1 ♔g7 and the black king invades.

Similarly, a threat to the enemy queen is very forceful – unless your opponent threatens to take your queen with check.

ASEEV – HICKL
Munich 1991-92

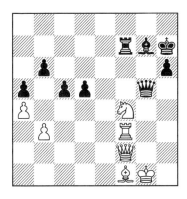

White to move

A piece down for three pawns, Black has excellent compensation. But, carried along by his calculations, he has just played ...♕g5+, intending to meet 1.♗g2?? with 1...♗d4. After White played the correct...

1.♔h1

...Black passed up an excellent, practical move of precaution (2...♔g8, getting the king off a checking diagonal and protecting his rook).

1...	♗d4??

How can this be bad? After all, it's highly forcing.

2.♘h3!   **1-0**

But this is more forcing, as 3.♖xf7+ is threatened, and 2...♗xf2 3.♘xg5+ hxg5 4.♖xf7+ clears the board.

Now we'll examine a slightly more elaborate example. It is not just a case of "He threatens my queen, but I threaten mate in two." The element of force is still present but it is of a long-range nature.

FATALIBEKOVA – RANNIKU
USSR Women's Championship 1974

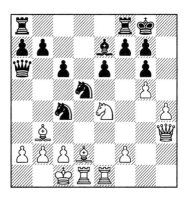

White to move

Black's centralized knights appear just as strong as White's bishops – perhaps more so, when you realize that Black is threatening 1...♗a3 (2.bxa3? ♕xa3+ and mates). But White also has a strong plan involving the opening of the h-file. Only through an accurate examination of the position will White realize whose threats have greater force.

1.♖h1!   **♗a3?**

Better defensive chances are offered by 1...♘xd2 so that ...♘f4 can be played later. But Black saw that after 1...♗a3 she cannot be stopped from a powerful capture on b2.

2.h5!   ♘xb2

This certainly looks powerful. But force can often be deceptive.

3.hxg6!

White may also be winning with 3.h6!. As so often happens, Black has overestimated the power of a discovered check.

3...   ♘xd1+
4.♔xd1   fxg6
5.♕xe6+   ♖f7
6.♕xg6

And **1-0** after **6...♖d8 7.♘f6+ ♖xf6** (7...♔f8 8.♖h8+ ♔e7 9.♕e4+ ♔d6 10.♖xd8+) **8.gxf6.** Black's threats were not illusions – they were forceful. But White's were more so.

Our final example helped decide a U.S. Championship:

BENJAMIN – KAMSKY
U.S. Championship 1991

1.e4 e5 2.♘f3 ♘c6 3.♗b5 a6 4.♗xc6 dxc6 5.0-0 ♕d6 6.d3 ♘e7 7.♗e3 ♘g6 8.♘bd2 c5?! 9.♘c4 ♕e6 10.♘g5 ♕f6 11.♕h5 ♗d6

White now begins a powerful forcing sequence involving two pawn sacrifices.

12.f4!   exf4
13.e5!   ♘xe5
14.♗xf4!   ♘xc4

This appears to win a piece, but White has a surprise at the end. Now 15.♖ae1+ isn't sufficiently forceful since Black can avoid immediate disaster with 15...♔d7!.

15.♗xd6	**♕d4+**
16.♔h1	**♘xd6**

There is a strong temptation here to capture on f7 (17.♘xf7 ♘xf7 18.♕xf7+ ♔d8 19.♖ae1 and against 20.♕e7# Black is lost, e.g. 19...♕d6 20.♕xg7 ♖e8 21.♖xe8+ ♔xe8 22.♖f7; or 19...♕d7 20.♕f8+!).

But White saw that 17.♘xf7 has a curious flaw to it: 17...0-0 is a legal move! Not only is it legal, it eliminates all tactical dangers. So White played...

17.♖xf7??

...which threatens all sorts of murderous discovered checks of great force. But this spoiled his brilliancy because of...

17...	**♕g4!**

White's discovered checks are meaningless now and he has nothing to show for his sacrificed material. He resigned on move 30.

Yet in the diagram there is a win, provided White recognizes the power of force. After 17.♖ae1+!, Black can lose either quickly with 17...♔d8 18.♘xf7 (transposing to the 17.♘xf7 ♘xf7 tree limb) or more slowly with 17...♔d7 18.♘f3! and 19.♘e5+.

Opening a Pandora's Box

Most middlegames are quiet. They become charged with energy only when one player makes a threat or two. His opponent counters with a greater threat and the two sides throw ideas at each other until they run out. Then the tactical energy spills off and a new period of calm is reached.

Therefore, provoking one of these showdowns of force is a high-risk enterprise. Savielly Tartakower alluded to this when he spoke of unleashing "the combinational genie." The possibility of a surprise you hadn't counted on increases dramatically.

SHAMKOVICH – BOTTERILL
Hastings 1977-78

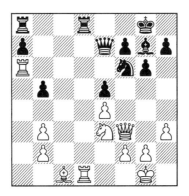

Black to move

White has greater piece activity but also some weaknesses. Black can prepare an invasion of the vulnerable queenside or center with 1...♖xd1+ or 1...♖ac8. Instead:

| 1... | ♖d4? |

Black chose this precisely because it was more forceful. He foresaw what he called the "dreadful force" of the next series of moves.

| 2.♖xd4 | exd4 |
| 3.e5! | |

Here we go. The knight on f6 is attacked, ♕xa8+ is threatened, and ♘d5 is looming. Black has one good reply.

| 3... | ♖c8! |

Since 4.♗d2 ♕xe5 favors Black, White's hand is also forced.

| 4.exf6 | ♖xc1+ |
| 5.♘f1 | ♕e1 |

Each of the moves since 2.♖xd4 was forced. But now Black pays for having made the position dynamic. Neither White's obvious threat (fxg7) nor Black's (...♕xf1+) is particularly devastating. But:

6.♖xa7!

Black said later that he underestimated this move when he began the force-fight with 1...♖d4, but he might have just overlooked it completely. Such an oversight is understandable in a sharp position. After 6.♖xa7, White threatens ♕d5xf7+ or fxg7/♕xf7#.

Black can delay matters with a few checks (6...♕xf1+ 7.♔h2 ♕g1+ 8.♔g3), but they are soon over and White then has all the threats (including 9.♖a8+ ♗f8 10.♖xf8+ ♔xf8 11.♕a8+ and mates).

In the game, Black went on the defensive with **6...♗f8** and lost directly: **7.♕d5 ♕e6 8.♕xd4! ♕e2 9.♖a8!** (threatening ♕d6 or ♕b4) **9...♖xf1+ 10.♔h2 ♖xf2 11.♖xf8+!** (more forceful, of course, than a queen move) **11...♔xf8 12.♕c5+! 1-0** because of 12...♔e8 or 12...♔g8 13.♕c8+.

Of course, when a position is *already* dynamic, it seems to make no sense to play quiet moves. But it would be a mistake to exclusively look for the forcing candidates.

J. POLGÁR – GRANDA ZÚÑIGA
Madrid 1992

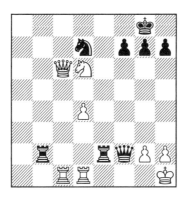

White to move

Black's knight can go to f8 to meet simple back-rank threats and his own threat of ...♕xg2+ prevents 1.♕xd7. Yet White has a significant advantage, and the way to maximize it is simply 1.♖g1!, threatening the knight.

The knight cannot be protected and can only go to f8. Then 2.♖cf1 ♕xd4 3.♖xf7 yields excellent winning chances (3...♖b8 4.♖gf1 ♖e6? 5.♖xf8+! ♖xf8 6.♖xf8+ ♔xf8 7.♕c8+ ♔e7 8.♘f5+ ♔f7 9.♕xe6+! and wins).

1.♖f1??

This is forceful, but opens up Pandora's Box. Both sides now have potentially vulnerable back ranks.

1...   ♕xg2+??

A counter-blunder that led to a quick loss: 2.♕xg2 ♖xg2 3.♖c8+ ♘f8 4.♖xf7! ♖xh2+ 5.♔g1 ♖hg2+ 6.♔f1 and Black's defeat was

111

assured. It was all the more embarrassing in that Black now had the advantage.

The way to exploit White's too-forcing move is 1...♖bc2!! because 2.♖xc2 ♕xf1 is mate and 2.♖xf2 ♖xc6! leaves White's rooks dangling. White's best, in fact, is 2.♕a8+ ♘f8 3.h3, although it is Black who has the edge after 3...♖xc1 4.♖xc1 ♕xd4.

In the following example, White rejects a non-forcing defensive move, which he sees leads at best to a draw, in favor of an aggressive defense that appears to refute a sacrificial attack. But when you walk into such a forcing situation, where it is possible to calculate with a greater degree of accuracy, then you had better meet that standard of accuracy.

ALBURT – SHIRAZI
U.S. Championship 1983

1.d4 c5 2.d5 ♘f6 3.♘c3 g6 4.e4 d6 5.♘f3 ♗g7 6.♗e2 0-0 7.0-0 ♘a6 8.♘d2 ♘c7 9.a4 e6 10.♘c4 exd5 11.exd5 b6 12.♗f4 ♗a6 13.b3 ♖e8 14.♗f3 ♘h5! 15.♗d2 ♗xc4 16.bxc4 ♕h4 17.♗e2?! ♗e5

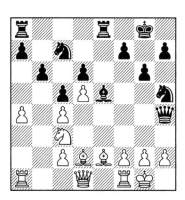

With his last two moves, Black advertises his willingness to sacrifice pieces for mate.

18.g3   ♘xg3

19.hxg3 ♗**xg3**

Now White has a choice of defenses. First, he can capture on g3. This gives Black an immediate perpetual check as well as the possibility of a mate if he can get another piece to the kingside. The greatest demerit to 20.fxg3 is that it is passive, leaving Black with the opportunity to work out a winning continuation or grab a draw if he can't find one.

On the other hand, White can try 20.♔g2, threatening 21.fxg3 as well as 21.♖h1. This has the advantage of forcing matters.

20.♔g2??

As it turns out, this is a blunder because White, in his zeal to force matters, has overlooked...

20... ♕**h2+**
21.♔f3 ♗**xf2!**

This move wins quickly. The bishop can't be taken (22.♖xf2 ♕h3+ 23.♔f4 g5+ 24.♔xg5 ♖e5+, etc.). And the forcing defense of 22.♗f4 fails to 22...♖e3+! 23.♗xe3 ♕g3+ and mate next.

22.♖g1 ♖**e5!**

And **0-1** after **23.♗d3 ♗xg1 24.♘e4 ♖f5+.**

With 20.♔g2, he took the risk of allowing his king to be lured forward, thinking that by forcing matters he wouldn't allow Black time to add to his attacking army. (In fact, back at the diagram White chose 18.g3 over 18.h3 because he counted on 20.♔g2.)

Had he reviewed his thinking accurately at move 20, White would have found that 20.fxg3! ♕xg3+ 21.♔h1 would have drawn since Black's other pieces are too far away to be of any immediate use.

The Limits of Force

Finally, it should be pointed out that "quiet" moves may also be forcing, and sometimes the apparently passive is better than the malevolently dynamic.

LUKÁCS – LÜCKE
Budapest 1991

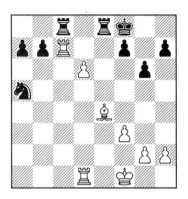

White to move

White is a pawn down but has excellent compensation in light of his superior minor piece, advanced rook, and passed pawn. Instinct tells him he should look for a forcing idea, since quiet play is likely to neutralize his compensation and lead to a victory for Black's passed queenside pawns.

But when he looks for forceful lines he finds that 1.♖d5 – which works after 1...b6 2.♖xa7 and 1...♖xc7 2.dxc7 b6 3.♖d8 – only draws after 1...♘c4 2.♖xb7 ♘e3+ 3.♔f2 ♘xd5 4.d7.

Better is 1.♖a1, so that 1...b6 2.♖xa7. White has to see that 1...♖xc7 2.dxc7 b6 loses to 3.♖c1 ♖c8 4.♗d3 and ♗a6. But White missed that and played...

1.♔g1!?

...which, in fact, is forceful because now 2.♖d5 ♘c4 3.♖xb7 is a winning line (no check with 3...♘e3).

1...   ♖xc7?

Black probably saw that his forcing 1...f5? fails to 2.♖xh7, threatening 3.d7. On the best defense, 1...♖ed8, White has only a minor edge.

2.dxc7   ♔e7
3.♗xb7!   1-0

Because of 3...♘xb7 4.♖e1+ ♔d7 5.♖xe8 ♔xe8 6.c8♕+.

Sometimes you need to maneuver your thinking midway between the most forceful and the least. The following example helps demonstrate this:

BENKO – BYRNE
U.S. Open 1964

1.e4 e6 2.d3 d5 3.♘d2 ♘f6 4.♘gf3 b6 5.e5 ♘fd7 6.g3 c5 7.♗g2 ♕c7 8.0-0 ♘xe5? 9.♘xe5 ♕xe5 10.c4 ♕d6? 11.cxd5 exd5 12.♘c4! ♕d8 13.♕h5 ♗b7

White has just played four moves in a row of varying force and is in the mood to push the action along. Now he has to make a choice. With 14.♘e3 he will threaten a pawn, and in fact must win it since 14...d4?? loses to 15.♗xb7.

The alternative is a forcing move like 14.♖e1+ or 14.♗g5. White can mix the two ideas together with 14.♗g5 ♗e7 15.♖fe1, but he has to find a good follow-up after 15...♘c6.

After the game White explained that he gave up on this last tree, and played the inferior **14.♘e3** instead, because he examined only one continuation after 14.♗g5 ♗e7 15.♖fe1 ♘c6, what he called the "Morphy-style" 16.♖xe7+ ♘xe7 17.♖e1.

But then he saw that 17...0-0 18.♗xe7 could be met by 18...♖e8!, after which 19.♗xd8 ♖xe1+ 20.♗f1 dxc4 is decidedly unclear.

White was correct to reject the violent "Morphy" line in favor of 14.♘e3?!, which led to a solid advantage and, in fact, to a win in another ten moves. But he missed the best branch – the middle-of-the-road branch – which would have won a piece immediately: 14.♗g5 ♗e7 15.♖fe1 ♘c6 16.♘e5!.

Force in Action

Finally, let's examine a full game that illustrates the dangers of misjudging force. The game shows how an obscure master missed an opportunity to mate a former world champion in less than 30 moves, then went on to lose because of a variety of calculation errors.

TAN – SMYSLOV
Petrópolis 1973

1.e4 d6 2.d4 ♘f6 3.♘c3 g6 4.♗c4 ♗g7 5.♕e2 c6 6.e5 ♘d5 7.♗d2 0-0 8.♗b3 a5 9.a4 dxe5 10.dxe5 ♘a6 11.♘f3 ♘c5 12.♗xd5 cxd5 13.♗e3 ♘e4 14.♗d4 ♘xc3 15.♗xc3 b6 16.♕d2 ♗a6 17.h4! ♕d7 18.h5 ♕g4 19.0-0-0! ♕xa4 20.♔b1 ♖fc8 21.♖h4 ♕e8 22.hxg6 hxg6 23.♖dh1 ♖c4

White has sacrificed a pawn for a promising kingside attack. Black's last move, threatening to diminish the enemy army by a trade of rooks, compels White to weigh the various choices: He can block the fourth rank with 24.♗d4, 24.♘d4, or 24.g4. Or he can retreat his rook to h2 or h3. But these are all inferior because they lack force.

24.♖h7?!

Yes, this is superior to the moves just mentioned: It carries more power in the form of the threatened 25.♖xg7+ ♔xg7 26.♕h6+ and mate next. But at the same time, White fails to consider the most forceful line – that is, moving the rook one square farther and giving check.

Once you spot 24.♖h8+! ♗xh8 you have to examine 25.♕h6. This threatens mate on h8, but runs out of steam after 25...♗g7. Therefore, you should look for a more forceful second move, and find it in the form of 25.♖xh8+! ♚xh8 26.♕h6+ ♚g8:

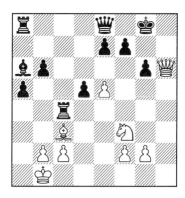

Position after 26...♚g8 (analysis)

White is very close to delivering mate, and the final stage of calculation involves determining whether ♘g5 and ♕h7+ leads to that result. At first glance the double-rook sacrifice appears unsound because of 27.♘g5 e6! 28.♕h7+ ♚f8 29.♕h8+ ♚e7 30.♕f6+ ♚d7 and Black escapes, or 27.♘g5 e6 28.♘h7 ♖f4!.

But if you refine the sequence a bit with 27.e6! first, the game is over. After Black meets the threat of mate on h8 with 27...♖xc3 or 27...f6, White has the pretty and effective 28.♘g5!!. Mate is then unstoppable.

Meanwhile, back in the game, Black met the threat of 25.♖xg7+ with ...

24... ♕f8
25.e6

There is more than one idea for continuing the attack. With Black's queen now blocking the king's evacuation route, White can triple major pieces on the h-file, followed by ♖h8+. This has the drawback of calling for three "quiet" preparatory moves (e.g., 25.♖h2, 26.♕e1, and 27.♕h1, or perhaps the more accurate 25.♕g5 and ♕g3-h2). But it's not obvious how Black can defend against this slow buildup (25.♕g5 d4 26.♕h4! f6 27.e6).

Instead, White opts for the more forceful idea, threatening 26.♖h8+ ♗xh8 27.♖xh8# or 26.♖xg7+.

25...   **♖xc3**

This can be called semi-forcing, since White must either capture on c3 or come up with a more forceful move of his own. Because there are checks and mate threats of various kinds in this position, the force-power of 25...♖xc3 is relatively low.

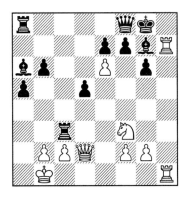

26.exf7+?

This is forceful but for only one move. White appears to have played this move without an idea in mind – a very dangerous policy. He could, of course, have simply played 26.bxc3. But that might have turned the initiative over to Black.

If he had looked a bit more deeply, White might have found 26.♘g5!, which threatens to win the queen with 27.exf7+. Then 26...fxe6 is clearly unsatisfactory because of 27.♘xe. So he would focus attention on 26...f6, and then 27.♕xc3, preparing to win with 28.♕h3 and 29.♖h8+, looks good. But 26...f6 27.♘f7! and 28.♖h8+ is better. It wins outright.

This is the second win White missed for failing to search for force.

26...	♕**xf7**
27.bxc3?	

White misses a third opportunity and plays instead a quiet recapture. What are the more forceful tries in the position? The chief candidates are the attacks on the queen (♘g5 and ♘e5). The idea is to drive the queen away from the defense of two key squares, g7 and d5. Consider the consequences of 27.♘e5!:

a) If Black abandons g7 with 27...♕e6, he allows 28.♖xg7+! ♔xg7 29.♕h6+ ♔f6 (forced) 30.♕xg6+! ♔xe5 31.♖e1+ and wins.
b) If Black abandons d5 with 27...♕f6 or 27...♕f5, he allows 28.♕xd5+ and 29.♕xa8+.
c) If Black tries a desperado, meeting force with force, and tries 27...♖xc2, then 28.♕xc2 ♕f5! may kill the attack. But 28.♖xg7+! wins, since 28...♔xg7 29.♕h6+ bags the queen, and 28...♕xg7 29.♕xd5+ ♔f8 allows 30.♖h8+ ♕xh8 31.♕f7#.

27...	♖**d8**
28.♘e5	

One move late, now that d5 is covered.

28...	♕**f6**

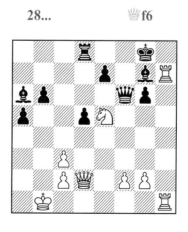

29.f4?

A final failure. White tries to consolidate with quiet moves, but the inadequacy of this policy is shown by the rest of the game: **29... d4! 30.g4?!** (30.♖7h6! wins) **30...♗b7! 31.♖1h3 ♖d5 32.cxd4 ♕d6 33.♕h2** (33.♖h8+ ♗xh8 34.♖xh8+ ♔g7! leads to nothing) **33...♕b4+ 34.♔a2 ♕a4+ 35.♖a3 ♕xd4 36.♖xg7+ ♔xg7** and, as he played **37.♖h3,** White's flag fell. **0-1**

What could he have done? The diagram position calls for force, and one likely policy is 29.♘g4!, forcing Black to choose between the losing 29...♕d6 30.♖xg7+! ♔xg7 31.♕d4+ e5 32.♘xe5 ♕f6 33.♖h6 or 29... ♕xc3 30.♕xc3 ♗xc3 31.♖xe7, when White's rooks are suddenly very strong on the seventh rank (31...♗g7 32.♘h6+ ♗xh6 33.♖xh6 ♖d6 34.♖hh7).

With a healthy appreciation of force, the aspiring calculator is ready for the meat and potatoes of calculation – the counting out and evaluating of variations in the tree of analysis.

Chapter 5

COUNTING OUT

"Everyone complains of his memory, and no one complains of his judgment."

–La Rochefoucauld

Once we've examined the tactical and strategic ideas in a position and have assessed the forcing moves, we move into a different realm. This is the more familiar form of calculation, the mental processing of tree branches. The most important questions to ask in this process are:

1) What is the final position in each sequence like? Is one more favorable than others? In short, how do we evaluate the branches of a tree?

2) Am I sure they are the *final* positions? After my intended two-mover, can I say "and wins"? In short, when can I stop calculating?

3) Do I have the right move order? Can the idea be improved by a different sequence?

4) Is there an escape route? If I begin a forcing sequence that runs four moves and suddenly realize after two moves have been played that I've made an oversight, can I bail out?

The Bottom Line

The most common misunderstanding about the powers of chessplaying computers – by experienced players as well as by novices – is that machines calculate more efficiently than humans. They don't.

They can't, because they lack a human's greater skills of intuition and evaluation. We can turn our attention to the most likely moves and responses and ignore the others. We don't have to work every variation out to mate.

"A master's strength is in the evaluation of a position," wrote Mikhail Botvinnik. You can have the *Stockfish* capacity to instantly analyze a candidate 15 moves deep. But if you conclude after those 15 moves that White is better when in fact Black has the edge, all your work is wasted.

In computer-only tournaments of the 1980s, much of the success of the champion program *Deep Thought* lay in its superior powers of evaluation. It won more than a few games from positions that its opponent had forced, considering them favorable, if not winning, when in fact they were unfavorable.

RIBLI – PLANINC
Portorož/Ljubljana 1975

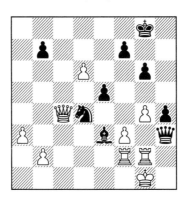

Black to move

White has the advantage of the double exchange (two rooks for Black's two minor pieces). But Black has what Bobby Fischer used to call "a juicy position." Black is the one with the threats, pins, and tactical ideas. Moreover, Black has just passed the time control so he can choose at his leisure between the various candidates (1...♘xf3+, 1...♗xf2+, 1...♕xf3).

Instead, Black calculated one line out to the natural end position, a position where the tactics are over and there seem no great issues left to be resolved. He quickly went into:

1...		♘xf3+
2.♔f1		♘d2+

White's reply is forced and his rooks become disconnected.

3.♖xd2		♕h1+
4.♔e2		♗xd2

Here Black concluded that with 5...♕e1+ and mate threatened, White must play 5.♔xd2, after which 5...♕xg2+ puts Black a pawn ahead in a queen-and-pawn endgame.

All quite true. But Black is not better; in fact in the end position he is worse. What he failed to remember is that the number of pawns in such an ending is often not as significant as how far they are advanced. In other words, he didn't evaluate the 5...♕xg2+ end position properly.

And the result was **5.♔xd2 ♕xg2+ 6.♔c3 ♕g3+ 7.♔b4 e4??** (loses; 7...♕e3! is unclear) **8.♕d4!** and the powerful d-pawn decided the game quickly: **8...♕e1+ 9.♔a4 b5+ 10.♔xb5 ♕f1+ 11.♔b6 ♕f4 12.♔c6 ♕g5 13.d7 ♕d8 14.♕b6 ♕f6+ 15.♔b7 ♕e7 16.♔c8! 1-0.**

This was an important lesson for Black to learn, particularly since he can win from the diagram if he searches further and finds 1...♗xf2+!. That requires a bit more computing time than 1...♘xf3+ because the tree of analysis gets wider and longer: After the bishop's capture, White has two ways of retaking on f2, and in each case the issue remains in doubt longer than the five moves that Black examined with 1...♘xf3↑.

But it would have paid off: 1...♗xf2+ 2.♔xf2 ♕xf3+ 3.♔g1 h3! 4.♖f2 ♕xg4+ 5.♔h1 ♕e4+ 6.♔h2 ♘f3+ and wins; or 2.♖xf2 ♘xf3+ 3.♖xf3 ♕xf3 and the white king's position makes this queen-and-pawn endgame a win for Black: 4.d7 ♕d1+, or 4.♕c8+ ♔g7 5.d7 h3! 6.♕c2 ♕xg4+.

First Step: Count the Pieces

In most evaluations, you'll be guided by the material situation. At the end of the main variation you will need to know who is ahead and by how much. The simplest way to do this is to count up what's left on the board at the end of the line.

Sound easy? Maybe so, but consider this example. Black not only misevaluates a variation materially, he doesn't even count the pieces on the board correctly when he resigns.

VERBER – MIKENDA
Haifa 1970

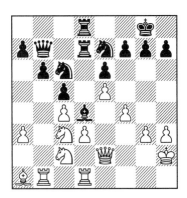

White to move

This comes from the last World Student Olympiad that was won by the United States. The Americans won by a single point – perhaps this one.

1.♘e4	♗xa1
2.♘xc5!?	

White appreciated that he has a poor game positionally because of the backward d-pawn and Black's ability to occupy d4. So, instead of the routine recapture (2.♖xa1 ♘f5 and ...♘cd4), he converts a slow strategic struggle into a dynamic, tactical one.

2...	♛a8
3.♘xd7	♘d4!

After 3...♘d4, Black has all the winning chances because White's knight is trapped on d7. The result of 4.♘xb6 axb6 is rough material equality (two pawns and a rook for two minor pieces), but the pieces would be much stronger than the rook. Black's choice, 3...♘d4, is even better.

4.♛e4!?	♘xc2
5.♛xa8	♖xa8
6.c5	

This manages to free the d7-knight, and it also confuses Black. Somehow in the Austrian's calculations he convinced himself that he has *lost* material over the last five moves. He sees that he's minus a rook and remembers taking an enemy piece. But instead of realizing that he has won two pieces for the rook, he thinks he has lost the exchange. There followed:

6...	♘e3
7.♖e1	

White commits his own error. With 7.cxb6! he preserves a large advantage.

7...	♗d4
8.cxb6	axb6
9.♘xb6	1-0

Of course, we know how to count the material on the board. But in a visualized position – a position not actually on the board – it is hardly easy. There are two basic ways of figuring out the status of material at the end of a mental variation:

The first, somewhat clumsy, method is to review the variation in your head, adding up the captured pieces by White and then the ones captured by Black along the way.

The alternative is to run through the sequence in your head until the end position and then "see" the remaining pieces.

Let's consider how this works in practice. Even in a battle of world champions, one can mess it up.

CAPABLANCA – ALEKHINE
Nottingham 1936

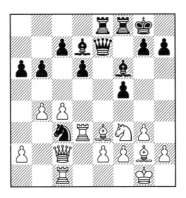

Black to move

1...	f4?

"A miscalculation of a somewhat peculiar kind," wrote Alexander Alekhine. He thought he was winning two exchanges. Instead, he gives up three pieces for the rooks.

2.gxf4   ♗**f5**

3.♕d2　　　　**♗xd3**
4.exd3

It was now time for Black to cut his losses by bailing out of his original combination. He should play 4...♘a4 (after which 5.d4 gives White an excellent, but not yet won, position). However, Alekhine went on to lose the game because he failed to count accurately.

Had Alekhine employed the count-up method, either at this point or back when he was weighing the merits of 1...f4, he might have sounded like this:

"Well, I will win one of his rooks for a bishop when I play 2...♗f5. Then he'll give up his rook for the knight on c3, I'll recapture with the bishop on f6, and he'll make the last capture. Hmmm. I know it often turns out badly when your opponent makes the last capture.

"What's the score? I'll have taken both of his rooks and he'll have gotten my f-pawn, plus one, two... no! three minor pieces. I know from experience that three pieces are almost always better than two rooks. So I have to play something else."

Had Alekhine employed the alternative method, visualizing the final position, he might have sounded like this:

"Let's see, after 1...f4 2.gxf4 ♗f5 3.♕-somewhere ♗xd3 4.exd3, suppose I allow him to continue 5.♖xc3 ♗xc3 6.♕xc3. What's left on the board?

"Well, we both have queens. And nothing has happened to my two rooks while both of his are gone. Hold on! I don't have any minor pieces left. How many does he have? He hasn't moved any of them. The bishop is still on e3, the bishop on g2, and the knight on f3. And I've also given up a pawn. The final score sounds even, but it must be bad for me."

Alekhine apparently used neither method. He played **4...c5?** and, after **5.♖xc3 ♗xc3 6.♕xc3 ♕f6 7.♕xf6 gxf6 8.♘d2!**, the true material picture was clear to everyone. The minor pieces swept into power with **8...f5 9.b5 a5 10.♘f1 ♔f7 11.♘g3,** and Black resigned shortly.

Sometimes when a lot of material is traded off, or when your opponent is losing something heavy, such as his queen, we become blinded.

ONOPRIENKO – LIBERZON
USSR Armed Forces Championship 1966

1.e4 c5 2.♘f3 e6 3.d4 cxd4 4.♘xd4 a6 5.♘c3 ♕c7 6.♗d3 ♘c6 7.♗e3 ♘f6 8.0-0 b5 9.♘xc6 ♕xc6 10.♕f3 ♗b7 11.a3 ♗c5 12.♖fe1 d6 13.♗g5 ♘d7 14.♕h3 ♘e5 15.♖ad1 0-0

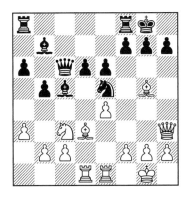

Here White sees what appears to be a winning move:

16.♘d5

It threatens both a knight fork at e7 that wins the queen, and a check at f6 that leads to a very strong attack. "And, of course, on 16...exd5 White plays 17.exd5, attacking the queen and threatening mate on h7," White says to himself.

But this is not so simple.

16...   exd5!

17.exd5 ♘xd3

Black's last move eliminates the mating bishop and forces White to continue:

18.dxc6 ♘xf2

White had calculated this far: he's won the queen for two minor pieces and threatens a bishop. But his own queen is hanging and he will likely lose a rook by discovered check. There is nothing "of course" about the position.

19.♕f3 ♗xc6!
20.♕xc6 ♘xd1+
21.♔f1 ♘xb2

Here is where the real calculation ends and the counting-up begins. The score reads: White has won a queen for a knight, a rook, and a pawn. Material is roughly even.

But, as Botvinnik used to point out, the "evaluation function" is not just a matter of adding two plus two. Sometimes you're dealing with material apples and strategic oranges that can't be added. The reason is that evaluation has a material component, but also a positional one.

Here White has several problems. His a-pawn is weak, his king is insecure, and he has no natural defense to an assault along the c-file.

The game actually saw **22.♖e4 ♘c4 23.♕d5 ♗xa3 24.♕d3 ♗c5 25.♖h4 f5 26.♕h3 h6 27.♕f3 ♖ae8 28.♗c1 ♖e4!,** and White fell apart in a few moves: **29.g3 ♖xh4 30.gxh4 f4! 31.♔g2 ♗e3 32.♗a3 ♘d2! 33.♕d5+ ♖f7 0-1.**

A more recent example shows how this kind of error can be made as early as move 9:

TAIMANOV – ZAICHIK
Leningrad 1989

1.♘f3 f5 2.d3 ♘c6 3.e4 e5 4.♘c3 ♘f6 5.exf5 d5 6.d4 exd4 7.♘xd4 ♘xd4 8.♕xd4 ♗xf5 9.♗g5 ♗xc2?

This is an error. Black made it knowing that White could begin a dangerous sequence with 10.♖c1 and then 11.♗xf6 ♕xf6 12.♕e3+ and ♘xd5. But Black convinced himself that White couldn't play it because of a surprise he intended at move 13.

10.♖e1!	**♗g6**
11.♗xf6	**♕xf6**
12.♕e3 +	**♔f7**
13.♘xd5	**♗b4+**

Consistent with his last move. Black hopes to win the queen with 14...♖he8. White promptly obliges.

14.♘xb4!	**♖he8**
15.♗c4+	**♔f8**
16.0-0!	**♖xe3**
17.fxe3	**♗f5**
18.g4	

White's moves have been virtually forced since move 13. But the final position of Black's combination must be greatly in White's favor despite the loss of his queen.

The game, in fact, lasted only ten more moves: **18...g6 19.gxf5 ♔g7 20.♘d5 ♕e5 21.fxg6 hxg6 22.♖f3,** and White won.

Even in relatively simple positions, with no strange material imbalances, a strong player can make horrible misevaluations. This is particularly common in endgame transitions.

ULIBIN – I. GUREVICH
Santiago 1990

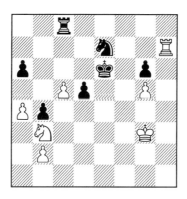

White to move

Let's evaluate: First, material is equal. Second, both sides have passed pawns but White's is a bit further advanced. White's rook and knight are a bit more active than Black's, but Black has the more useful king.

Bottom line: unclear. Normally, an "unclear" label is not a problem. Afterward, an annotator may decide to update his evaluation, changing from the equal sign at move 12 to the plus-over-equals, denoting a slight advantage to White, at move 20. But the players don't have to do this in the course of a game.

However, in this situation an evaluation is important because White has a relatively easy, forcing draw if he wants one: 1.♘d4+ ♚e5 2.♘f3+. Black cannot avoid the repeat of the position without incurring problems, e.g. 2...♚e6 3.♘d4+ ♚d7 4.♘b3 ♖f8 5.♘d4.

When you have the opportunity to force matters into a particular result (a win or draw), you should analyze the alternative with exceptional caution. However:

1.♘d4+	♚e5
2.♖xe7+?	♚xd4
3.♖e6	

White saw this far and concluded he was better. In fact, he is closer to losing than to winning.

3...	♔**c4**
4.♖xg6	♔**b3!**
5.♖xa6	♔**xb2**
6.♔f4??	

The final mistake. 6.♖d6! holds the draw.

And with his king able to support both passed pawns – unlike White's – Black won easily: **6...♔c3 7.♖h6 d4 8.g6 b3 9.g7 ♖g8 10.♖g6 b2 11.♖g1 ♖xg7** and White resigned shortly. White threw away this game because of gross misevaluation.

Finding the bottom line is not only part of processing variations: It can also play an inspirational role. When evaluating a seemingly forced line of play, the position may reveal to us a superior alternative.

AZMAIPARASHVILI – YUDASIN
USSR Championship 1986

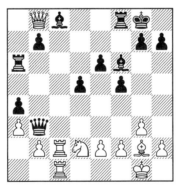

Black to move

White has just retreated his attacked knight from c4 to d2, simultaneously threatening the enemy queen and ♖xc8. He appears to be on the verge of winning:

1...   ♗**d7**

At a moment like this, when a player is at the decisive point of the game and emotions are naturally peaking, we can understand how White might bang down 2.♕xf8+ and then 3.♘xb3.

But, as students of calculation, we cannot excuse him. Because after 2...♔xf8 and 3...axb3 White, although up the exchange, is not winning. He is not even better. In fact, he stands worse.

His rooks can dominate the only open file but lack significant targets (♖c7 is met by ...♗c6). His bishop is locked in at g2 by Black's center pawns. Black, however, can attack a significant target – b2 – while bringing his king toward the center to advance his pawns.

White understood this and so he looked for a better move than 1.♕xf8+. He realized that he needed a new idea. And, as so often happens in chess, when you look, you find.

2.♖c8!!   **1-0**

A hard move to spot, but working out the lines is easy (2...♕-moves 3.♖xf8#; 2...♖xc8 3.♖xc8+ ♗xc8 4.♕xc8+ ♔f7 5.♘xb3; 2...♗xc8 3.♘xb3 and White has won a queen for a rook).

Many errors are made in evaluating positions with material equality, or what appears to be equality. Unless the two sides have exactly the same pieces left on the board, there is some difference in the value of their armies.

For example, the first book you read about chess told you that when you give up two pieces for a rook and a pawn (or two pawns), material is roughly even. This is rarely true in practice. Often the minor pieces are much better, particularly in an active middlegame. And sometimes the rook is winning, particularly in an ending with only a few pieces left or when there are passed pawns on both wings.

EVANS – ROSSOLIMO

U.S. Championship 1965

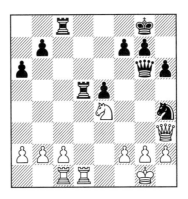

Black to move

Both of Black's rooks and his knight on h4 are under attack. But rather than begin defensive measures with 1...♖xd1+, he found a combination – in fact, it helped win the best-played-game prize in this event. The idea of exploiting the back rank (1...♖xc2) is not very difficult to find. Working out the combination to its end is much more of a challenge. This is because the main line is five moves long and requires finding an inspired "quiet" second move.

But many a strong master would have played something else even if they saw all five moves. They would have rejected the combination simply because they could not appreciate how well Black stood at the end.

Let's see:

1...   **♖xc2!**

So far, so good: 2.♖xc2 allows mate in one (2...♖xd1) and 2.♖xd5 allows mate in two. The real question is what happens after 2.♕xh4.

2.♕xh4   **♖d4!!**

A terrific move. Its strength is hard to foresee in the diagram but the variations are easy to work out at this point:

a) Protecting the knight with 3.f3 allows 3...♕xg2#.

b) Taking either rook allows the same back-rank mates as after 1...♖xc2.

c) Any quiet move allows Black to play ...♕xe4 and remain a pawn ahead, e.g. 3.h3 ♖xc1 4.♖xc1 ♕xe4, or 3.♖a1 ♕xe4.

That leaves one "loud" move:

3.♕d8+	♖xd8
4.♖xd8+	♔h7
5.♖xc2	♕xe4

Now examine what we have left:

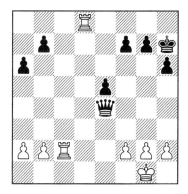

In terms of material, Black has won a queen and a pawn for two rooks. According to the primers, material is equal. There is a good reason for that judgment. If the white rooks were able to attack the same black pawn and Black were forced to defend it with his queen and king, the result of a liquidation beginning with rook takes pawn and queen takes rook would be a dead-even material ending with just pawns and kings left.

But the position in the diagram is not even. The rooks are not coordinated, while both 6...♕xc2 and 6...♕e1# are threatened. That means 6.♖c1 is forced, and Black has time to begin mobilizing his extra pawn and king before White can double his rooks against a target. Eventually, the black king can shepherd a passed pawn to a square on which White will have to begin the liquidating combination.

Black is the only one who can win such a position. This important realization – the evaluation of the end position – is what crowned a prize-winning game.

It lasted some 40 more moves but the power of the queen was evident after **6.♖c1 ♕e2 7.♖b1 f5! 8.♖dd1 e4 9.♖e1 ♕c4 10.a3 ♕a2! 11.g3 ♔g6 12.♔g2 ♕b3 13.♔g1 ♕a2 14.♔g2 ♔f6 15.f3 ♔e5 16.fxe4 fxe4 17.h4 ♕b3 18.♔h3 ♕c2 19.♖ec1 ♕f2 20.♖f1 ♕b6 21.♔g2 g6 22.♖f8 ♕b5 23.♖f2 e3 24.♖e1 ♔e4 25.a4 ♕c5 26.♔h3 b5! 27.axb5 axb5 28.♖f6 ♕e5 29.♖f8 ♕e7 30.♖f4+ ♔d3 31.♖f3 ♔d2.**

When he saw this game published in a Soviet magazine, the great violinist David Oistrakh – a strong amateur player – exclaimed, "On a violin I could not have played better."

What Is Compensation?

Before we leave the subject of evaluation, we must acknowledge that players often go into sequences that leave them decidedly behind in material, but with plenty of that vague commodity we call "compensation."

YUSUPOV – KARPOV
Candidates' Match (4) 1989

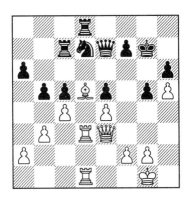

White to move

Black's last two moves, ...♖c7 and ...♘d7, begin a transfer of the knight from b6 to the kingside, either to f6 or perhaps to f8-e6-d4. Then White's absolute control of the d-file will be somewhat reduced and his winning plans curtailed.

It is moments like this when temporary opportunities arise.

1.♗xf7!!

This sacrifice was universally praised. Now on 1...♕xf7 White invades with the major pieces by 2.♕h3 and 3.♖d6.

1...	♔xf7
2.♕d2?!	

But this was sharply criticized. When White decided to sacrifice, he well understood that he would keep total control of the open file. But what else did he have in return for a bishop besides a single pawn?

It appears that even against a former world champion, White did not think he had to foresee a specific winning sequence in order to make such a sacrifice. What he saw was that Black couldn't extricate himself from the pin and achieve king safety.

Afterward, annotators found a number of improvements for White, such as 2.♖d6!, followed by the invasion of the queen to f5, via f3 or h3. Then after 2...♖dc8 3.♕f3+ ♔e8 4.♕f5 or 2...♖cc8 3.♖xh6 ♘f8 4.♖d5! White is close to a winning position, although in this last line 3... ♘f6 would have left matters unclear.

The game actually continued **2...♔e8 3.♕a5 bxc4 4.bxc4** and now instead of 4...♖c6 and 5...♕e6 with a solid position, Black blundered with **4...♖cc8? 5.♕a4! ♖c7? 6.♕xa6 ♖b8 7.♕g6+ ♔f8? 8.♖f3+ 1-0.**

Even though the attack and defense were both flawed, White's original decision was quite correct. He had compensation even though he did not specifically see how to use it.

A great master of evaluating such positions was Mikhail Tal:

TAL – LETELIER
La Habana 1963

1.e4 e5 2.♘f3 ♘c6 3.♗b5 a6 4.♗a4 d6 5.c3 ♗d7 6.d4 ♘ge7 7.♗b3 h6 8.♘h4 g5? 9.♕h5 ♖h7 10.♗xg5 exd4 11.f4 ♕c8 12.f5 dxc3 13.♘xc3 ♘e5 14.♗f6 ♘g8 15.♗xe5 dxe5

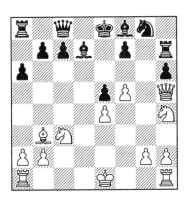

Many players of less than Tal's strength could have calculated the next three moves in advance. But few of them would have forced the play as the former world champion does here. His genius lay not in the length of his variations, but in the evaluation of positions such as the one that occurs three moves later, at 18.♘d5.

16.♘g6

This was more or less expected. There were only a few forcing moves to consider. One of them, 16.♗xf7+, doesn't quite work, and another, 16.♕g4, permits what we will call an "attack-defense" response, 16... ♘f6!, that halts White in his tracks.

16...   ♗d6

Tal's threats were 17.♘xf8, to set up the king for attack, and 17.♘xe5. Clearly, 16...fxg6 17.♕xg6+ was out of the question.

17.♗xf7+!   **♔xf7**

It isn't hard to spot 17...♖xf7 18.♘h8!. After the king moves, there are a number of discovered checks with the knight. Yet Tal played:

18.♘d5!

In reaching this position from the diagram, Tal disregarded the material imbalance (a bishop for a pawn) and the absence of specific positional compensation, but regarded the white knights, supported by the major pieces following 19.0-0, as sufficient to engineer a mating attack.

It's impossible for humans to calculate much further than 18.♘d5 with any degree of certainty. Tal relied on general principles, his instincts, and the consideration of a few likely continuations. The most obvious defensive moves either fail outright (18...♘f6? 19.♘xe5+) or allow more attacking pieces to join in (18...♔g7 19.0-0).

18...	**♔g7**
19.0-0	**♘f6**
20.♘xf6	**♔xf6**
21.♘xe5!	

Now we again have a position that can be calculated with some certainty (21...♗xe5 22.♕g6+; 21...♔xe5 22.f6+). Tal's decision at moves 16-18 is soon proven correct.

Compensation, then, is in the eye of the beholder. Whereas some players would never consider the position after 18.♘d5 acceptable for White because there are no concrete variations that show White winning, Tal reasoned the other way: There are no concrete variations that show Black consolidating.

21...	**♕e8**
22.♘xd7+	**♖xd7**
23.e5+!	**♗xe5**

And Black resigned after **24.♕xh6+ ♔f7 25.♖ae1 ♖d5 26.♕h7+ ♔f6 27.♖e4! ♗d4+ 28.♔h1 1-0** (28...♕xe4 29.♕g6+ ♔e7 30.f6+).

Is it Over?

When an amateur allows his opponent to play a strong combination, chances are that he either completely overlooked the possibility of a combination or misevaluated the final position.

But when a master allows a strong combination, it isn't necessarily because he and his opponent disagree about the nature of the end position. Rather, the two players may be considering two *different* end positions because one player stopped calculating the key line too soon.

TIMMAN – KARPOV
Montréal 1979

1.c4 ♘f6 2.♘c3 e5 3.♘f3 ♘c6 4.e3 ♗e7 5.d4 exd4 6.♘xd4 0-0 7.♘xc6 bxc6 8.♗e2 d5 9.0-0 ♗d6 10.b3 ♕e7 11.♗b2 dxc4! 12.bxc4 ♖b8 13.♕c1 ♘g4 14.g3 ♖e8 15.♘d1

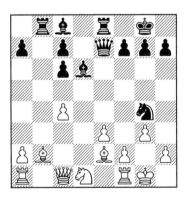

White is now lost, though it doesn't look that way. In fact, it won't be clear for several moves. But he has made a series of minor errors (10. cxd5 and 11.b3 was more exact, and 15.♗f3 was also better than what was played).

Jan Timman's fatal error was allowing the following combination, which he realized was coming. White had calculated 15...♘xh2 "to the end," but misjudged where that end was.

15...   ♘xh2

"Timman foresaw this move, of course," his opponent said later.

16.c5!

Timman saw the main line, which was not very original but would have been quite effective (16.♔xh2 ♕h4+ 17.♔g2 ♕h3+ 18.♔g1 ♗xg3 19.fxg3 ♕xg3+ 20.♔h1 and now 20...♖e4! wins, e.g. 21.♖f4 ♗h3!).

But he concluded that Black could not play 15...♘xh2 because of 16.c5!, which deflects the bishop. On 16...♘xf1 White takes the bishop first and, next move, the trapped knight.

16...   ♘xf1

Unfortunately for Black, the bishop cannot be diverted (16...♗xc5 17.♔xh2!).

Karpov might have tried the finesse 16...♗e5 17.♗xe5 ♘xf1, since White, with a bishop attacked, doesn't have time to capture on f1. There could follow 18.♗f4 g5 19.♗xf1 gxf4 20.exf4 with unclear results. But he has better.

17.cxd6

White saw this far... and stopped. He had good reason to: Black's queen and knight are both attacked, and one of them will be taken next move. White's kingside remains pretty much intact despite the loss of the h-pawn, and he has attacking ideas of his own, such as ♕c3.

White probably figured he stood much better in this position. Did he miss something?

17...   ♘xg3!

Yes, he missed the only forcing move in the position (18.dxe7 ♘xe2+ and 19...♘xc1 puts him the exchange and a pawn down). Timman probably saw it coming after 16...♘xf1, but by then it was too late.

18.fxg3   ♕xd6

This is where the calculation begun at 15...♘xh2 really ends. The difference is considerable from, say, the consequences of 17...♕xd6 18.♗xf1. In this case, White's king defense is a mess and he has one pawn less than expected. Moreover, his pieces are too late in arriving at the kingside (19.♔g2 ♕h6! 20.g4 ♕g5), while Black's get there quickly (...♖e6 and ...♕h6).

Black saw this far, White did not. The rest of the game was anticlimactic: **19.♔f2 ♕h6 20.♗d4 ♕h2+ 21.♔e1 ♕xg3+ 22.♔d2 ♕g2 23.♘b2 ♗a6 24.♘d3 ♗xd3 25.♔xd3 ♖bd8 26.♗f1 ♕e4+ 27.♔c3 c5! 28.♗xc5 ♕c6 29.♔b3 ♖b8+ 30.♔a3 ♖e5 31.♗b4 ♕b6 0-1.**

The moral is that you must not only evaluate a position correctly – you must evaluate the correct position.

There should be two general guidelines to the question, "How far is far enough?"

The first is to calculate as many moves ahead as it takes to reach a conclusion. The conclusion may be as definite as, "and White wins." Or it could be as vague as, "and I prefer my position," as Tal might have said in the earlier example in this chapter.

Second, you should calculate until the forcing moves are over.

Generally, the stronger a player's sense of what constitutes an advantage, the easier it is for him to calculate because he can reach a firmer conclusion and therefore stop after looking just a few moves ahead. Computers have to look much further.

LARSEN – PORTISCH
Siegen 1970

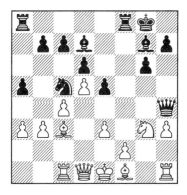

Black to move

It's not hard to pinpoint the squares that will figure prominently in Black's calculations: f2 and e4. One is protected only by the white king, the other only by a knight. Out of this comes the idea of 1...♖xf2!.

1...	♖xf2!
2.♔xf2	♘e4+

The game went on for two more moves, but it could have lasted at least five more if White had insisted. Yet Black did not really have to see any further than 2...♘e4+ in order to decide upon 1...♖xf2.

The reason is that judgment would tell him that 1...♖xf2 has to be sound in such a position. The knight check guarantees Black that he will get a piece back. Therefore, he'll have approximate material equality at move three. In addition, he can see that there will be checks and threats after that point.

The judgment that comes with experience tells him that: (a) he will have enough material compensation for the exchange; and (b) he'll be considerably better off than in the diagram in terms of positional considerations.

Black could, of course, examine all those checks and threats, as well as possible White defenses, to verify his evaluation of the 2...♘e4+ position. The lines are relatively easy to work out: White cannot move his king to g2 (3...♕xg3#) or e2 (3...♘xg3+). That leaves e1, which invites a strong 3...♕xg3+, and the only other legal move, which White played. By examining this far, Black would be able to conclude that he is not only well off after 1...♖xf2, but winning.

The point, however, is that in practical terms, Black didn't have to see that much when he decided on his move in the diagram.

3.♔g1	♕g3+
4.♗g2	♕xe3+
0-1	

There are at least three winning moves now (5...♘xc3, 5...♗h6 and a check on f4, and 5...♘f2).

A more elaborate version of the same principle is:

REORL – PALME
Austrian Championship 1977

1.c4 c5 2.♘c3 ♘c6 3.♘f3 e5 4.e3 d6 5.d4 ♗g4 6.♗e2 ♘f6 7.0-0 cxd4 8.exd4 ♗e7 9.♗e3 0-0 10.♖c1 ♖e8 11.h3 ♗h5 12.dxe5 dxe5 13.♕b3? ♘d4! 14.♘xd4 exd4 15.♖fd1 ♗c5 16.♗xh5 ♘xh5 17.♘e2?

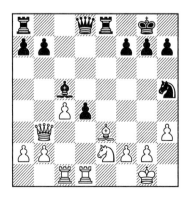

White is trying to exploit the pin on the d-pawn. He might have played 17.♗xd4 ♗xd4 18.♘b5, but rejected that because of 18...♗xf2+, and in the resulting equal-material position White has a vulnerable king.

Nevertheless, the move he preferred, 17.♘e2, is bad, particularly since it allows a queen sacrifice whose soundness does not require much calculation.

17...	**dxe3!**

We tend to label every queen sacrifice as "brilliant." This one is not.

The tactical idea is fairly simple. A novice can recognize that in the diagram position Black cannot defend his d-pawn. A better-than-novice would know to look for a tactical way out of the d-pawn problem. And a less-than-master would recognize that the only tactical way out is a sacrifice.

So once Black gets the idea, the rest is the processing of variations. The tree of analysis is a narrow one. But how tall it stands depends on how long Black wants to examine it.

18.♖xd8	**exf2+**

Now 19.♔f1 appears best in order to protect the knight. The alternative is 19.♔h2 ♖axd8 20.♕f3 (20.♘-moves invites a strong ...♖e1), after which there are several forcing methods but the simple 20...g6 leaves White hard-pressed to meet 21...♖d2, e.g. 21.g4 ♖xe2! 22.♕xe2 ♗d6+ and a knight fork wins the queen.

19.♔f1	**♖axd8**

Should Black have looked this far? Should he have stopped when he saw that he had rook, bishop, and pawn for the queen and retained attacking chances with ...♖d2 or ...♖xe2?

20.♕f3	**♘f6**

21.♘g3	♖d2!

Or this far? That is, until he realized White could do little about his threats of doubling rooks on the second rank or on the d-file, e.g. 22.♖b1 ♖xb2.

22.♕c3	♖ed8
23.b4	♖d1+
24.♖xd1	♖xd1+
25.♔e2	♘e4!

0-1

Or did he figure it all out to the end, i.e. 26.♘xe4 f1♕# or 26.♕e5 ♖e1+ 27.♔d3 ♘xg3 and queens with check.

Any answer could be correct depending on the confidence and evaluation skill of the calculator. Many grandmasters would play 17...dxe3 on instinct and stop looking after 19...♖axd8, realizing that the position offers excellent compensation for the queen and would be better than any variation in which Black just loses the pinned d-pawn.

Other players do not trust such short-run evaluations, and would work out the variations at least as far as 21...♖d2. (And there are still others who do not trust *long* variations because they feel there's bound to be a mistake.)

This example should be contrasted with others in which you must reach the end. The nature of such positions requires you to calculate a long series of thrusts, parries, and counter-thrusts to the end – and be absolutely sure that it is the end.

BARDA – KERES
Moscow 1956

1.d4 ♘f6 2.c4 e6 3.♘c3 ♗b4 4.e3 b6 5.♗d3 ♗b7 6.f3 c5 7.♘e2 cxd4 8.exd4 ♘c6 9.♗e3 d5 10.0-0 dxc4 11.♗xc4 0-0 12.♕d3 ♕e7 13.a3 ♗xc3 14.♘xc3 ♖fd8 15.♖ad1 ♖ac8 16.♖fe1?

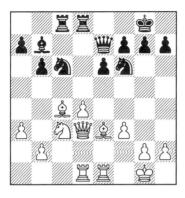

White, realizing that Black's last move contains the threat of 16... ♘e5, calculates a forcing series of replies that appears to refute that knight move.

But Black has calculated further...

16...	♘e5!
17.dxe5	♖xd3
18.exf6	

White counted on this when he took no precautions against 16...♘e5. If Black now takes time to defend his queen, 19.♗xd3 will give White two pieces and a rook for his own queen.

18...	♖xd1
19.fxe7	♖xe1+
20.♔f2	

White undoubtedly saw this far – five moves ahead – when considering his 16th move. Almost certainly he assumed Black would now move the attacked rook (e.g., 20...♖h1) to retain his material edge. But then 21.♗b5! queens the e-pawn.

Remember that there are two criteria for determining when a sequence is over. Often a player will consider one criterion (it's over when you can reach a clear conclusion, such as "White is winning after 20...

♖h1 21.♗b5") and under-appreciate the other (it's over when the forcing moves are absolutely over).

20...   ♖xe3!

This is what White missed. He stopped looking for forcing moves and permitted this final desperado twist. After **21.♔xe3 ♖e8**, White recognized his material deficit, and realizing that this was the true end of the sequence begun by 16...♘e5, he **resigned**.

In both of these examples, the tree was tall and very thin. But decisive, game-winning combinations aren't the norm. The branches of most trees don't have to be analyzed in great detail. The following example illustrates why:

ANAND – YE JIANGCHUAN
Kuala Lumpur 1989

1.e4 c5 2.♘f3 e6 3.d4 cxd4 4.♘xd4 ♘f6 5.♘c3 d6 6.g4 h6 7.♖g1 ♘c6 8.h4 h5 9.gxh5 ♘xh5 10.♗g5 ♘f6 11.♗e2 a6 12.h5 ♗d7 13.♕d2 ♗e7 14.0-0-0 ♕c7 15.h6 gxh6

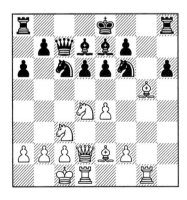

Here White began a combination:

16.♗xf6   ♗xf6

17.♘f5!

The tree unveiled by this yields at least five branches of consequence. Let's consider their sizes:

a) 17... "pass" – a nonviolent move, such as 17...♖d8. All such moves are met by 18.♕xh6 (18...♖xh6?? 19.♖g8#), re-establishing material equality but with Black's king trapped in the center. After 18...exf5, White renews the mating net with 19.♘d5! when not only Black's queen but the f6-bishop and (as a result) the h8-rook are all threatened.

b) 17...0-0-0 at least removes the king from the center, but after White sees 18.♘xd6+ and 19.♘xf7 he knows that his advantage may even be greater than in (a) lines. Actually, he has to look one move further to see that 19.♘xf7 ♗xc3 20.♕xc3?? ♕f4+! wins for Black but that 20.bxc3 wins easily for White.

Here, White had to look to move 20 in the longest subvariation, but it ends in a winning material edge.

c) 17...♗g5 is a natural counterattacking move since 18.♘xd6+?? loses to 18...♕xd6! and White is pinned up. However, White meets the bishop move with 18.f4.

After 18...exf5 19.fxg5 or 19.♘d5 followed by 20.fxg5, how much further does he have to calculate? It's a matter of taste, but many masters would see that White will, at worst, be a pawn down after 20.fxg5, and know that a knight on d5 is more than worth such a pawn. They would stop calculating as soon as they saw 18.f4.

d) 17...♗e5 also looks reasonable. But by the same token as (c), White can stop looking past move 18 when he sees 18.f4.

e) **17...♗e7** was the game continuation but it is again fairly easy to see that 18.♘xe7 gives White excellent prospects however Black retakes. If White wants to, he can work out ideas such as 18...♔xe7 19.♖g3! followed by ♕f4/♖f3 or ♖d3xd6, or 18...♘xe7 19.♖g7 or 19.♕xd6.

f) Finally, there is 17...exf5, after which 18.♘d5 is the natural continuation. Unless Black wants to return the piece immediately, 18...♕d8 is the only response. This is the most important variation we have to calculate because it is the only one that leaves White *behind by a significant amount of material.*

Yet, it turns out to be also one of the shortest limbs. Once White finds 19.♕xh6!! he need see only that 19...♖xh6 20.♖g8 is mate and that anything else allows either 20.♘xf6+ or 20.♕xh8+! ♗xh8 21.♖g8#.

The game actually continued (17...♗e7) **18.♘xe7 ♔xe7 19.♖g3 b5 20.♕f4 ♖ad8 21.♕h4+ ♔e8,** and White won soon after **22.♗xb5! ♘e5 23.♗e2 ♕c5 24.♗h5 ♖f8 25.f4 ♘c6 26.e5 d5 27.♗xf7+! ♖xf7 28.♖g8+.** (Q.E.D.)

The reverse side of missing an opponent's move after the apparent end of a sequence is missing your own strong move. That's just as embarrassing.

Many a winning combination is rejected by players when they find a surprising tactical response for their opponent. But often when your opponent has such a stunning move at his disposal, the position is so explosive that you have an equally stunning counter.

SHORT – MILES
Brighton 1984

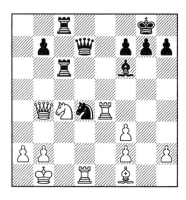

White to move

White saw that 1.♘b6 forks major pieces and wins at least the exchange. But when he rechecked his variation, he found a surprise answer: 1...♘e2!, which (a) threatens 2...♖c1+ and mate, (b) threatens 2...♕xd1#, and (c) allows him to meet 2.♗xe2 with a mixture of the first two ideas (2...♕xd1+! 3.♗xd1 ♖c1#).

Very pretty, and White might have counted himself lucky for noticing 1...♘e2 in time. That's why he actually played **1.a3?.**

But after the game he must have felt differently when 1.♘b6 ♘e2 2.♕f8+!! was pointed out: 2...♔xf8 3.♘xd7+ and 4.♗xe2 wins a piece; 2...♖xf8 3.♘xd7 attacks pieces at e2 and f8 and also wins material.

As a result of this failing, many calculated sequences never get started at all. A player gets a very good idea, then halts abruptly when he sees "the refutation."

KOVAČEVIĆ – THIPSAY
Thessaloniki 1988

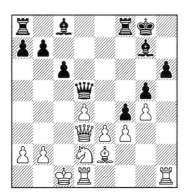

White to move

Here, for example, White has two tempting ideas. One is to get his bishop somehow on the b3-g8 diagonal, winning the pinned queen. The other idea is the opening of the h-file via ♖xh6.

He first examines quiet methods of exploiting the first idea (1.♕c3) and rejects them as insufficient (1...b5). Then he puts the two ideas together and sees 1.♖xh6 with the idea 1...♗xh6 2.♕g6+ followed by ♗c4 (2...♗g7 3.♗c4; 2...♔h8 3.♕xh6+ ♔g8 4.♗c4).

But when he looks further and sees the reply 1...♗f5, what happens then?

There is a strong temptation to drop the matter entirely and look for another move in the diagram. The sequence 1.♖xh6 ♗f5 appears to be a perfect case of a mildly forcing move (1.♖xh6) being refuted by a more forceful counter. After 1...♗f5 White loses his opportunity to play ♕g6+. On 2.gxf5 ♗xh6 or 2.e4 ♗xh6 3.exd5? ♗xd3 or 2.♕c3 b5 (3.♖xc6 ♖ac8!), White's original plan is in tatters.

Nevertheless:

1.♖xh6!	♗f5!
2.e4	♗xh6
3.gxf5!	

White correctly looked further after noticing 1...♗f5. He didn't search for a sparkling counter-refutation, but merely kept his head and evaluated the position after 3.gxf5 as being strongly in his favor. In fact the game ran its natural course quickly. Now 3...♕xa2 4.e5 followed by 5.♖h1 or 5.f6 decides the game.

3...	♕d7
4.♘c4	♗g7
5.♘e5!	♗xe5
6.♕b3+	1-0

Because of 6...♔g7 (6...♕f7 7.♗c4; 6...♖f7 7.dxe5 and 8.♗c4) 7.dxe5 ♕c7 8.♕e6 followed by ♖d7+ or ♕g6+.

It should be stressed that it takes great skill to sense when a variation is over and when there is still a bit of life in it. The absence of forcing moves is a good key to the location of an end position. But often there are devastating "quiet" moves that drastically alter matters.

FIGLER – DUBININ
USSR Correspondence Team Championship 1979

1.d4 ♘f6 2.c4 e6 3.♘f3 ♗b4+ 4.♘bd2 b6 5.a3 ♗xd2+ 6.♗xd2 ♗b7 7.g3 ♘c6 8.♗e3 d5 9.♗g2 dxc4 10.♘e5 ♘d5 11.♘xc4 ♕d7 12.♗c1 0-0-0! 13.e3 h5 14.b4 e5 15.dxe5 b5 16.♘a5 ♘xa5 17.bxa5 ♕f5 18.♕b3

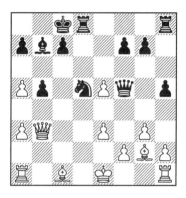

Black almost certainly intended 18...♘c3, attacking the queen, the unprotected g2-bishop, and the mating square d1 all at once. The knight move would also regain Black's lost pawn (19.e4 ♕xe5).

After 18.♕b3, however, White can meet 18...♕xe5 with 19.♗b2. Now 18...♘c3 doesn't seem to work because, after 19.♗xb7+ and 20.♕xc3, White can answer the terrible 20...♕f3 simply by castling. Right?

18...   ♘c3!

Wrong. Since this was a correspondence game, Black had the luxury of simply setting up the position after 21.♕xc3 on his board to search for a response, no matter how "quiet." A trained calculator should be able to do the same, since the first few moves are so forcing that the "false end position" after 21.♕xc3 is relatively easy to visualize.

19.♗xb7+   ♔xb7
20.a6+   ♔c8
21.♕xc3

There is no safety in 21.0-0 because of 21...♘e2+ 22.♔g2 h4, threatening 23...h3+ and mates.

21...   **♕f3!**

Here White played the meek **22.♗b2** and resigned a few moves after **22...♕xh1+ 23.♔e2 ♕d5.** But why didn't White just castle at move 22, covering both d1 and h1?

Because Black, to his credit, realized that just because there are no captures, checks, or mate-in-one threats after 21.♕xc3, it is not the end of the action. After 22...h4! there is no defense to 23...h3 and 24...♕g2# (23.♖e1 hxg3 24.fxg3 ♖xh2!). Even though White has an extra piece, a weakened enemy king position, and two free moves to do it, there is nothing to be done on the kingside or queenside.

Move Order

The other key element of variation processing is the order of moves. Suppose the tactical ideas you are working with include a pin of the queen and a knight fork. You can use one idea or both. But if both, which comes first?

After all, if you are working with forcing moves, you are often in a position to determine not only the matters being disputed at the board but also the sequence in which these matters come up for debate.

Let's begin with a simple tactical idea arising out of an old opening trap:

1.d4 d5 2.c4 c6 3.♘f3 ♘f6 4.♘c3 e6 5.e3 ♘bd7 6.♗d3 ♗d6 7.e4 dxe4 8.♘xe4 ♘xe4 9.♗xe4 0-0 10.0-0 e5? 11.dxe5 ♘xe5 12.♘xe5 ♗xe5

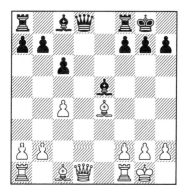

At first glance the position seems to defy a search for ideas. Everything of White's, except the c-pawn, is on an analogous square as Black's, but on the other side of the board. And everything of Black's, except the bishop on e5, is protected. How can anything be happening in such a quiet, symmetrical position?

The answer is that White has the only significant advantage here: It is his turn to move. Perhaps he can attack the bishop and also something else.

Asking yourself questions like that produces 1.♕h5. It threatens the bishop and also 2.♕xh7#. Is that decisive? No, because there is a defense that meets both threats: 1...f5!.

White should look further. Not further into 1.♕h5 f5, and not for different ideas. He should look for a different way of using the ♕h5 idea. There are only a few good ideas in a position, so you shouldn't reject them hastily.

Here White can revive the double attack on h7 and e5 by using a different order: 1.♗xh7+! ♔xh7 2.♕h5+ ♔g8 3.♕xe5. This order wins a pawn, not a piece as White hoped to do with 1.♕h5. But it has the advantage of being more forceful than the queen move. And that makes it work.

Now examine a slightly different version. Remove Black's f-pawn and put it on d4. We see that 1.♗xh7+ works here, too, but again only wins a pawn. The best move order now is 1.♕h5!, which wins (1...♕f6 loses outright to 2.♗xh7+! ♔h8 3.♗g6+ ♔g8 4.♕h7#, and 1...♖e8 allows 2.♗xh7+ ♔f8 3.♗g6 with decisive threats).

The difference between the right and the wrong order can be brutal as well as embarrassing:

PÉTURSSON – KORCHNOI
Wijk aan Zee 1990

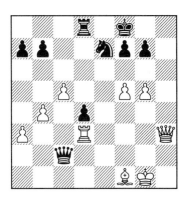

White to move

This occurred two moves before the time control, and if White had found the correct order, the game probably would not have lasted much longer. The two ideas in the position are the check on h8 and the advance of White's f-pawn (attacking the knight and cutting off the king's escape square). After 1.♕h8+ ♘g8 2.f6 gxf6 3.gxf6, Black loses at least a piece. But in time pressure:

1.f6?!   ♘g6!

White found nothing more than a draw after **2.♕h7? gxf6 3.gxf6 ♕c1.** But he missed two more wins: 4.♖g3! followed by ♖xg6! would have won and, earlier, so would 2.♖xd4!. The moral: If you get the move order right at first, you won't have embarrassments like these later on.

Move order can be a minefield, but it can also be an ally in unlocking the tactical secrets of a position.

KERES – SPASSKY
Göteborg 1955

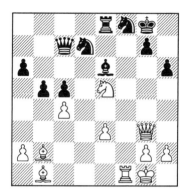

White to move

White has a wonderful game here, with two crisp bishops cutting through the air that leads to the kingside. The natural idea that suggests itself is an attack on g7, using the forcing nature of a mate threat. Black's minor pieces play no role in the defense of that square. Any move of White's knight would open the b2-g7 diagonal and threaten mate.

But each of those knight moves would also permit 1...♕xg3, squelching the threats. White might be able to extract an endgame edge with the *Zwischenzug* (in-between move) 1.♘xd7 ♕xg3 2.♘f6+, but 2...gxf6 3.hxg3 ♗xc4 is not at all clear.

But White knew his position deserved more than an endgame edge. And he didn't need to find a new idea:

1.♕xg7+!!   1-0

The main – in fact, the only real – variation is a nice one. It runs 1...♔xg7 2.♘xd7+ ♔g8 3.♘f6+ ♔f7 4.♘d5+, winning back the queen at the profit of a piece.

You can praise Paul Keres for his magnificent tactical vision, but, technically, all he did here was to re-order his moves – ♕xg7+ before ♘xd7, not after.

Differences in move order may determine whether a combination works or fails. Or it may mean that the superior order leads to a decisive result rather than just a significant advantage.

Sometimes we shortchange ourselves by taking in the wrong order:

SOKOLOV – STURUA
USSR Young Masters Tournament 1984

1.e4 e5 2.♘f3 ♘c6 3.♗b5 a6 4.♗a4 ♘f6 5.0-0 ♗e7 6.♖e1 b5 7.♗b3 d6 8.c3 0-0 9.h3 ♘b8 10.d4 ♘bd7 11.♘bd2 ♗b7 12.♗c2 ♖e8 13.♘f1 d5 14.♘xe5 ♘xe4?

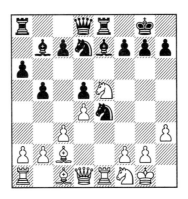

Here White played **15.♘xf7 ♔xf7 16.♖xe4.** Both of his moves were awarded exclamation points because of 16...dxe4 17.♗b3+ ♔f6 18.♕h5 g6 19.♕h6 and wins, or 17...♔g6 18.♕g4+ ♗g5 19.♘g3.

The problem with this bit of brilliance is that after 16.♖xe4 Black played **16...♘f6** and was able to put up stiff resistance before eventually conceding. Is there a better way, something that leads to more than just a pawn-up middlegame?

What takes some of the sting out of White's combination is that White played his most forceful move first and Black could ignore the less forceful 16th. Suppose we change matters a bit: first 15.♖xe4 dxe4 (on 15...♘xe5 16.♖xe5, White remains a knight ahead) and now 16.♘xf7.

Now the consequences of 16...♔xf7 are exactly the same as in the line 15.♘xf7 ♔xf7 16.♖xe4 dxe4 because we have transposed exactly. The difference is that the second sequence ends with 16.♘xf7, a move that attacks Black's queen. After a queen move, the addition of 17.♗b3 and a discovered check looks like it should be quickly decisive, e.g. 16...♕c8 17.♗b3 ♔f8 (else 18.♘d6+) 18.♕h5 ♘f6 19.♘g5!!.

But when you change the order, you usually change the opportunities for both sides. Black should have certain chances in the second order that he doesn't get in the first. If we look further we'll find them: After 16...♕b8! 17.♗b3 c5 White can regain his material, but no more. For example, 18.♗e6 ♘f8; or 18.♘e5+ c4 19.♘xd7 ♕c7; or 18.dxc5 ♘xc5 19.♘d6+ ♔h8!.

Conclusion? The order chosen by White was best.

Now let's examine a more sophisticated example, which further illustrates the double-edged sword of sequence. Here it spoils a golden opportunity for a little-known player to defeat a world champion.

GRIGORIAN – KARPOV
USSR Championship 1976

1.d4 d5 2.c4 e6 3.♘c3 ♗e7 4.♘f3 ♘f6 5.e3 0-0 6.b3 b6 7.♗b2 ♗b7 8.♗d3 c5 9.0-0 cxd4 10.exd4 ♘c6 11.♕e2 ♘b4 12.♗b1 dxc4 13.bxc4 ♗xf3 14.gxf3! ♕xd4 15.♘e4 ♕d8 16.♖d1 ♕c7 17.♘xf6+ ♗xf6

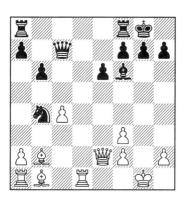

This position, arising out of a then-popular opening, had been endorsed by theoreticians but not really tested over the board. White has sacrificed one pawn, and the health of his other pawns, for a kingside attack. The ideas in the position include ♗xh7+, ♕e4, and ♗xf6, and even some supplementary help from ♔h1 followed by ♖g1+.

Okay, so much for the ideas. Time to start processing the variations. We might look first at the lines involving ♕e4. Suppose we break up the kingside with 18.♗xf6 gxf6 19.♕e4, how does Black protect h7? The obvious answer is 19...f5 and on 20.♕h4 he can stop the attack dead with 20...f6.

But is there a better way of using the ♕e4 idea – that is, a better move order? Yes, and it lies in the immediate 18.♕e4 since the ...f7-f5 defense is now impossible and 18...g6 allows 19.♗xf6 at a time when it wins the bishop.

Does this mean that 18.♕e4 wins outright? No, because a further examination shows that Black can just move his king rook, vacating f8 for his king. The position after 18...♖fd8 19.♕xh7+ ♔f8 is hard to evaluate: Material is now even, but White's pawns are still a mess and it's not clear whose king is in greater jeopardy.

White turns instead to a familiar idea. Remember Lasker–Bauer and Kuzmin–Sveshnikov from Chapter 2? Well, a relative of the two-bishop sacrifice lurks under the facade of this position. White played:

18.♗xf6　　　　gxf6
19.♗xh7+

Very nice. Now 19...♔xh7 20.♕e4+ ♔g7 21.♕g4+ and 22.♔h1! give White a crushing attack (e.g., 21...♔h8 22.♔h1 ♕c5 23.♕h4+ and 24.♖g1+). And on 19...♔h8 White plays 20.♗e4 ♖ad8 21.♔h1 with a very strong game.

19...　　　　♔g7!

This is what White overlooked. When examining the diagram position, he failed to see that the g7 square would be available. He continued the game desultorily with **20.♖d4 ♖h8 21.♖g4+ ♔f8 22.♕b2 ♖xh7 23.♕xb4+ ♕c5 24.♕d2 ♖c8** and lost not only his golden opportunity to upset a world champion, but the game as well (0-1, 40).

We might say that this was an error of visualization, like those we'll consider in Chapter 8. But here it was mainly a mistake of move order, because White could have avoided the ...♔g7 defense had he played the right sequence: 18.♗xh7+!, and if 18...♔xh7 then 19.♕e4+ and 20.♗xf6 (with ♕g4+ and ♔h1 as he had planned). Black would have to avoid this with the unpleasant 18...♔h8 or some other indifferent defense, leaving him with doubtful chances of survival.

Serendipity and Sequence

The juggling of move orders is a fine example of the serendipity at work that we saw in Chapter 3.

VYZHMANAVIN – NOVIKOV
USSR Championship 1990

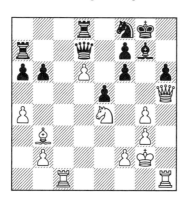

White to move

White toys with a few ideas in this position (1.♘xf6+ ♗xf6 2.♕xh6, and 1.♖c7 ♖xc7) and finds that neither seems to get anywhere. But what about 1.♕xf7+, he wonders.

Then on 1...♕xf7 2.♗xf7+ ♔xf7 White has 3.♖c7+ ♖xc7 4.dxc7 ♖-moves 5.♘d6+! and wins.

Unfortunately, there are several holes in this sequence. For one, Black need not capture on move 3 but can play 3...♖d7!. Furthermore, he can refute the combination very simply with 2...♖xf7!.

But the idea doesn't go away and White wonders about a different order. Try 1.♕xf7+ and 2.♖c7. Then 2...♖xc7 is answered by 3.dxc7 ♖-moves 4.♗xf7+ ♔xf7 5.♘d6+, or 3...♕xb3 4.cxd8♕.

Ah, but there's another flaw: 2...♕xb3!, leaving Black ahead a queen for a rook.

One last try and three is a charm: **1.♖c7!!** and now 1...♖xc7 2.♕xf7+! ♕xf7 3.dxc7 transposes into the most favorable of the previous lines.

In fact, after 1.♖c7, Black **resigned.** Another Soviet grandmaster later told the winner, "I looked at the position for ten minutes and couldn't understand what happens on 1...♖xc7."

Sometimes, of course, it doesn't matter whether you play A before B or B before A. But perhaps three times out of four you will find there is a significant difference. Here's another example of how juggling ideas and sequences allows a player to be brilliant.

HONFI – BÁRCZAY
Kecskemét 1977

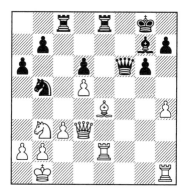

White to move

In this position White played **1.c4** to drive the knight back, at the risk of opening up the long diagonal that leads from f6 to b2.

Most masters shown Black's position would look first at 1...♘a3+. It meets the threat to the knight with a gain of time. The only problem is that 2.bxa3! is a simple refutation (because 2...♕a1+ allows 3.♘xa1!).

So Black tries to find a way to use the ...♘a3+ and ...♕xb2 ideas both. And there it is: **1...♖xc4! 2.♕xc4 ♕xb2+!!** and wins (3.♖xb2 ♘a3+ 4.♔-moves ♗xb2+ 5.♔xb2 ♘xc4+ and 6...♖xe4).

Orders and Options

In the last few pages we considered how changing the sequence of events can lead to distinctly different results. But what happens when it seems you can reach exactly the same end position by different routes? Which road do you take?

This is a crucial matter because, as noted earlier, each move order creates its own options for the opponent.

If it seems that your opponent will get those options anyway, you want to place them at the least dangerous point. Usually this means *before* you are fully committed. In other words, give him choices at the beginning, not the end.

BOEY – FILIP
European Team Championship 1972

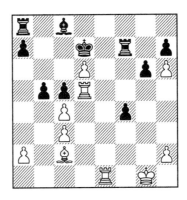

White to move

White has a temporarily dominant position but must act quickly before Black coordinates his forces with 1...♗b7 and a move of his a8-rook. There doesn't appear to be anything significant in 1.♖xc5 ♔xd6! 2.♖d5+ ♔c7 or in other semi-quiet lines.

As he calculates them, however, White sees that the unused resources in the position are his king and advanced hpawn. It takes too long to bring the king into significant action. But what about getting the h-pawn moving?

That can be done by 1.♖e7+, exchanging rooks, followed by ♗xg6. If Black then takes the bishop, White queens. (Do you see how?)

Think about the correct order of moves for a minute or two here before reading on.

The right way of doing things is:

1.♗xg6!   **hxg6**

2.♖e7+	**♖xe7**
3.dxe7+	**♚xe7**
4.♖d8!!	**1-0**

The sacrifice of the rook is necessary to queen since 4.h7 fails to 4...♗b7. After 4.♖d8, however, White will promote (4...♚xd8 5.h7, or 4...♗b7 5.♖xa8 ♗xa8 6.h7) and then sweep the board of black pawns.

But the key to this combination was not the pretty 4.♖d8; it was the order of the earlier moves. Why did White start with the bishop capture? The reason is that even though it is a sacrifice it is the least forcing move in the series.

The reason is that it is a bit less forcing than the rook check. After 1.♖e7+ ♖xe7 2.dxe7+ ♚xe7, White would then play 3.♗xg6 and after 3...hxg6? 4.♖d8!, we reach the game – the same end position.

However, in this order Black has plenty of other third moves, such as 3...♗e6 followed by ...♗xd5 or ...hxg6 or ...♖g8. Black has more choices in this order. Only 1.♗xg6 produces the optimum result.

The matter of force and sequence becomes even more important in defensive calculation:

GELLER – MATULOVIĆ
Skopje 1968

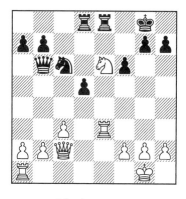

Black to move

White appears to stand better because of his more advanced knight and better pawns. But **1...d4!**, dissolving the weak d-pawn, should lead to a dead-even game. In fact, because it seizes the initiative (by making a forcing move) it also creates land mines for White to step into.

One of those mines is fairly obvious: 2.♘xd8? is clearly going to be answered by 2...dxe3. Then 3.♘xc6 is the only way to avoid the loss of a piece. Black would then have a choice between the most forceful 3... exf2+ or the equally promising recapture on c6, either of which leaves Black with better placed pieces.

White's real choice is between 2.cxd4 and 2.♘xd4. They lead to the same position after 2.cxd4 ♘xd4 3.♘xd4 ♕xd4 or 2.♘xd4 ♘xd4 3.cxd4 ♕xd4, with dead equality. So the exact calculator seeks the one that allows his opponent the fewest alternatives. A strong grandmaster, White chose what he thought was the "most forceful." He chose 2.cxd4, perhaps because it retains the threat of 3.♘xd8 and averts such side lines as 2.♘xd4 ♖xe3!?.

But **2.cxd4??** allowed another possibility: **2...♖xe6! 3.♖xe6 ♘xd4!**, after which Black wins a piece in all variations (4.♕c4 ♘xe6; 4.♖xb6 ♘xc2).

One final example to show how difficult defensive calculation can be when your opponent is juggling several ideas:

VINSNES – KRASENKOW
Rilton Cup 1990

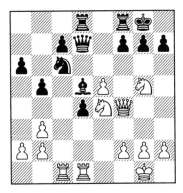

Black to move

Black appreciated that he was under pressure on both wings with several tactical ideas at work against him. Those ideas include (a) the knight sacrifice ♘f6+; (b) the attack on h7 or a knight sacrifice there; and (c) the elimination of a key defensive piece, the black knight, by way of the exchange sacrifice ♖xc6.

With all that in mind, Black examined a few key variations and, finding them harmless, played:

1...   ♕e7?

This attacks the e-pawn, which can only be defended by the humble retreat 2.♘f3. Black understood that he was allowing 2.♕f5 but saw that 2...♗xe4! 3.♘xe4 ♕xe5! and 3.♕xe4 ♕xg5 4.♖xc6 ♕h5 was nothing to fear.

He was chiefly concerned, however, with several different move orders employing the ideas mentioned above. The first is 2.♘f6+ gxf6 and now 3.exf6 is easily met by 3...♕e5! (4.♕h4 ♕f5).

White can prevent that queen centralization by the different sacrificial order 2.♖xc6 ♗xc6 3.♘f6+ gxf6 – still forced – 4.exf6. But then 4...♕e2! saves the day. (Note that it was White's first move that created a new opportunity for Black: White's rook is hanging at move 5.)

So Black examined yet another sequence: 2.♘f6+ gxf6 and now 3.♘xh7 with the threat of 4.♘xf6+ and the idea of meeting 3...♔xh7 with 4.♖d3 and 4.♖h3+. But this can be met by 3...♘xe5! and then 4.♘xf6+ ♔g7 5.♘h5+ ♔g6!.

As much as he shuffled the moves around, Black saw no explicit danger. Unfortunately, he missed the one move order that punishes him:

2.♖xc6!   ♗xc6
3.♘f6+   gxf6

On 3...♔h8, White wins with 4.♘gxh7!.

4.♘xh7!!

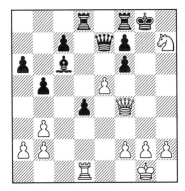

This is the sequence of ideas that eluded Black. Now 4...fxe5 allows
5.♘f6+ ♕xf6 6.♕xf6 with a won endgame.

4...	♔xh7
5.♕h4+	♔g7
6.♕g4+	♔h8
7.♖d3	♗e4

Last hope (8.♕xe4?? f5!?).

8.♖h3+	♗h7
9.♕f5	1-0

Bailout

One of the special tricks of calculation technique is being aware of
escape routes that appear in the tree of analysis. These enable a player to
bail out of a long variation before the end position. For example:

WIRTHENSOHN – HÜBNER

Swiss Championship 1991

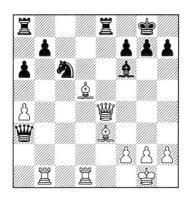

White to move

Black's last move, ...鼉fe8, sets all sort of alarms for White. It is, of course, a forcing move that attacks the white queen. But it invites the question: "What squares lose protection as a result?"

The pertinent answer is f7. Being an aware calculator, White examined **1.♗xf7+! ♚xf7** and the natural follow-ups 2.♖xb7+, 2.♕c4+, and 2.♕d5+. He eventually found that **2.♕c4+!** was best, since 2...♚f8 3.♗c5+ is bad for Black and 2...♖e6 allows 3.♖xb7+ ♘e7 4.♗c5 ♕c3 5.♖xe7+! or 3...♗e7 4.♗c5.

So White could be fairly certain that after beginning the combination with 1.♗xf7+, he would face a position with **2...♚g6!**. Is there anything clear after that? White wasn't sure. He played the bishop sacrifice anyway, because he had spotted a bailout: After 2...♚g6, he could repeat the position with 3.♕g4+ ♚f7 (obviously forced) 4.♕c4+! ♚g6.

And if he couldn't find anything to be confident about after that, White knew he could just repeat the position again and claim a draw. (In fact, there is a very good continuation: 3.♖b3! ♕e7 4.♕g4 + with excellent winning chances, e.g. 4...♚f7 5.♖d7 or 4...♗g5 5.h4 h5 6.♕g3!).

Of course, even with a bailout opportunity you must calculate the consequences of the main line accurately if you decide to go into it. Here is a similar example:

LJUBOJEVIĆ – SMYSLOV
Petrópolis 1973

1.e4 c6 2.d4 d5 3.exd5 cxd5 4.c4 ♘f6 5.♘c3 e6 6.♘f3 ♗e7 7.♗f4 dxc4 8.♗xe4 0-0 9.0-0 ♘c6 10.♖c1 a6 11.a3 b5 12.♗a2 ♗b7 13.d5!? exd5 14.♘xd5 ♘xd5 15.♗xd5 ♖c8 16.♖e1 ♗f6! 17.♗d6! ♖e8

Clearly 17...♕xd6?? 18.♗xf7+ was impossible. White now studied the position at some length and played **18.♗xf7+?! ♔xf7 19.♕d5+ ♔g6.**

He has a draw, if he wants it, with 20.♕d3+. The **key line is 20...♔h6 21.♖xe8 ♕xe8 22.♕f5 ♘e5 23.♕f4+ g6! 24.♕xf6 ♕g6.**

But White refused the bailout and went in for **20.♖xe8? ♕xe8 21.♕d3+ ♔f7 22.♖e1,** hoping to bring the rook decisively into play.

However, he was lost soon after **22...♘e7!** (23.♕b3+ ♗d5 24.♖xe7+ ♕xe7 25.♕xd5+ ♕e6; or 23.♗xe7 ♗xe7 24.♘e5+ ♔g8 25.♕b3+ ♔f8 26.♕e6 ♖c7; or 23.h4 ♕d8).

Bailouts do not always lead to forced draws, of course. Sometimes when you're midway through the tree leading to a major advantage, you realize there's a major flaw in your analysis and you have to bail out with only an equal position. So be it.

Usually, bailouts occur in forcing lines.

GIPSLIS – VAN WELY

Gausdal 1992

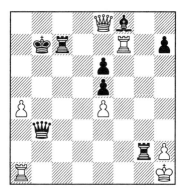

White to move

Here White, with the initiative, has just delivered a rook check at f7 and Black found the only reply, ...♖c7. What next?

White, an experienced grandmaster, makes a remarkably naive move, **1.♔xg2??**. It lacks any forcing power whatsoever and permits Black a myriad of checks. Black found 1...♕c2+ and suddenly White saw that 2.♔g3 ♕d3+ 3.♖f3 allows 3...♖g7+ and wins. The game continued **2.♔h3 ♕d3+ 3.♔h4 ♕xe4+ 4.♔h3 ♕e3+ 5.♔g2 ♕d2+! 6.♔g3 ♕g5+ 7.♔h3 ♕h5+ 8.♔g3**, and now **8... ♕g6+!** with 9...♖xf7 wins, although 10.♖b1+! still puts up some resistance.

What should White have done? He should have examined 1.♖xc7+ ♔xc7 2.♕f7+!. He could have seen that 2...♔b6 now allows 3.♔xg2 when 3...♕b2+ can be met by 4.♕f2 + and White wins.

But the main reason White should have played the 2.♕f7+ line is that on 2...♔c6, the only other reasonable alternative, White could assure himself of at least a perpetual check with 3.♕e8+. With this bailout option he could have guaranteed the same result (a draw) as his best chance after 1.♔xg2??.

In fact, after 2...♔c6 White does not have to bail out but can continue the game with 3.♔xg2, after which he has some winning chances following 3...♕b2+ 4.♔h3 ♕c3+ 5.♔h4 ♕xa1 6.♕xf8.

Calculating in Stages

One of the most widely reprinted gems of calculation in chess history was a combination played by a future world champion, Mikhail Botvinnik, against a past one, José Capablanca.

BOTVINNIK – CAPABLANCA
AVRO 1938

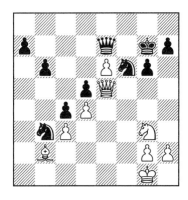

White to move

White began a 12-move combination that ran **1.♗a3! ♕xa3 2.♘h5+! gxh5 3.♕g5+ ♔f8 4.♕xf6+ ♔g8 5.e7!.** In the face of unstoppable mate, Black ran out of checks after **5...♕c1+ 6.♔f2 ♕c2+ 7.♔g3 ♕d3+ 8.♔h4 ♕e4+ 9.♔xh5 ♕e2+ 10.♔h4 ♕e4+ 11.g4! ♕e1+ 12.♔h5 1-0.**

But it wasn't until more than forty years later that Botvinnik revealed that he hadn't seen 12 moves ahead.

"I must admit that I could not calculate it right to the end and operated in two stages," he wrote. First he saw as far as 5.e7 and figured out that Black had no more than a perpetual check. That meant he could safely play the first stage (up to 6.♔f2) without risk of losing. Once that position arose on the board, he was able to find the white king's method of escape from checks.

Calculating in stages is a method of breaking down the unfathomable into bite-size chunks of analysis. A more recent example:

NUNN – FEDOROWICZ
Wijk aan Zee 1991

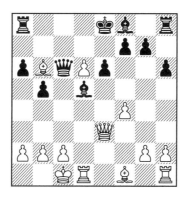

White to move

Here White saw the idea of exploiting the long diagonal with ♗e2 and ♖xd5, since ...exd5 is then illegal and ...♕xd5 allows ♗f3!, skewering Black's queen and rook. But the direct route, 1.♗e2 threatening 2.♖xd5, fails to 1...♖c8, forcing White to defend c2.

So White considered, and eventually played, a different order, which allows him a couple of bailouts. The first stage went:

**1.♖xd5!   ♕xd5
2.♗e2**

Now most moves lose quickly to 3.♗f3 or 3.♖d1. For example, 2...♕xd6 3.♖d1 ♕e7 4.♕c3! with 5.♕c6+ threatened; or 3...♕b4 4.♕f3 ♖c8 5.♕b7; or 3...♕b8 4.♗f3 ♗e7 5.♗c6+ ♔f8 6.♖d7, etc.

$$2... \qquad \text{♛xa2}$$

At this point, the end of the first stage, White can begin to calculate again, having foreseen that 3.♕c5 is good enough to lead to a favorable endgame (3...♕d5 4.♖d1! ♗xd6 5.♕xd6).

$$\textbf{3.♕f3!}$$

This begins a second stage. Key variations run 3...♖c8 4.d7+! ♔xd7 5.♕b7+ and 3...♕d5 4.d7+ ♔e7 5.♖d1 ♕xf3 6.d8♕+.

$$\textbf{3...} \qquad \textbf{♗xd6!}$$
$$\textbf{4.♕xa8+} \qquad \textbf{♔e7}$$

White need not have calculated this far, but if he did he could pause again before starting the third stage. One natural, but faulty, continuation is 5.♕xh8?? ♗xf4+ and mates.

Instead, White found **5.♕b7+ ♔f8 6.♗c5,** and if 6...♗xc5, then 7.♕c8+ picks up the bishop with check. The game actually ended with **6...♕a1+ 7.♔d2 ♕xh1 8.♕b8+ 1-0.**

As we've seen in this chapter, there are many intermediary steps the careful calculator performs before making his move. Some merely confirm the correctness of his tree of analysis (the bottom line, is it over?) while others (move order, bailout, calculating in stages) may simplify the process of calculating.

Chapter 6

CHOICE

"Half the variations which are calculated in a tournament game turn out to be completely superfluous. Unfortunately, no one knows in advance which half."

—Jan Timman

In an obvious sense, all chess moves are a matter of choice. But there are often critical points in a game in which you must choose between two or more moves that on first examination appear equally good. This is often true even when dealing with relatively simple, forcing positions.

LJUBOJEVIĆ – SZABÓ
Hilversum 1973

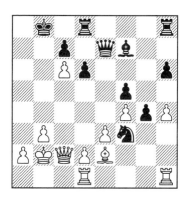

White to move

One idea stands out here: White should try somehow to get his queen to the mating square b7, probably via a check along the b file. White pursued this with:

1.♕c3   d5!

Now White saw that his intended 2.♕b4+ was stopped and that the alternative idea 2.♕a5 and 3.♕a6 allows the defense 2...♕f6+ and 3...♕xc6.

2.♖c1

Protecting the c-pawn and renewing the ♕a5-b5+ threat.

2...   d4!
3.♕a5   ♖d5

And Black has seized the initiative. After the game, White made a great effort to prove he had missed a win – and eventually he succeeded. But even if you know there is a simple win in the diagram, it's not so easy to find. Black claimed that after the game he asked 50 spectators their opinions of the position, and that all agreed 1.♕c3 was best. "Then I understood why Ljubojević found his move so natural!" he concluded.

Natural, but quite inferior to 1.♕d3!, which either mates immediately or avoids mate at the cost of the queen.

What happened was that White failed to appreciate that he had a choice. This is one of the many problems that arise in a game when we are faced with two or more equally attractive ideas.

More often when we make a bad choice it happens in a position that has C-H-O-I-C-E written all over it in capital letters. Then there is often a right move and a wrong move, or sometimes a good move and a better move. (And, sadly, in some positions only a bad move and a worse move.)

The worst mistake when confronted with a choice is to believe it doesn't make any difference which path is taken.

HAUCHARD – SHIROV
Santiago 1990

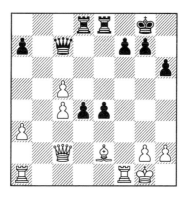

White to move

It used to be axiomatic for annotators to criticize that most common of choice errors with the words, "Wrong rook!" Here is a typical example.

White should play a rook to d1 so he can return his extra piece and eliminate the two terrible passed pawns when Black plays ...d4-d3. But which rook?

Not seeing any particular difference, White made the commonsense choice, activating his unused a1-rook and leaving his other rook on its half-open file. Yet that is a blunder.

> 1.♖ad1? ♕xc5
> 2.♔h1

Much better is 2.♗g4 d3 3.♕f2. (Black could have avoided this with 1...d3! 2.♗xd3 exd3 3.♖xd3 ♕xc5+ 4.♔h1 ♕f5!.)

> 2...   d3

3.♗xd3   exd3

If White had played 1.♖fd1!, he could now continue 4.♖xd3 and have some survival chances. But here 4.♖xd3 loses outright to 4...♕f5!!. There was a difference in rook moves in the diagram. (White ended up playing 4.♕c3 and lost after 4...♖e3!.)

Another case in point:

LJUBOJEVIĆ – LARSEN
Las Palmas 1974

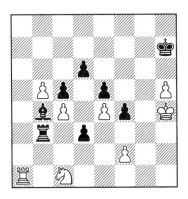

Black to move

White has just retreated his knight from e2. Both players have dangerous passed pawns, but Black has to spend a tempo to move his attacked rook before he can push his d-pawn.

Seeing little difference between the various rook moves, Black continued:

1...   ♖c3?
2.♘xd3!   ♖xd3
3.♔g5

White takes his time but knows that he is winning, with 4.♖a7+ or 4.b6. The immediate 3.b6 allows 3...♖b3 and 4...♗-moves.

3...	♗a3
4.b6	

4.♖b1! wins right away.

4...	♖b3
5.b7	♖xb7
6.♖xa3	

And White won the rook ending without further incident. But, going back to the diagram, we can see that there is a significant choice to be made. And once we see that, we are closer to finding that 1...♖a3! turns a loss into a win (2.♖xa3 d2!).

(White can make it a bit harder with 2.b6! d2 3.b7 d1♕ 4.b8♕ – but not 4.♖xa3 ♔h6! – 4...♕h1+ 5.♔g5, although after 5...♕g2+ he must lose.)

The loser in that game, Bent Larsen, once said that when mentally examining a sequence – that is, without looking at a board – you often don't actually "see" a position in your mind until you have to make a choice.

Visualization of a sequence, he added, is not a case of watching a "moving picture" that advances one frame at a time. In most calculating, you make moves quickly in your mind without trying to picture the entire board. "Then, maybe you stop after a few moves in a critical line, since now there's a choice. And then maybe you 'see' the position."

In other words, choice becomes a stop sign.

MARSHALL – RUBINSTEIN
Bad Kissingen 1928

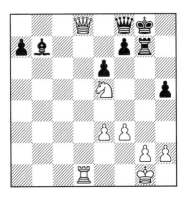

White to move

White is confronted with a broad but pleasant choice. He can offer to play an endgame, or force one (with 1.♖d7 or 1.♕xf8+). Or he can threaten to win with a queen move that prepares 2.♖d8, such as 1.♕a5, 1.♕f6, or 1.♕h4.

The ♖d8 idea seems the most natural, but which is the proper queen move? Each seems to have its pluses and minuses. For example, 1.♕a5 has the added benefit of threatening the a-pawn. And with 1.♕h4 White threatens the h-pawn as well as ♘d7-f6+ (e.g., 1...f6 2.♘d7; or 1...♗d5 2.♘d7).

White chose **1.♕f6?!.** But after **1...♕c5!** he lost his way. White would be mated after 2.♖d8+ ♔h7 3.♘xf7? ♕xe3+. (He had to reverse the order with 2.♘xf7 ♕xe3+ 3.♔h1, because then 3...♗d5 favors him after 4.♘h6+ ♔h7 5.♘f5!.)

In the game, White continued **2.♕d8+.** But Black avoided the repetition of the position with **2...♔h7! 3.♕d3+ f5** and soon had a winning superiority: **4.♘d7 ♕e7 5.e4** (5.♘e5!=) **5...fxe4 6.fxe4** (6.♕b5 and Black is only slightly better) **6...♗c6! 7.e5+ ♔h8 8.♘f6 ♕c5+ 9.♕d4 ♖xg2+,** etc.

What goes into making a choice? If we could count on 100% accuracy in our calculations, we'd naturally choose the line that leads to the greatest advantage.

But in the real world, we can't rely on such certainty. More often we're faced with situations like this:

ROGERS – SHIROV
Groningen 1990

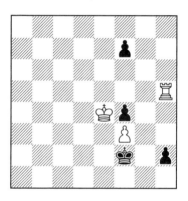

Black to move

Black saw two apparently equivalent methods of clinching the draw. The more elaborate way is 1...♔g3!, a classy waiting move that forces White to remove one of his well-placed pieces. After 2.♖h8, for example, Black has 2...f5+! 3.♔xf5 ♔xf3 4.♖xh2 ♔g3 and 5...f3, with a certain draw.

But that's a lot of calculating, and it leaves White with considerable options. After the game, Black explained that he wanted something "simpler," something with a shorter tree and a more clear-cut end position. So, even with plenty of time on his clock he chose:

1...	♔g2??
2.♔xf4	h1♕
3.♖xh1	♔xh1

4.♔g3!

Now it was easier to calculate variations, but unfortunately for Black there was only one. It goes 4...♔g1 5.f4! ♔f1 6.f5! (not 6.♔f3 f5! 7.♔e3 ♔g2) 6...♔e2 7.♔f4 ♔d3 (7...f6 8.♔e4 ♔f2 9.♔d5) 8.♔e5 ♔e3 9.f6! and Black, with his king sealed off, cannot avoid the loss of his pawn and the game.

In that example, seeking the "simpler" and faster option did Black in. But in other situations, the temptation to play something more forceful turns out to be fatal.

V. CHEKHOV – AZMAIPARASHVILI
USSR Team Championship 1981

1.d4 d5 2.c4 e6 3.♘c3 ♗e7 4.♘f3 ♘f6 5.♗f4 0-0 6.e3 c5 7.dxc5 ♗xc5 8.♕c2 ♘c6 9.♖d1 ♕a5 10.a3 ♘e4? 11.cxd5 exd5 12.♖xd5 ♘xc3 13.bxc3 ♕xa3 14.♘g5! g6 15.♗c4 ♗f5 16.♖xf5!

This sacrifice can be made quickly by calculating in general terms – if you are confident of your evaluation skills. White can say to himself, "For the price of the exchange I destroy his king position, pick up the pawn at f5, and have a dangerous attack against h7." (Actually, if he calculates more precisely White may become discouraged by realizing that 16...gxf5 17.♕xf5 fails to 17...♕xc3+.)

16...	**gxf5**
17.0-0	**♘e7**
18.♗e5!	**♗d6**

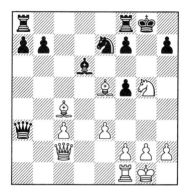

Stop sign. White must choose between retaining his bishop – 19.♗d4 and if 19...♗c5 then 20.♗f6 – and going for the immediate kill with 19.♕e2 and 20.♕h5. Exchanging on d6 and then 20.♕e2 and 21.♕h5 is not a serious option because Black's queen can then defend the kingside easily.

In light of what happens, it would be easy to explain that White did not examine 19.♗d4 sufficiently. Actually, he saw that it was a winning move, with variations such as 19.♗d4 ♕a5 20.♕e2 f4 (necessary, to defend h7) 21.♕h5 ♕f5 and now 22.♗d3! is strong.

19.♕e2

But he played this because it was "more convincing."

19...   ♗xe5
20.♕h5   ♔g7!

And this was the simple move he overlooked. White's error was in part visual – not seeing that the king could go to a square that in the diagram is covered by a bishop.

After **20...♔g7 21.♕xh7+ ♔h6,** White missed **22.♘xf7!** and allowed Black to survive in the endgame.

A third criterion, besides the forcefulness and length of a variation, is the clarity of its end position:

KORCHNOI – UDOVČIĆ
Leningrad 1967

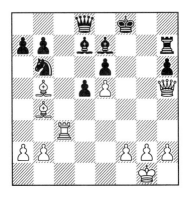

White to move

Having sacrificed a piece for a brutal attack, White has good reason to look for the knockout blow. But there is nothing to be gained from 1.♖f3+ ♔g8.

So White begins to weigh the alternatives, which are 1.♖g3, with ♕g6 and ♗d2xh6+ in mind, and the immediate 1.♕g6 with ♖f3+ or ♖g3 coming up. Both moves have their benefits, but only one leads to a win.

1.♕g6!

This is superior to 1.♖g3 ♗xb4! 2.♕g6 ♖f7! with a likely perpetual. White had expected 2...♕g5, after which he has a decisive material edge (3.♖xg5 hxg5 4.♕xh7 ♗xb5). But as the winner explained later, "I did not want to play with a queen against three enemy pieces."

After 1.♕g6, the only way to defend against both 2.♕xh7 and 2.♖f3+ is:

1...	♖g7
2.♕xh6	♗xb5?

$$3.\underline{\mathbb{Z}}g3 \qquad 1-0$$

Black should have played 2...♔g8 3.♖h3 ♔f7, but White still wins by trading off all four bishops and overpowering the king with his major pieces (4.♗xd7 ♕xd7 5.♗xe7 ♕xe7 6.♕h8! ♕g5 7.♖f3+ ♔e7 8.♕f8+ ♔d7 9.♕d6+).

Even though this variation is much longer than the 1.♖g3 alternative, it is much preferable because it actually wins.

Tactical vs. Technical vs. Positional

Sometimes choice is a matter of style. Two paths may lead to end positions of the same value but one way will be selected by tacticians, another by positionally oriented, or endgame oriented, players.

Aron Nimzowitsch is remembered today chiefly for his imaginative – and, by the standards of his day, bizarre – approach to strategy. But he was also a formidable tactician and calculator and had a fine grasp of pragmatic play. He explained his approach to making choices after his great tournament success at Karlsbad 1929.

NIMZOWITSCH – TARTAKOWER
Karlsbad 1929

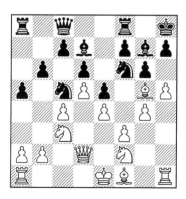

Black to move

White threatens the win of a piece with h5-h6, as well as the dangerous opening of the h-file. Black responded:

1... gxh5

And Nimzowitsch began to calculate. He saw quickly that, with 2.♗xf6 ♗xf6 3.♕h6, his threats of 4.♕xf6+ and 4.♕xh5 and 5.♕xh7# would force 3...♗g7 4.♕xh5 h6.

Then the natural way of continuing the attack would be 5.g5. He concluded that that would be strong enough to force Black to play 5...f5!. And that created a stop sign for Nimzowitsch.

He realized there would then be a perfectly good positional plan of 6.gxf6 followed by ♗f1-h3xd7 and the exploitation of the light squares. Or he could win material and continue the mating attack with 6.gxh6.

"All this is extremely complicated," Nimzowitsch wrote, "and therefore I played after no longer than five minutes' thought **2.♗xf6 ♗xf6 3.♖xh5 ♗g7 4.♘h1!**." This required very little calculation and ensured a big positional edge once the knight reached h5.

White's practical approach paid off, as he won soon after **4...f6 5.♕h2 h6 6.♘g3 ♔h7 7.♗e2 ♖g8 8.♔f2** followed by ♖g1 and ♘h5.

In the next, much more elaborate example, White also believes he is close to a win and begins to calculate in greater depth:

DOLMATOV – LERNER
Tashkent 1983

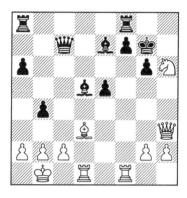

White to move

| 1.♘f5+! | gxf5 |
| 2.♕g3+! | |

The choice between this and 2.♗xf5 ♖h8! 3.♕g3+ ♔f8 or 2.♕xf5 ♖h8 was not difficult to make. Black's next move is forced, since here 2...♔h8 allows 3.♖xf5! and a quick mate.

| 2... | ♔h6 |

Clearly, White must take on f5 now or very soon. But how? There are two winning lines here, and as White put it afterward, one is for tacticians and the other for pragmatists.

Pragmatists might choose 3.♗xf5 with threats of 4.♖xd5 and 4.♕h3+. Then the defensive try 3...♗xa2+ 4.♔xa2 ♕c4+ 5.♔b1 ♕h4 covers several key kingside squares. But if you visualize that position well, it's not hard to see that White then wins with 6.♖d6+! (6...♗xd6 7.♕xh4).

Therefore, Black has to vary his move order with 3...♕c4, after which 4.♕h3+ ♕h4 5.♕xh4+ ♗xh4 6.♖xd5 leaves White with a pawn-up endgame. The win then is almost a technical matter but it is fairly certain (6...f6 7.♖d7 or 6...♗f6 7.♖d6 ♔g7 8.♗e4, etc.).

Bottom line: With best play, 3.♗xf5 leads to a certifiable win that will require several more moves of work.

Tacticians, on the other hand, may prefer a shorter road to victory. It requires a series of forcing moves beginning with 3.♖xf5, which threatens ♕h3+, ♕g4+, and ♖h5#. Black needs a flight square and the best way to make one is 3...♖g8.

Then 4.♖h5+! is the only way to keep the initiative, but with a bit of hard calculating the win can be found: 4...♔xh5 5.♕h3+ ♔g5 (not 5...♗h4 6.♕f5+ ♗g5 7.g4+ ♔h4 8.♕h7+ ♔xg4 9.♖g1+, etc.), and now 6.♕f5+ ♔h6 7.♕h7+ ♔g5:

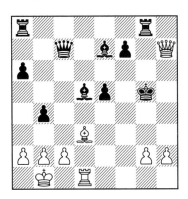

Position after 7...♔g5 (analysis)

With the king lured up to its fourth rank, White can close off the escape routes with 8.♖f1!, e.g. 8...♗e6 9.h4+ ♔g4 10.♕e4+ ♔h5 11.g4+! ♔xh4 12.♕h1+ and mate in a few moves.

"Unfortunately," White recalled, "there just wasn't enough time to allow the calculation of all this." So he played a third line, which appeared to be an improvement on the first line.

3.♕h3+?!   ♔g7

4.♗xf5

Now 4...♕c4 does nothing to block the kingside threats. However, with a change in move order Black gets a superior version of the pragmatists' line above.

4...	♗xa2+!
5.♔xa2	♕c4+
6.♔b1	♕h4
7.♕e3	♖ad8

Black prevents the ♖f3-g3 knockout and prolongs the game quite a bit. White managed to find the only winning plan now (8.♕xe5+ ♗f6 9.♕c7 ♖xd1+ 10.♖xd1 ♕f2 11.♗e6!) and eventually won the endgame. But he had chosen the last and least of the three winning paths.

Defensive Choice

In calculation we have to recognize stop signs both in our own forcing lines and in our opponent's. Failure to recognize such stop signs even occurs in prepared opening analysis, as in this curious case:

HÜBNER – KORCHNOI
Interpolis 1987

1.e4 e5 2.♘f3 ♘c6 3.♗b5 a6 4.♗a4 ♘f6 5.0-0 ♘xe4 6.d4 b5 7.♗b3 d5 8.dxe5 ♗e6 9.♘bd2 ♘c5 10.c3 ♗e7 11.♗c2 ♗g4 12.♖e1 ♕d7 13.♘f1 ♖d8 14.♘e3 ♗h5 15.♘f5 0-0 16.♘xe7+ ♘xe7 17.b4 ♘a4

Black had examined this opening in some detail before the game and, as one of the world's foremost tacticians, considered the tempting candidate move of a bishop sacrifice on h7.

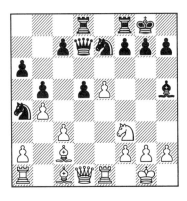

18.♗xh7+!   ♔xh7
19.e6

Now when he saw the position appear on the board, Black rechecked his previous analysis. Clearly, 19...fxe6 is bad because of 20.♘g5+ ♔g8 21.♕xh5 or 20...♔g6 21.g4, with a winning position in either case.

Black's intention when analyzing the position at home was to insert the *Zwischenzug* 19...♗xf3. Then 20.♕xf3 would allow him to play 20...fxe6 safely, with a fine game.

The crucial line occurs, of course, when White answers 19...♗xf3 with something more forceful, and that's why Korchnoi planned on 20.♕c2+ ♗e4 21.♖xe4 and now 21...fxe6!. Despite the availability of any number of discovered checks, Black's position is safe and quite sound.

But while studying the position for 50 minutes at the board, Black suddenly realized that White has a choice at move 20. He could play 20.♕d3+! instead of 20.♕c2+, with the significant difference that 20...♗e4 allows 21.♕h3+, followed by winning the queen. So...

19...   1-0

It's tempting to head into variations in which your opponent has the least choice. But, as we should know by now, this is a double-edged sword.

KUPREICHIK – SVESHNIKOV
Kuibyshev 1986

1.e4 c5 2.♘f3 ♘c6 3.♘c3 e5 4.♗c4 ♗e7 5.d3 ♘f6 6.♘g5 0-0 7.f4 exf4 8.♗xf4 d6 9.0-0 h6 10.♘f3 ♗e6 11.♕d2 d5 12.exd5 ♘xd5 13.♗xd5 ♗xd5 14.♗xh6!? gxh6 15.♕xh6

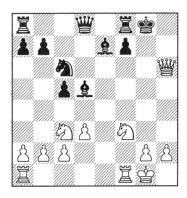

White has two pawns for his sacrificed bishop, but no immediate threats. A rook lift to g3 or h3 would be a dangerous threat, but it is at least three moves away. Black therefore has a broad choice, chiefly centering either on a forceful defense eliminating possible attacking pieces (15...♘d4) or on the slower addition of more defensive pieces (15...♗e6 and 16... ♗f5).

In fact, in the postmortem analysis, Black was winning most of the variations that continued with 15...♗e6, e.g. 16.♘e4 ♗f5 17.♘fg5 ♗xe4 18.♘xe4 ♕d4+ 19.♔h1 ♕g7, and so forth.

15...	♘d4?
16.♘xd4	♗g5

Black intended this *Zwischenzug* rather than 16...cxd4 17.♘xd5 ♕xd5 because then White has time for ♖f3-g3+.

17.♕h5	**cxd4**
18.♘xd5	**♕xd5**

It never occurred to Black that there would be a significant choice here. After all, he is the one doing the threatening (with 19...♗e3+, winning the queen). The quiet 19.♔h1 would allow an easy defense with 19...♔g7 and 20...♖h8.

19.♖f4!!

Now Black is virtually lost. On 19...f6 there follows 20.♕g6+ and ♖f3-h3#. Against **19...♖ae8 20.h4 ♖e5 21.hxg5 ♖xg5 22.♖g4!** (the game continuation) Black collapsed quickly: **22...f6 23.♖f1 ♔g7 24.♖xf6! ♔xf6 25.♕h6+ ♔e7 26.♖xg5 1-0.**

Summing up, we should remember certain basic rules of choice.

1) Choices exist in every position, and if we don't look for alternatives we're shortchanging ourselves.

2) There are pluses and minuses to each alternative, and it is the calculator's task to recognize and weigh them.

3) There is no single criterion for making a choice. The criteria may be tactical, practical, technical, or any number of others.

4) Our opponents get to make choices, too, and we should try to limit them.

Finally, a bit of serendipity: In studying our opponent's options we sometimes develop new ideas for ourselves. But in doing so we also create new options for our opponent:

MECKING – O. RODRÍGUEZ
Las Palmas 1975

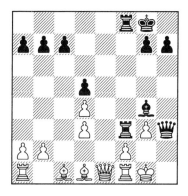

Black to move

Black has sacrificed a bishop for a kingside attack that has reached its apex. If there is going to be a time for hard calculation, it is now. Unfortunately for him, the direct mating ideas, such as 1...♖xg3+ and 1...♖8f5, don't work. (In the latter case, White simply answers 1...♖8f5 with 2.♕e8+.)

Black therefore studied the only other violent try in the position, 1...♖xf2. He saw that 2.♖xf2 ♕xg3+ 3.♔f1 ♗h3+ was strong for him (4.♔e2 ♖e8+ 5.♔d2 ♖xe1 6.♔xe1 ♕g1+ 7.♔e2 ♗g4+).

Therefore, he needed to correctly evaluate the consequences of the defensive queen sacrifice 2.♕xf2! ♖xf2 3.♔xf2 ♕h2+ 4.♔e3. He saw that 4...♕h6+ was a sure draw and that 4...♕xg3+ 5.♗f3 ♗xf3! 6.♖xf3 ♕e1+ 7.♔f4 h6, followed by advancing the kingside pawns, was a winning try.

But as he studied the situation, Black concluded that White could not strengthen his position. For example, ♗xf3 allows ...♗xf3 and mate on g2. So he figured his choice was between 1...♖xf2 and some other move that improves the position for ...♖xf2 on the following move.

1...	h5??

2.♗g5!

With this, White not only stops 2...h4 but also prepares to seal off the kingside with 3 ♗h4. Black now has no choice but to capture on f2. Yet he finds that White's last move has made a major difference.

2...	♖xf2
3.♕xf2	♖xf2
4.♖xf2!	

And White consolidated smoothly since Black, without control of h4, lacks a perpetual check. The game ended with **4...♕xg3+ 5.♔g2 ♕e1+ 6.♔h2 ♗xd1 7.♖d2! 1-0.**

Resignation was a bit premature, but the outcome is fairly certain after 7...h4 8.♗f4 g5 9.♗e5 g4 10.♖axd1 g3+ 11.♔h3, because White's king is safe and his pieces are ready to overwhelm the queen.

What is striking about this example is that Black failed to see the most significant differences between (a) the immediate 1...♖xf2 and (b) the preparatory 1...h5. Had he done so, he would have found (c) 1...h6!, which would have won quickly. By creating *Luft* – while not allowing 2.♗g5 – Black creates the powerful threat of 2...♖8f5 and 3...♖h5, as well as an improved version of the ...♖xf2 idea.

Clearly, there are a lot of ways to miscalculate, and in the next two chapters we'll take a closer look at them.

Chapter 7

MONKEY WRENCHES

"Nothing is more disturbing than the upsetting of a preconceived idea."

–Joseph Conrad

We can think of calculated variations as if they were mechanical devices, with elaborate systems of connecting parts (sub-variations), with demands for fuel and energy (material and force), and with stop-and-start controls and the like. But any mechanism can be thrown out of kilter by a monkey wrench. This chapter deals with the monkey wrenches.

The most common ones are:

a) Assumption
b) Quiet move
c) Destruction of the guard
d) *Zwischenzug* (in-between move)
e) Attack-defense
f) Desperado

Assumption

It is impossible to calculate well without making certain assumptions. A master will think to himself, "I go there and he must reply such-and-such. Then I play the rook check and he must go to the e-file. Then I play such-and-such and I win a piece." Those "musts" are his assumptions.

When you begin to recheck variations, it is essential to firm up those assumptions, to make sure that the "musts" are really "musts" and not merely "most likelies."

An embarrassing case, which helped doom an elite GM's chances of becoming world champion, was this:

NISIPEANU – IVANCHUK
FIDE World Championship 1999

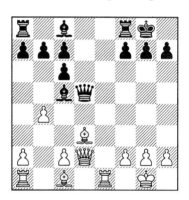

Black to move

Black played the astonishing **1...♗xf2+??**. Since Black would be winning after 2.♔h1 ♗xe1, he knew this was the decisive point in the game.

Yet he assumed White would play 2.♔xf2 and allow 2...♕d4+ followed by 3...♕xa1.

When White replied **2.♕xf2!** instead, he **resigned**.

A more elaborate, but also fatal, example of faulty assumption was:

BALCEROWSKI – KRANTZ
Stockholm 1966

1.d4 ♞f6 2.c4 g6 3.♞c3 ♝g7 4.e4 d6 5.f3 0-0 6.♝e3 e5 7.d5 c6 8.♛d2 cxd5 9.cxd5 a6 10.0-0-0 ♜e8 11.♚b1 ♞bd7 12.♞ge2 b5 13.♞c1 ♞b6 14.♝d3 ♝d7 15.g4 ♜b8 16.♝g5 ♞c4 17.♝xc4 bxc4 18.h4 ♜b7 19.h5 ♛c7 20.hxg6 hxg6 21.♝h6

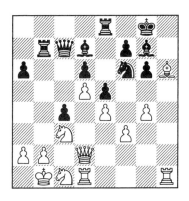

21...   ♜eb8?

Black decides against the cautious 21...♝h8 in favor of a combination. If White captures on g7 now, Black will give up his rooks for White's queen and b-pawn. Black's moves are all checks in this variation until he has time to retake on g7 (22.♝xg7 ♜xb2+ 23.♛xb2 ♜xb2+ 24.♚xb2 ♚xg7), so he has reason to have faith in his assumptions.

**22.♝xg7!   ♜xb2+
23.♚a1!!**

But Black is betrayed by those very assumptions. Now 23...♜xd2 24.♝xf6 sets up a mate on h8 that can be delayed but not avoided. And since 23...♚xg7 24.♛h6+ also leads to mate there, Black vainly played on with **23...♞h5 24.♛h6 f6 25.gxh5** and got mated after all: **25...♝e8 26.♛h8+ ♚f7 27.♛f8#.**

That was a fairly striking, but complex, example with a lot of pieces on the board. Yet very good players can make very bad errors of assumption with only a few legal possibilities to consider:

SPIELMANN – DURAS
Karlsbad 1907

White to move

Rudolf Spielmann, who ranked among the world's best players for three decades, gave this as an example of a "chess accident." The endgame would be drawn at virtually any level of skill. But in this particular encounter of grandmasters, White responded quickly to Black's checking move...

1.♖f4??

...because he wanted the game over quickly. He saw, of course, that 1...♖xf4+ 2.♔xf4 was a classic example of the opposition – and a book draw. But the game was over too quickly:

1...	**♔g5!**
0-1	

After 1.♖f4, how many moves for Black were there for White to consider? Basically, only three: (1) the exchange of rooks, (2) a lateral retreat, such as 1...♖a5, and (3) the winning reply.

It wasn't that White had misevaluated the forced result of 1...♔g5 (2.♖xf5+ ♔xf5). As a master he would have instantly known it was a win for Black. The reason White lost was that he didn't consider 1...♔g5 at all.

For a more recent example on a slightly busier board:

KARPOV – AGDESTEIN
Match (1) 1991

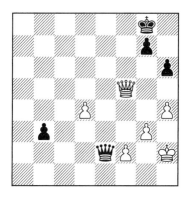

White to move

White has an extra pawn but Black has considerable compensation because his b-pawn is further advanced than White's d-pawn. White can see, quite plainly, that 1.♕d5+ and 2.♕xb3 leads to a hopeless draw (2...♕xf2+ and 3...♕xd4).

The mistake here is astonishing because it was made by the outstanding example in our time of a practical calculator. Knowing that he could force a draw, Anatoly Karpov rushed headlong into a variation that turned out to lose quickly. How did this happen?

1.d5??

It happened because White counted on Black's replying 1...b2. "After all," he might have asked himself, "what other useful move does Black have?" There would follow 2.d6 and now **either** 2...♕d1 3.d7 b1♕ 4.♕xb1 ♕xd7 or 2...b1♕ 3.♕xb1 ♕xf2+ 4.♔h3 leaves White with good technical chances of scoring a full point.

1...   ♕c2!

A relatively simple move, but the simplest of moves are often overlooked when we make false assumptions. Black now wins a tempo to advance his passer. The game ended with:

2.♕f3	b2
3.d6	b1♕
4.d7	♕bd1
5.♕a8+	♔g7
0-1	

Usually when we make a faulty assumption, it happens because we count on our forcing move's being met by an obedient reply (1...♖xf4+? in the Spielmann example, or 1...b2? in the Karpov case). This mental sloppiness occurs quite often when we give checks, the most forcing moves of all.

HODGSON – WOLFF
Preston 1989

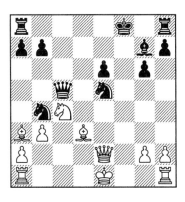

White to move

White is in serious trouble because of the double attack on his d3-bishop and because of the vulnerability of his a1-rook on an exposed diagonal. He could have searched for a tricky response such as 1.0-0-0! after which anything might happen (although after 1...b5! he appears to be lost). However, White saw a forcing line and played it.

1.♘xe5?   ♗xe5
2.♕f2 !

Neat: After the exchange of queens, Black's pinned knight hangs with check. Unfortunately...

2...   ♔g7!

And resignation was in order because 3.♕xc5 ♘xd3+ wins material. White actually played **3.♗c4** and resigned after **3...♕xf2+ 4.♔xf2 ♘c2 0-1.** As Grandmaster Eduard Gufeld once said of one of his own faulty assumptions, "I forgot that chess is not checkers – and captures are not obligatory!"

False assumption is one of the most serious dangers to a calculator because it carries with it more than just a heavy penalty on the board. There is also a *psychological* price to pay.

Once you realize you've made an assumption mistake, you start second-guessing yourself. And when you start doubting your assumptions, you are half-beaten. This doubting may linger into the next game, or for several games. Each time you begin to calculate you may feel yourself questioning your conclusions because you remember that mistaken assumption of the past.

At the board, suddenly realizing that you've made a wrong assumption can absolutely derail your train of thought.

ELISKASES – HENNEBERGER
Libverda 1934

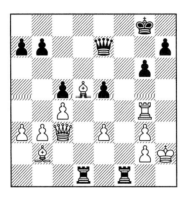

Black to move

Here White has a slight material edge but Black's connected rooks threaten mate on h1. White has allowed the rooks to penetrate because he calculated the effect of his last move, **1.♗d5+.**

Wherever the king moves, White can release the mate danger:
1) 1...♔h8?? 2.♕xe5+ and mates;
2) 1...♔g7 2.♕xe5+ ♕xe5 3.♗xe5+ ♔h6 (3...♔f8 4.♖f4+ trades a pair of rooks) 4.♖h4+ ♔g5 5.♗f4+ and 6.♔h3.
3) 1...♔f8 2.♖f4+! ♖xf4 (2...exf4 3.♕h8#) 3.exf4 and 4.♕xe5 must win.

All very neat. White must have been congratulating himself when:

1...   **♕f7!!**

Stunned, White quickly responded...

2.♗xf7+   **♔f8!**

...but now realized that the only way to avoid mate was to resign. In the postmortem he realized that his 2.♗xf7+?? was a blunder. If he had studied the position more fully he would have seen 2.♖xg6+!, which frees a square for his g-pawn (2...hxg6?? 3.♗xf7+ and 4.g4 wins) and forces 2...♔f8 3.g4 ♕xg6 4.♕xe5!, after which White's threats are so much greater than Black's that a draw would likely result.

Faulty assumption also occurs frequently with recaptures. As we noted in Chapter 4, captures, particularly of the more valuable pieces, are among the most forcing of moves. But there are severe limits to their power to compel:

YUSUPOV – SHORT
Barcelona 1989

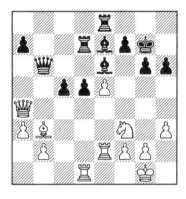

White to move

White's positional idea – the attack on d5 – has become a tactical idea because of the pin on Black's d7-rook. With that in mind, White continued:

1.♖xd5??

White is certain to escape with the pawn (or more) after 1...♗xd5 2.♕xd7 or 1...♖xd5 2.♗xd5 ♖d8 3.♗xe6 ♕xe6. He mistakenly assumes Black must take on d5 immediately.

1...   ♖ed8!

But here there was nothing to do but resign, as a piece is lost (2.♖xd7 ♗xd7 3.♕c4 ♗c6!).

And while we are usually more careful about wrong assumptions when we are doing the forcing, it is another matter entirely when performing defensive calculation.

DREEV – ANAND
Candidates' Match (1) 1991

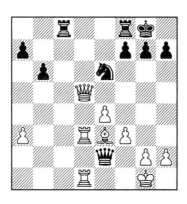

White to move

Black has just played ...♕e2, threatening 1...♖c2. White continued:

1.♕d6??

So that the queen can retreat to g3 and defend after 1...♖c2. "Of course, if Black puts a rook on d8 I can play 2.♕xd8 and mate him on the last rank," White probably said to himself. However:

1...	**♖cd8!**
2.♕xd8	**♘xd8!**

And White soon resigned.

Advanced Assumption

Perhaps the most common assumption error, as we've seen, involves the "I-check-him-and-he-must-go-there" situation. Naturally, there are many versions of this. We often assume that the other player will give us a check, or that he cannot allow us to queen a pawn or somesuch. We come to that mistaken conclusion perhaps because it would be consistent with his previous move or because it just looks natural.

ZSU. POLGÁR – BELYAVSKY
Munich 1991

1.d4 f5 2.♗g5 g6 3.♘c3 d5 4.e3 ♗g7 5.h4 c6 6.♗d3 ♕b6 7.♖b1 ♘d7 8.♘f3 ♘gf6 9.h5 ♘e4 10.hxg6 hxg6 11.♖xh8+ ♗xh8 12.♗xe4 fxe4 13.♘h4 ♔f7 14.♕g4 ♘f8 15.♕g3 ♗e6

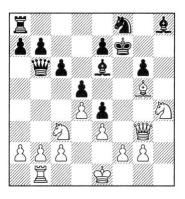

White has been playing for the last four moves with the intention of penetrating on the kingside with her queen. She can do that now with 16.♕f4+ ♗f6 17.♗xf6 and 18.♕h6, but decides instead to go after the g6-pawn.

With 16.♗h6, White threatens 17.♗xf8 and 18.♕xg6+ or 18.♘xg6. Of course, Black does not have to recapture on f8 at move 17. But if he doesn't, he'll just be a piece down, right?

16.♗h6?	♗f6

17.♗xf8   g5!!

Surprise: By agreeing to remain temporarily a piece down, Black traps two enemy pieces on the kingside. Even after **18.♗h6 gxh4 19.♕h2,** White was lost: **19...c5! 20.♘e2 ♕a5+ 21.♔f1 ♕xa2 22.♖e1 ♕xb2,** etc.

Another example of a mistakenly assumed check:

DOLMATOV – MAKARICHEV
Palma de Mallorca 1989

1.e4 e5 2.♘f3 ♘f6 3.d4 ♘xe4 4.♗d3 d5 5.♘xe5 ♘d7 6.♘xd7 ♗xd7 7.0-0 ♕h4 8.c4 0-0-0 9.c5 g5 10.f3 ♘f6 11.♗e3 ♖g8!? 12.♘c3 g4

Black thought over his last two moves for about an hour, and this had a typical psychological effect on his opponent. White examined the most natural defense (13.♕e1 g3 14.hxg3 ♖xg3 15.♘e2). He stopped his calculations when he located the most dangerous variation (15... ♖xg2 16.♔xg2 ♕h3+ 17.♔g1 ♗d6!) and then found a fine refutation – 18.cxd6 ♖g8+ 19.♗g5!!, after which the white king escapes by way of the newly cleared f2-e3-d2 route.

Had he examined the position a bit deeper, he would have chosen 13.g3!, and if 13...♕h3 then 14.f4 ♘h5 15.♕e1! with a solid defense.

13.♕e1?   g3

White most expected 13...♕h5. Now he rechecked his variations, discovered his error – and also found there were no good bailouts available.

14.hxg3   ♖xg3
15.♕d2

What he saw too late was that 15.♘e2 is met, not by the assumed rook sacrifice (15...♖xg2+?), but by the improvement 15...♗d6!, after which 16.♘xg3 ♗xg3 threatens the queen as well as mate on h2. After 16.cxd6, Black wins with 16...♖xg2+ 17.♔xg2 ♖g8+ 18.♗g5 ♖xg5+ 19.♘g3 ♗h3+ or 18.♘g3 ♕h3+.

15...	**♗xc5!**
16.dxc5	**♖dg8**

Now there is no defense to ...♖xg2+ since 17.♖f2 allows 17...♖h3 and 18...♖h1+. White actually played **17.♖fd1 d4 18.c6 dxe3 19.cxd7+ ♔d8** and **resigned** in view of 20.♕e2 ♖xg2+ 21.♕xg2 ♕f2+!.

Assumption errors often go hand-in-hand with move-order errors:

TSESHKOVSKY – GUFELD
Vilnius 1975

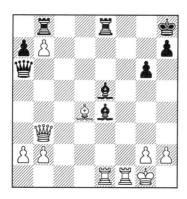

White to move

White is temporarily a piece behind but he can regain it with 1.♖xe4, and the endgame after 1...♗xd4+ 2.♖xd4 ♕xb7 3.♕xb7 ♖xb7 4.♖d2 is excellent for him.

But White correctly believed he deserved more than a mere pawn-up ending. The geometry of Black's defenses got him thinking of a mixture of the ideas ♗xe5+ and ♖f8+. But in which order?

207

White can win with 1.♖f8+! ♖xf8 2.♗xe5+, which forces 2...♖f6, and then the simple 3.♗xb8. Perhaps he saw only 3.♕f7, which appears stronger, but then gave up on the combination when he saw the reply 3...♕b6+ 4.♔h1 ♗xg2+! 5.♔xg2 ♕f2+ and it is Black who wins.

So he reversed the order:

1.♗xe5+?   ♖xe5
2.♖f8+?

It was time to bail out with 2.♕c3!, after which White retains an advantage – but no win – following 2...♕b6+ 3.♖f2 ♕c5 4.♕xc5 and 5.♖xe4.

2...   ♖xf8
3.b8♕

And here White looked into Black's eyes as if expecting him to resign (3...♖xb8 4.♕xb8+ and 5.♕xe5+). Instead Black made a move that defends everything and also makes decisive threats.

3...   ♕f6!
4.♕xa7   ♗d3!

Even with two queens, White cannot defend the trio of squares e1, f1, and f1.

5.♕d1   ♖xe1+

And **0-1** because 6...♕f1+ forces mate. Situations like this should be a warning to all calculators.

Quiet Move

One of the things we assume most often when we calculate is that forcing moves are going to follow forcing moves until the sequence is over. But often it is a non-forcing move, a "quiet" move, that makes a combination work. Or it can be a quiet move that refutes a sequence.

This is particularly dangerous when it is your opponent who is doing the forcing (or non-forcing) and you have to figure out when to stop calculating a sequence.

ŠPAČEK – MOTWANI
Luxembourg 1990

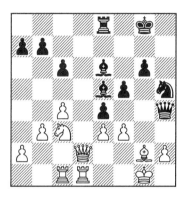

White to move

To fend off the attack on the dark squares, White played 1.f4, fully aware of the possibility of a sacrifice.

1.f4	**♘xf4**
2.exf4	**♗xf4**
3.♕f2	

So far, so calculated. Now on 3...♕xh2+ 4.♔f1 ♗g3 5.♕xa7, or 4...♗xc1 5.♖xc1 (or 3...♗xh2+ and 4...♗g3), Black has compensation for a sacrificed piece but White also has excellent defensive chances.

3...	**♕h6!**

An easy move to miss because it is (a) a retreat and (b) a non-check in a position rife with more forceful moves. Yet a quick look will show that the threats of 4...♗e3 and 4...♗xc1 are so dangerous that White has only one move.

4.♕e1	♕xh2+
5.♔f1	♗xc1
6.♖xc1	e3

The advance of the c- and f-pawns quickly decided: **7.♘e2 f4 8.♘g1 ♗g4 9.♖c2 e2+! 10.♖xe2 ♖xe2 11.♘xe2 f3**, etc.

Now let's examine how early in the game an error may be made:

KRUPPA – BAREEV
USSR Club Championship 1988

1.e4 e6 2.d4 d5 3.♘c3 ♘f6 4.e5 ♘fd7 5.f4 c5 6.♘f3 cxd4 7.♘xd4 ♕b6 8.♗e3

With his last move, White not only prepares to discover an attack on the black queen (e.g., 9.♕d2 ♘c6? 10.♘xe6) but also dares his opponent to grab the b2-pawn, which must have been Black's intention when he played 7...♕b6.

After 8...♕xb2, White's knight is hanging on c3, and moving it doesn't seem to generate dangerous compensation (9.♘a4 ♕b4+ 10.c3 ♕a5).

Therefore, the variation to consider most carefully is 8...♕xb2 9.♘db5!, which threatens both 10.♖b1, trapping the queen, and the check on c7.

Bareev, however, found an adequate defense in 9...♕b4, which extricates the queen from any trap, prepares to defend c7 with 10...♕a5, and maintains an attack on c3, so that 10.♘c7+ ♔d8 11.♘xa8? allows a strong counterattack with 11...♕xc3+ 12.♗d2 (12.♔f2 ♗c5) 12...♕c5.

Black, who within a few years had become one of the world's best players, looked for other dangerous 10th and 11th moves in this last, key variation, and then confidently went ahead:

8...	**♕xb2?**
9.♘db5!	**♕b4**
10.♘c7+	**♔d8**
11.♗d2!	

A devastating "quiet" move, which wins a decisive amount of material. Black either loses the trapped rook or, as Bareev chose, drops his queen to **11...♔xc7 12.♘b5+ ♕xb5 13.♗xb5.** Black missed 11.♗d2 because it seems to be so lacking in force, merely a defensive move, protecting c3.

Finally, when provoking a combination that leaves your opponent with a myriad of threats, it is very dangerous to overlook a quiet move:

VAGANIAN – GELLER
New York 1990

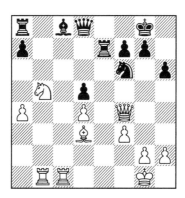

Black to move

White's last move, 1.♕f4, prepares a knight invasion at c7. But after examining this in some depth, the veteran grandmaster playing Black calculated this forcing line: 1...a6 2.♘c7 g5!, since 3.♕xf6 ♖e1+ 4.♖xe1 ♕xf6 5.♘xa8 ♕xd4+! and 6...♕xd3 gives Black at least equality.

1...	**a6?**
2.♘c7!	

Any other move renounces any chance for advantage. Now 2...♘h5 allows White to retain the edge with 3.♕h4.

2...	**g5**
3.♕xf6	**♖e1+**
4.♖xe1	**♕xf6**
5.♔h1!!	

This is the quiet move Black either underestimated or overlooked entirely. His rook cannot escape (5...♖a7 6.♖e8+ ♔g7 7.♖xc8! threatening ♘e8+). So Black played:

5...	**♕xd4**
6.♖bd1!	**♔g7**
7.♘xa8	

And Black resigned shortly after 7...♕a7 8.♖c1 (8...♕xa8 9.♖e8). White may have been merely lucky, not seeing 5.♔h1 in the diagram position any more than Black did. But Black made the crucial error by forcing matters into an area he was not certain of.

Destruction of the Guard

Another common monkey wrench that can upset a careful calculation is the elimination of a crucial piece. Typically, that piece is captured, overworked, or lured elsewhere.

Calculators should be particularly wary about this when they are "stretching" their own pieces, that is, linking several of them together in a fragile, tactical tether.

ADAMS – SHIROV
Biel 1991

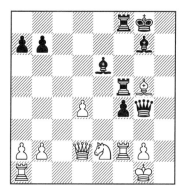

White to move

White is a pawn up but he clearly has kingside problems, with 1...
♜xg5 and 1...f3 threatened. He decides to solve two problems with one
move:

1.♗xf4?

This seems to make sense because each White piece is protected by
another one. But in precisely this kind of position there is the danger that
one piece will be deflected.

1...   **♗c4!**

A very simple move, with an elementary threat to win a piece by 2...
♗xe2. White searches and searches for an antidote. But there is none
(2.g3 ♗xe2 3.♕xe2 ♜xf4!), and White resigned after **2.♗e3 ♜xf2
3.♗xf2 ♗xe2 0-1.**

Naturally, when you raise the stakes by initiating a sequence that involves a lot of hanging or sacrificed material, the price of miscalculation
rises. So does the amount of material your opponent is willing to give up
in order to eliminate the one piece that makes your sequence work.

Case in point:

TAL – KORCHNOI
USSR Championship 1958

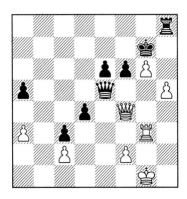

White to move

In this early game between future stars, White holds the initiative but his advanced pawns appear to be at a standstill. White saw he could draw with 1.♕f3, since Black cannot allow the queen to penetrate at b7 and would have to play 1...♕d5. Then 2.♕f4! (or even 2.♕xd5 with a drawn endgame) 2...♕e5! would repeat the position.

But it also occurred to White that he had a choice here, and he opted for a combination that, since it was forcing, he thought was probably better than 1.♕f3.

1.h6+?	♖xh6
2.♕xh6+?	♔xh6
3.g7	

And the pawn cannot be blocked, so Black must take a perpetual check, White thought. However...

3...	♕xg3+!

And, with a three-pawn edge (4...♔xg7), Black won easily. White built his combination on the existence of two elements, the rook and g7-pawn. What he overlooked was that if either element was eliminated, even at the cost of Black's queen, White's position would collapse.

A key element, essential to a sequence, may even be the existence of a flight square.

SHISHOV – ZAGORYANSKY
Riga 1953

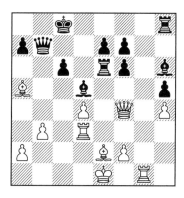

White to move

Here we have a disguised version of a back-rank mate. White's queen is attacked. But he also sees that 1.♕xh6 ♖xh6 2.♖g8+ and 3.♖d8 is a mate. What can go wrong with such a forcing line?

1.♕xh6??   ♖xe2+!

And Black wins because the king can go safely to e6 after 2.♔xe2 ♖xh6 3.♖g8+ ♔d7 4.♖d8+. White misread the position in the diagram by not recognizing that a vital element of the combination – the unavailability of e6 – was only temporary.

215

Zwischenzug

Zwischenzug is a German word that means "in-between move" – in between the assumed moves of the expected sequence. Like sand in the cogs of a machine, a *Zwischenzug* can interfere with, slow down, or completely halt the wheels of the mechanism.

M. GUREVICH – GELLER
Helsinki 1992

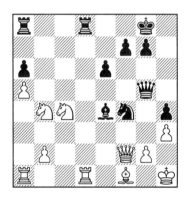

Black to move

Having sacrificed a piece, Black plays the natural follow-up:

1...	♘xh3
2.♕e3	

Now 2...♕f5 3.♖d4! offers little. So Black should simply grab some material back with 2...♖xd1 3.♖xd1 ♕xe3 4.♘xe3 ♘f2+ 5.♔g1 ♘xd1 6.♘xd1. In the resulting ending, White's two minor pieces are only a bit better than Black's rook and two pawns.

2...	♕xe3??

But this is just a blunder, overlooking the in-between move:

3.♖xd8+!	1-0

Black does not get to fork the king and rook now and will have only two pawns for a piece in a lost endgame.

Note incidentally that, after the correct 2...♖xd1, White can insert his own *Zwischenzug* with 3.♕xg5, which is more forcing because the capture of a queen carries greater weight than that of a mere rook. But then Black has an even more forcing reply, 3...♖xf1+!, which leaves him two pawns ahead.

The consequences of missing a *Zwischenzug* are rarely mild. Often they turn a very simple maneuver into a shambles. When you're increasing the tension in a position – that is, when your pieces must coordinate precisely – or when your material is hanging all over the board, or your king is walking the plank, you must make sure there are no surprises.

LJUBOJEVIĆ – KASPAROV
Linares 1991

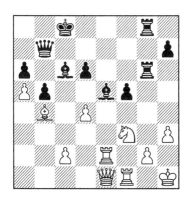

Black to move

White has just played 1.d4, trying to slow down Black's attack. With 1...♕g7, and if 2.♕f2 then 2...♖g3!?, Black's initiative stays on track. But the world champion thought he saw a more forceful route.

1...	♖xg2??

$$2.\Xi xg2 \qquad \Xi xg2$$
$$3.\mathbb{\dot{\Xi}}xg2 \qquad \mathbb{W}g7+$$
$$4.\mathbb{\dot{\Xi}}h1$$

And White, a rook ahead, should have won quickly. (He later blundered.) But what did Black overlook when he sacrificed his rook?

The answer came in the postmortem analysis when Black explained that he had been counting on 2...$\mathbb{\dot{Q}}$xf3 (not 2...Ξxg2). But in rechecking his tree limbs at move two he saw that 2...$\mathbb{\dot{Q}}$xf3 3.Ξxf3 $\mathbb{W}$xf3 loses to the elegant *Zwischenzug* 4.$\mathbb{W}$c3+!! $\mathbb{W}$xc3 5.Ξxg8+, followed by 6.$\mathbb{\dot{Q}}$xc3.

Moral: You can afford to overlook *Zwischenzugs* in quiet positions, but not when you've just sacrificed a rook.

A *Zwischenzug* must meet two criteria: (a) it must be sufficiently forcing to prevent the sequence from continuing normally, and (b) as a result, the sequence cannot achieve its intended objective.

The absence of either criterion renders the *Zwischenzug* harmless. A *Zwischenzug* that can safely be ignored is useless. And a forcing but irrelevant insertion – such as the familiar "spite check" that a player often tries just before resigning – succeeds only in lengthening the game by a move or two. Computers used to be notorious *Zwischenzug* fanatics, throwing material at their opponents' pieces in a sacrificial orgy to delay being mated.

NIEMALA – TAL
Riga 1959

1.d4 $\mathbb{\dot{Q}}$f6 2.c4 c5 3.d5 e6 4.$\mathbb{\dot{Q}}$c3 exd5 5.cxd6 d6 6.e4 g6 7.f4 $\mathbb{\dot{Q}}$g7 8.$\mathbb{\dot{Q}}$f3 0-0 9.$\mathbb{\dot{Q}}$e2 Ξe8 10.e5 dxe5 11.fxe5 $\mathbb{\dot{Q}}$g4 12.e6 fxe6 13.0-0 exd5 14.$\mathbb{\dot{Q}}$xd5 $\mathbb{\dot{Q}}$e6 15.$\mathbb{\dot{Q}}$c4 $\mathbb{\dot{Q}}$e5 16.$\mathbb{\dot{Q}}$g5! $\mathbb{\dot{Q}}$xf3+ 17.$\mathbb{W}$xf3 $\mathbb{W}$xg5 18.Ξae1 Ξf8!

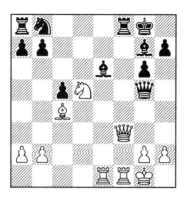

Here White has three plausible moves. The first, which requires less calculation, is 19.♕e4, attacking the e6-bishop and indirectly threatening b7 and the undeveloped rook at a8 (e.g., 19...♗f5 20.♘e7+ ♔h8 21.♘xf5 gxf5 22.♕xb7). But 19...♘c6! 20.♕xe6+ ♔h8 favors Black.

The second alternative, which calls for White to look a bit further, is the queen sacrifice 19.♕xf8+ ♗xf8 20.♖xe6, which however fails to 20...♘d7 21.♘c7 ♔h8 22.♘xa8 ♕g4 23.b3 b5!.

White chose a third sequence, which starts out relatively quietly and then picks up force.

19.♖xe6

Now on 19...♖xf3 he inserts a *Zwischenzug* – 20.♖e8+! – with consequences such as 20...♔f7 21.♘c7+! ♔f6 22.♖xf3+, or 20...♗f8 21.♖xf3, winning in either case.

| 19... | ♗d4+! |

Black gets the first opportunity to play a *Zwischenzug*. It meets the forcing requirement (being a check), and it also makes a difference in White's intended sequence by clearing g7 for Black's king.

| 20.♔h1 | ♖xf3 |
| 21.♖e8+ | ♔g7 |

22.♖xf3	♕c1+
23.♗f1	♘c6!

Black could have won through other means, but this seizes the initiative and finishes off nicely. The game ended with **24.♖xa8 ♘e5 25.♖ff8 ♘g4** (also winning is 25...♘f7) **26.♖f3 ♘f2+ 27.♔g1 ♘e4+ 0-1.**

A *Zwischenzug* is a double-edged sword. By inserting a surprise move into a forcing sequence you increase the chances of being surprised yourself:

WHEELER – POVAH
London 1977

1.c4 e5 2.♘c3 ♘f6 3.♘f3 ♘c6 4.g3 ♗b4 5.♗g2 0-0 6.0-0 e4 7.♘g5 ♗xc3 8.dxc3 ♖e8 9.♘h3 h6 10.♘f4 b6 11.♗e3 d6 12.♗d4 ♘e5 13.b3 ♗b7 14.♕c2 ♕d7 15.♖ad1 ♕f5

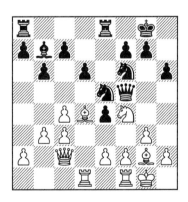

16.♘d5	♘xd5
17.♗xe4?	

This *Zwischenzug* deserves a better fate. It is more forcing than 17.♕xe4 ♕xe4 18.♗xe4, which also gives White a pin on the d5-knight but leaves Black free to liquidate favorably with 18...♘xc4!.

17...   ♛h3!

What did White miss in this game? Perhaps he overlooked the strength of this move, which threatens mate (18.♗xd5 ♘g4). Or maybe he saw this far and overlooked that 18.♗xe5 (eliminating a key part of the mating attack) allows 18...♘f6!.

18.♗g2

Or perhaps he saw all of the above and just counted on this *Zwischenzug,* which appears to drive the queen back (18...♛h5 19.cxd5 ♘g4 20.h3).

18...   ♛xg2+!

Black can vary the move order with 18...♘f4 (19.♗xh3 ♘xh3#; 19.gxf4 ♛xg2#; 19.♗xb7 ♘g4). But the text is prettier and at least as fast: 19.♔xg2 ♘f4+ 20.♔g1 ♘h3#.

Attack-Defense

Calculation involves a rhythm of thrusts and parries. You threaten his rook, he defends it. You check his king, he moves it. You surround his bishop, he tries to break out of the web. In each case, the player with the initiative is doing the threatening and the opponent is doing the responding. This is what makes counting out easy: the comfortable, reliable rhythm.

But suppose you make a threat and your opponent responds with a move that not only defends against your threat, but makes a threat, or threats, of its own. Suddenly, your forcing sequence is halted. Now he is doing the forcing.

KHALIFMAN – SPEELMAN
Munich 1992

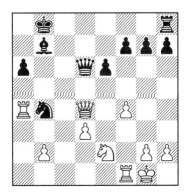

Black to move

White's last move, 1.♕xd4, offers Black a poor endgame, which he naturally rejects. Nevertheless, Black should have sat on his hands before playing...

1...   ♕c6??

If this is as good as it looks (threatening mate on g2 as well as the rook on a4), Black is winning outright. But it's a chimera.

2.♕xg7!   1-0

Black did not see that the queen defends g2 on this square – as well as threatens 3.♕xh8+.

That example was caused by a visualization problem: Black didn't foresee that a piece could attack h8 and at the same time defend g2. In the next case we have a different kind of oversight, an attack-defense move met by an attack-defense move.

IVKOV – LARSEN
Candidates' Match (4) 1965

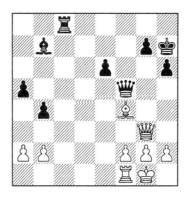

White to move

It's a quiet position in which Black's pieces are more active but a draw seems virtually inevitable because of the bishops of opposite colors. After 1.♗e5 and a subsequent ♖d1, White should hardly lose.

1.a3??

He decides to eliminate a pair of pawns before playing ♗e5.

1...	**♖c4!**
0-1	

What did White overlook? He saw 1...♖c4, of course, but assumed that he could just threaten mate with 2.♗e5, defending against the threat while threatening mate.

The surprise to him was 2...♖g4!, which meets his attack-defense move with one of Black's own. It not only defends against the threatened mate on g7 but wins through an attack on g2.

The attack-defense problem becomes more common as your tactical ideas get more sophisticated and the sequence takes on more finesse. The possibilities for being surprised multiply.

LAPIKEN – RESHEVSKY
U.S. Open 1955

1.e4 c5 2.♘f3 d6 3.d4 cxd4 4.♘xd4 ♘f6 5.♘c3 g6 6.♗e3 ♗g7 7.f3 0-0 8.♕d2 a6? 9.0-0-0 b5 10.a3 ♗b7 11.g4 ♘c6 12.h4 h5!? 13.gxh5 ♘xh5 14.♖g1 ♔h7 15.♔b1 ♕c8 16.♘d5! ♘xd4 17.♗xd4

Black has good prospects in the endgame – if he can reach it – because of the weakness of White's kingside pawns. But we're more interested in what happens as the minor pieces are liquidated.

17...   ♗xd5

Black visualizes a distant position in which the only minor pieces left are his good knight and White's less-than-wonderful light-squared bishop.

18.♗xg7   ♗a2+

The point of this forcing finesse is to bring the queen into a better view of the world on e6. There is also a positional benefit in denying White the opportunity to capture on d5 with a pawn, creating potential pressure against e7 via the e-file.

White gets no time to carry out his own threat, 19.♕h6+ and mate next, because Black's last move is a check, as will be 19...♕e6 after White takes the bishop on a2.

19.♔xa2   ♕e6+

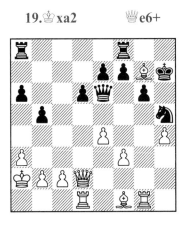

20.♔b1	♔xg7
21.♗e2	♖h8
22.♖g5	♕f6
23.♖dg1	e5!

And after 24...♘f4 he was on the road to victory. But he was very lucky, since he was quite lost after 19...♕e6+.

Had White found 20.♗c4!, Black could have quietly resigned. The only way then to protect his queen and also avoid 21.♕h6+ is 20...♕xc4+. But then 21.b3! closes the diagonal for good, and threatens the queen once more.

One further example shows that sometimes a double attack can be met by a double defense.

KHOLMOV – ANIKAEV
Rostov-on-Don 1976

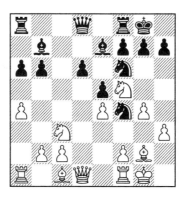

White to move

Black has just dropped a knight onto f4 – and it was a blunder.

1.♗xf4	exf4
2.e5!	

A double attack that wins a piece. White threatens 3.exf6 as well as 3.♗xb7.

2...	♗xg2

Black makes the best of a bad deal. White, a veteran grandmaster, can seal the win of material with 3.exf6 since if Black continues desperado-style with 3...♗xf1, he loses more material after 4.fxe7!.

3.♘xe7+?   ♕xe7
4.exf6

This appears to be the same thing as 3.exf6 but with extra force, since the queen is threatened, not just a bishop on e7.

4...	♕b7!

This is what White overlooked. Black protects both pieces at once. The game later ended as a draw.

Desperado

A further complication in a calculated sequence arises when one capture is met by another, setting off a chain reaction. Usually this involves mutual captures and a very short chain reaction: I play queen takes queen. You re-establish material equality by answering rook takes queen. I have no more captures and the chain ends.

But sometimes, even with several protected pieces on the board, we work out longer chains in which pieces that are about to be captured inflict as much damage as possible.

For example, in 1949 a new idea in the Scotch Game was introduced in the game Bogoljubow–Schmid, West German Championship: **1.e4 e5 2.♘f3 ♘c6 3.d4 exd4 4.♘xd4 ♘f6 5.♘c3,** and now **5...♘xe4?!:**

Subsequent analysis showed that White can obtain an edge with 6.♘xe4 ♕e7 7.f3 d5 8.♗b5 ♗d7 9.0-0. However, in the original game White responded:

6.♘xc6

Black cannot recapture on c6 because then 7.♘xe4 would win a piece. So he had to play:

6...   ♘xc3

Now if White recaptures on c3, Black will follow suit on c6 and remain a pawn ahead (remember, he took the e-pawn at move 5).

7.♘xd8☐   ♘xd1☐
8.♘xf7   ♘xf2

Actually Black can equalize more easily with 8...♚xf7, when material is even.

9.♘xh8   ♘xh1

There's nothing left to take and the desperado sequence is over. In the game White continued 10.♗d3? (10.♗e3!) and had the worst of it after **10...♗c5! 11.♗xh7 ♘f2 12.♗f4 d6.**

In this example, the marauding knights each played the role of desperado, a piece that seems doomed to be captured (even though neither knight actually was). And, being doomed, they were determined to scorch as much earth as possible.

Desperado situations need not last long, and a sequence doesn't always involve captures of the same kinds of material (pawn for pawn, piece for piece). When the captures are unequal, the "winner" of the sequence is usually the player who makes the most damaging capture.

TIVIAKOV – ØSTENSTAD
Gausdal 1992

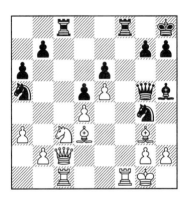

White to move

Here's an odd, though hardly unique, example of a double blunder by masters, thanks to desperado tactics. White finds a clever way to win a pawn and avoid the consequences of 1...♕e3+.

1.♘xd5??

This is based on Black's vulnerable first rank: 1...♖xc2?? allows 2.♖xf8#.

1...   **♖xf1+??**

2.♖xf1   **♕d8**

Of course, the exchange on f1 changed little: 2...♖xc2 3.♖f8#). The game ended with:

3.♗h4!   **♕d7**
4.♕c5!   **1-0**

But it would have been quite a different story if Black had found 1...♕xc1!, short-circuiting White's idea in all variations. Black then wins at least a piece.

If the same kinds of pieces are being captured, the player who makes the final capture is often the one who wins. This principle accounted for one of the shortest games ever lost in an Olympiad team tournament (it was lost by the artist Marcel Duchamp). The game Müller–Duchamp, The Hague 1928, went **1.c4 e5 2.♘f3 ♘c6 3.♘c3 ♘f6 4.d4 exd4 5.♘xd4 ♗b4 6.♗g5 h6 7.♗h4,** and now Black entered a faulty desperado sequence with **7...♘e4? 8.♗xd8 ♘xc3.** He counted on winning back the queen after 9.bxc3 ♗xc3+ or 9.♕d2 ♘e4, or on winning gobs of material compensation (9.♕b3? ♘xd4).

But he missed **9.♘xc6!,** and resigned after **9...♘xd1+ 10.♘xb4 1-0.** His opponent had made the first and last capture.

When invited into a desperado derby by your opponent, you need to keep a clear idea of when one of you can stop capturing and head for a tactical exit.

SPASSKY – TIMMAN
Montpellier 1986

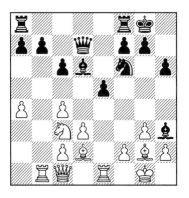

White to move

White played the seductive 1.♗xh6, based on the idea that after 1...gxh6 2.♕xh6 he is attacking both the f6-knight and the h3-bishop and may be able to force a perpetual check if matters become too complicated. For example, if he reaches the position after 2...♗xg2 3.♕xf6 ♗h3 and determines that 4.♖e4 or 4.♘e4 is unsatisfactory, White can bail out with checks on the g- and h-files.

1.♗xh6?   ♗xg2!

Perhaps only now did White see that 2.♕g5 ♕g4 3.♔xg2!, which wins a pawn, is not Black's best defense and that instead he can play 2...♘e8 3.♔xg2 ♕e6!, winning the bishop. (In the diagram it is very difficult to see how the bishop on h6 can become trapped.)

2.♗xg7

When in a desperado derby, do as the desperados do. Now 2...♔xg7 3.♕g5+ ♔h7 4.♕xf6 is a favorable line for White.

2...   ♘h7
3.♗xf8

It appears that everything has turned out well for White. He's gotten two pawns and a rook for a bishop. The desperado sequence can end now with 3...♝xf8 4.♚xg2, or 3...♝f3 4.♛e3, after which White wins.

3...   ♛h3!

But Black exits first and with a major threat (4...♝f3 and 5...♛g2#). The queen move not only makes the threat but also protects the g2-bishop. Unless White has a comparable move (defending the f8-bishop while meeting the mate threat), his gains will be much more modest.

4.♛h6

Or 4.♛e3 ♚xf8!? 5.♘e4 ♝xe4 6.♛xe4.

4...	**♝xf8**
5.♛xh3	**♝xh3**
6.♜xb7	**♘g5**

And although material is roughly equal, Black's pieces work together much better than White's. He won a long endgame.

It is crucial, in calculating such sequences, to keep two key points in mind:

a) What is the score (the material balance or imbalance) after each move?

b) Where does it end? That is, what will it look like at the time of the last capture?

It was a failure to answer the second question correctly that cost humanity a game in one of the first victories by a computer over a grandmaster.

MILES – DEEP THOUGHT
Long Beach 1989

1.d4 d5 2.c4 dxc4 3.e4 ♘f6 4.♘c3 e5 5.♘f3 exd4 6.♕xd4 ♗d6 7.♗xc4 0-0 8.♗g5 ♘c6 9.♕d2 h6 10.♗h4 ♗g4 110-0-0?

Black's last two moves contained a tactical point, allowing a desperado that White misses:

11...	**♗xf3**
12.gxf3	**♘xe4!**

As a result, the h4-bishop is *en prise* and White will not regain the pawn after 13.♘xe4 ♕xh4 14.♘xd6 because of 14...♖ad8 (15.♘f5 ♕xc4).

White may obtain some counterchances in that line (e.g., with 15.♕c3 and a later ♖hg1), but he decides he has to go into the full desperado because at the end of it he sees material equality.

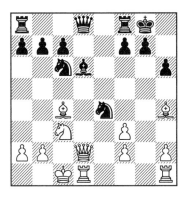

13.♗xd8?	**♘xd2**
14.♗xc7!	

The move White was counting on. His position will not be particularly pretty after 14...♘xc4 15.♗xd6 ♘xd6 16.♖xd6, or 14...♗xc7 15.♔xd2, but at least the number of pawns will be the same for each player.

14...   **♗xh2!!**

Wrong again. "I must admit I totally overlooked the decisive counter-desperado," Miles said after the game. By using this order of moves, Black wins a pawn. Clearly 14...♗xc7 15.♕xd2 ♗xh2?? loses a piece. But here 14...♗xh2 15.♗xh2 ♘xc4 or 15.♖xd2 ♗xc7 makes off with a pawn.

White consoled himself with **15.♗xh2 ♘xc4 16.♖d7**, but after **16... b6** he had scant compensation and lost in 38 moves.

Desperado calculation often seems like a totally new game, something like Loser's Chess, that offshoot of chess in which the players take turns trying to lose material to one another. It requires some of the most stringent calculation technique. You not only have to keep count of the quickly changing material situation, you must also keep an eye out for surprise moves that stop the chain reaction – in your opponent's favor.

A classic example of the last point is:

BIALAS – JOPPEN
West German Championship 1961

1.e4 c5 2.♘f3 ♘c6 3.d4 cxd4 4.♘xd4 e5 5.♘b5 a6 6.♘d6+ ♗xd6 7.♕xd6 ♕f6 8.♕c7 ♘ge7 9.♘c3 ♕e6 10.♗d3 b5 11.0-0? ♖b8!

This begins a game, not of Loser's Chess but of Trap the Queen. Having failed to ensure an escape route (11.♕b6), White is faced with an ominous 12...♖b7.

12.f4!   **♖b7**
13.♘d5!

A clever defense. Black can't play 13...♖xc7 because 14.♘xc7+ forks king and queen. And he can't capture on d5 because the c8-bishop hangs with check.

Moreover, White has a threat of his own: to trap Black's queen with 14.f5. The immediate 13.f5 loses to 13...♕f6!.

13...   0-0!

Black can make a desperado of his queen here with 13...♕xd5, hoping for 14.exd5 ♖xc7 15.dxc6 ♘xc6 (or even 14.♕xb7??, when 14...♕c5+! buys out of the chain reaction and gains time for 15...♗xb7).

But White has a better way of surrendering his own trapped queen after 13...♕xd5, and it's 14.♕xc8+ ♘xc8 15.exd5, so that on 15...♘b4 16.fxe5 ♘xd5 he can take command with 17.♗e4 and 18.♖d1.

14.f5

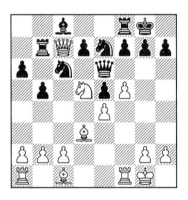

This is the position both sides have been playing for: White, because it's the best he can get; Black, because it's an easy win. Still, the win is tricky.

It comes from 14...♘xf5!, after which White has nothing better than 15.exf5 and then to resign after 15...♕xd5, since White's queen remains trapped.

A similar, but inferior, version of this is 14...♘xd5, which transposes into the easy win after 15.exd5? ♕xd5. The flaw in this thinking is that it leaves the black queen hanging while White takes over the tactical initiative.

14...	♘xd5?
15.♕xb7??	

Too greedy. White can recoup with 15.♕xc8! because 15...♖xc8 16.fxe6 re-establishes material equality and leaves Black with hanging material at d5 and f7.

15...	♕d6!!

Now this move wins. Black recognizes that it's time to halt the chain reaction of captures. When the music stops, White's queen is still trapped (16.♕a8 ♘c7). In the game, he actually played **16.♕xc8 ♖xc8 17.exd5 ♕xd5 18.♖d1,** but saw no point in continuing the struggle after **18...e4! 19.♗e2 ♕c5+ 20.♔h1 ♕f2! 21.♗f1 e3 0-1.**

Before we leave this wonderful example, let's consider what would have happened on 14...♕xd5 instead of the faulty 14...♘xd5 or the superior 14...♘xf5. Then, faced with the possibility of 15...♕c5+, which ends the chain reaction once and for all, White could not afford any additional captures such as 15.♕xc8 or 15.♕xb7. But he could have survived into the ending with 15.exd5 and 16.dxc6.

The basic dangers of desperado play are:

a) Overlooking a capture that allows your opponent to come out materially ahead when the chain reaction stops.

b) Allowing him to halt the carnage at an embarrassing moment (e.g., 15...♕d6!! above).

Chapter 8

OVERSIGHTS

"No plan survives contact with the enemy."
–Field Marshal Helmuth von Moltke

In the course of calculating you are bound to make oversights. You will simply overlook moves by your opponent that didn't seem possible when you first charted the course of the next few moves. Every player makes this kind of mistake sometimes.

But if you learn how to calculate properly, you can reduce the frequency and severity of oversights and avert crises before they occur on the board.

Of course, nobody guesses his opponent's next move 100 percent of the time. In fact, 50 percent is a pretty good figure to shoot for. The grandmaster who anticipates every move his opponent plays is a figure of myth.

Only during certain periods of a game – portions of familiar openings, textbook situations in the endgame, and during forcing combinations – can a player be reasonably certain of what will happen next.

The difference between winning and losing, however, is the nature of these very natural surprises. You may overlook a good knight maneuver or a timely defensive retreat. Those oversights usually won't cost you much. But you don't want to overlook knight-takes-queen-double-check.

LARSEN – PETROSIAN
Santa Monica 1966

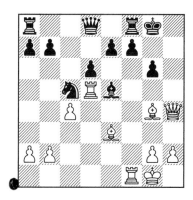

Black to move

A classic example of a major oversight occurs in this game. Black, then the world champion, is being pressed but is still several moves away from a crisis. He sees that he can beat off the attack with 1...e6, and also appreciates that the endgame that follows 2.♕xd8 ♖fxd8 3.♖xe5 dxe5 4.♗xc5 is not at all clear because Black's pawns are well centralized and mobile. But he plays:

1...	♘e6?
2.♖f3	

Now the threat of 3.♖h3 and 4.♕h6 is so dangerous that Black must calculate very carefully. He has a choice between:

a) kicking the enemy queen with 2...♗f6 (e.g., 3.♕h6 ♗g7 4.♕h4 ♗f6), and

b) taking the big risk with 2...f5 3.♖h3 ♔f7!.

237

From a practical point of view, it is much more comfortable to pick (a). The variations are easier to count out and you run less chance of mate. But, and this is the main point, even in (a) you have to make sure you aren't overlooking something big.

2...   ♗**f6?**
3.♕h6   ♗**g7**

And by "big" we mean a capture, a check or, in this case, a dangerous move that allows the queen to remain in mating proximity.

4.♕xg6!

Larsen saw this move when he played 2.♖f3, since otherwise he would have had to concede his plan was wrong and retreat the queen to h3 or h4. But Petrosian clearly had no idea this was in the air when he was choosing between 2...f5 and 2...♗f6.

The move 4.♕xg6 is one of the most famous in chess history, but, as both players readily acknowledged, its main lines were fairly simple to calculate. The rest of the game went **4...♘f4 5.♖xf4 fxg6 6.♗e6+.** Now 6...♔h7 7.♖h4+ ♗h6 8.♗xh6 leads to mate, so Black played **6...♖f7 7.♖xf7 ♔h8 8.♖g5 b5 9.♖g3** and **resigned** before the decisive rook check.

Once we become trained at chess tactics – when we readily recognize pins, skewers, back-rank mates, and the like – the number of our oversights will decline sharply. But they will never disappear completely. There are simply too many causes, especially psychological ones, to plague us. To reduce our oversights further, we have to recognize these causes.

Here's an instructive but typical example of a grandmaster overlooking a winning move of his own. He didn't find it because for once his instincts told him not to examine it.

CHRISTIANSEN – SHIROV
Biel 1991

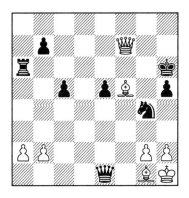

White to move

White, behind in material, has queen checks available at h7 and f8 but they don't seem to lead anywhere. His g1-bishop is pinned and useless. And he is faced with ...♘f2#.

Yet White has a simple winning move that threatens mate in two and that Black can only delay by sacrificing his pieces randomly.

1.h3?   ♖f6!

Black drew in a few moves when White was forced to take perpetual check. The winning move, found days later by Shirov, is 1.g3!!, threatening 2.♕f8+ ♔g5 3.h4#. But, as Black was the first to point out, it is an extraordinarily hard move to find.

Why? Because 1.g3 seems to invite danger. It opens a very dangerous diagonal leading to White's king. Without the bishop on e4, Black mates with 1...♕e4+. Psychologically, 1.g3 is the kind of move we would consider only after exhausting virtually every alternative.

Simple Visual Oversights

The most elementary – and most embarrassing – oversights are the one-movers, the strong moves that are so obviously good that we could not have dreamt of allowing them. But somehow we do: We allow an enemy piece to advance deep into our side of the board. Or we miss a strong retreat. Or we just have a blind spot.

KUPREICHIK – POLUGAYEVSKY
USSR Championship 1974

1.e4 c5 2.♘f3 d6 3.d4 cxd4 4.♘xd4 ♘f6 5.♘c3 a6 6.♗e2 e5 7.♘b3 ♗e7 8.f4 0-0 9.a4 ♘bd7 10.g4 d5 11.♘xd5 ♘xe4 12.0-0 ♘dc5 13.c4 ♘xb3 14.♕xb3 ♗c5+

For various reasons, White is reluctant to move his king. But his tactical antennae should be going up all around his side of the board after a check like this. Yet...

15.♗e3??　　♘d2!

This was a case of White's believing that on his side of the board he was relatively secure. Less explainable is the following, with pieces so close to one another.

P. POPOVIĆ – LJUBOJEVIĆ
Manila Interzonal 1990

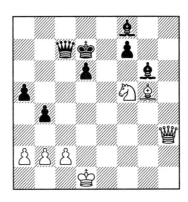

Black to move

Black has no convenient way out of the discovered check if he tries to win. So he tries...

240

1...	♕c4

White immediately notices that 2.♘e3+ fails to 2...♕e6. He then examines other discovered checks, rejecting each one when he sees they achieve nothing after the same 2...♕e6 (or, in the case of 2.♘d4+, a king move).

So he settles on the one discovery that actually accomplishes something:

2.♘xd6+??

This at least wins a pawn. However, White **resigned** before Black could play 2...♔xd6!.

Donald Byrne, a strong American amateur and coach of the 1950s and '60s, recommended that players always think about their positions mentally when away from the board. In this way you often "see" a move that your mind blocked out when you last examined the position with your eyes.

But when seated at the board, it pays to recheck every significant change in the position – every capture, sacrifice – by examining as many enemy responses as you feel comfortable with. I've known masters who, when considering a move that would likely force resignation, will consider every legal reply.

In this way few accidents like the following are likely to happen:

YERMOLINSKY – BRAUDE
New York 1992

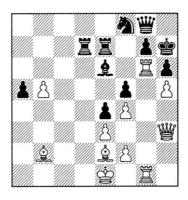

White to move

White, with a growing edge, has been attacking on the kingside for the last 20 moves, and for the last 15 Black's queen has been sitting passively at g8. But perhaps not as passively as you might think, because here White forgets about it and plays:

1.♖xe6??

He can win with a move like 1.b6 but was counting on the exchange sacrifice followed by 2.♕xf5+ as being a clearer win.

1...   ♕xe6!

White simply did not remember that the queen was still on the board. He played a few more moves and resigned.

Retreats

Psychologists have said that the kind of strong moves most likely to be overlooked are retreats.

Part of the momentum of calculation leads us to believe that "I advance there and he must advance there, or else I've improved my position." But when your opponent can take a well-developed piece and move it backward, we often blot that out of our consciousness and don't even try to evaluate it. We've trained our force-oriented calculating minds to look mainly for counterattacks and counterthreats.

A notorious example:

FISCHER – LARSEN
Santa Monica 1966

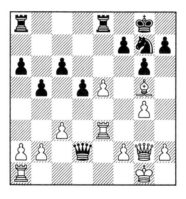

White to move

White has been working up an attack against the vulnerable dark squares but here avoids 1.♗h6 in favor of...

1.b3?   **b4!**

Now 2.cxb4 d4! would give Black the better chances. White thought briefly about the new situation and replied:

2.♕h3?   bxc3!
3.♕h6   ♘e6
0-1

What did Fischer overlook? It certainly wasn't 3...♘e6. No, according to his opponent, White had counted on the game ending with 3.♗f6 ♘e6 4.♕xh7+ ♚xh7 5.♖h3+ "and 6.♖h8#."

But this fails miserably to 5...♕h6!, a retreat that ends all threats. Once Fischer saw this, he went through the motions of 3.♕h6 but resigned when he realized how hopeless was his attack and how destroyed was his queenside.

An even simpler retreat cost Black an embarrassing defeat in the following:

KASPAROV – ANAND
Dortmund 1992

1.♘f3 d5 2.c4 c6 3.d4 ♘f6 4.♘c3 dxc4 5.a4 ♗f5 6.e3 e6 7.♗xc4 ♗b4 8.0-0 0-0 9.♕e2 ♘bd7 10.♘e5 ♖e8 11.♖d1 ♕c7 12.♘xd7 ♕xd7 13.f3 ♘d5 14.♘a2 ♗f8 15.e4 ♗g6 16.♕e1 f5?? 17.exd5! 1-0

What happened? Black didn't appreciate his opponent's last move and assumed that he could now play 17...exd5, simultaneously attacking the queen and the c4-bishop. When he realized that 18.♗e2! was legal, he resigned.

Even a short-range retreat, particularly to the side of the board by a centralized piece, is often overlooked. The following, coming in the middle of a close world championship match, was called "the blunder of the century."

KARPOV – KASPAROV
World Championship (11) 1987

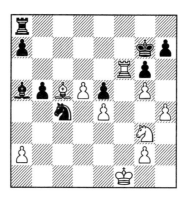

Black to move

Hyperbole aside, it is a perfectly natural occurrence. White, with a slight advantage, used his previous two moves to shift his rook from c2 to f6.

1...	**♗b6**
2.♖c6??	**♘a5!**

Winning the exchange and ultimately the game.

White was victimized by several psychological factors. First, he saw he was making progress with his last few moves and disliked the prospect of having to play 2.♗xb6 axb6! 3.♖f2.

Second, a5 had been occupied the previous move, so Black's moving a piece to that square did not readily occur to White. And, perhaps crucially, Black's key move withdrew his best-placed piece backward and to the side of the board.

Related to retreats is the problem of "short moves." When his rivals complained that they could never guess Anatoly Karpov's moves, it was often because they generally involved shifts of a piece one or two squares away.

KORCHNOI – SALOV
Amsterdam 1991

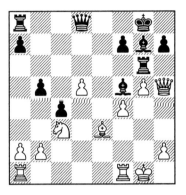

White to move

1.♘xb5??

And White resigned immediately when he saw Black's "short" reply.

1...   ♛e8!

This kind of oversight occurs most often with the most valuable pieces. Because the queen has such great mobility, we assume that our opponents will sweep it across the board.

Line Blocks

Another minefield for calculators lies in positions in which a key diagonal or file can be forcefully cut by a surprise move. We call these line blocks.

In the following example, the white knights might be a match for the enemy bishops if they could be anchored by some supporting pieces or pawns. To avoid retreating the attacked d5-knight, White tries to calculate a way out. The idea that occurs to him involves Black's vulnerable first rank.

TSESHKOVSKY – MILES

Palma de Mallorca 1989

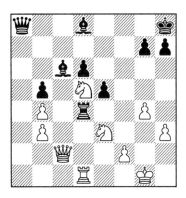

White to move

There is a good idea here, but White does not find it. It is 1.♖xd4 exd4 and then 2.♕f5, threatening mate, which gains time for 3.♘c7. Instead, White finds the attractive...

1.♖c1	♗xd5
2.♕c8	

This looks better. In fact, isn't White winning? What can Black do about the threat of 3.♕xa8 followed by 4.♖c8?

2...   ♖c4!!

That's what. By cutting his opponent's communications along the c-file, Black ensures he will remain a piece ahead (3.♕xa8 ♖xc1+ and 4...♗xa8; 3.♘xc4 ♕xc8; 3.♖xc4 dxc4).

The winner in the last example had a similar experience with the white pieces. This time, in an even more perilous position, he found a way to cut communications on a diagonal.

MILES – PRITCHETT
London 1982

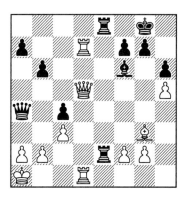

Black to move

Despite White's domination of the d-file and pressure on f7, it is Black's attack that arrives first. He can win directly with the simple 1...♕c2 2.♖b1 ♖e1, e.g. 3.♕xf7+ ♔h8 4.♖dd1 ♗xc3!.

But Black saw the idea of the bishop capture in another scheme...

1...   ♗xc3

...which seems to win even faster, as ...♗xb2+ cannot be averted. However:

2.♕xf7+   ♔h8

Correct here is 2...♔h7!, when Black escapes after 3.♗e5 ♕xd7! 4.♕xd7 ♗xe5!, since White can't play 5.♕xe8 (no check!) 5...♗xb2+!.

3.♗e5!!   1-0

An incredible final move and an easy one to overlook. Actually, it is quite logical, since it's the only way to defend b2. It works by cutting communication along the e-file and the long diagonal, since otherwise 3...♖2xe5 4.♕xg7# or 3...♗xe5 4.♕xe8+ and mates.

What made White's third move so hard to visualize is the chess blindness that occurs on heavily fortified squares. Your mind tells you that such a move as 3.♗e5 is not worth a second's consideration in any sub-variation because the square is defended by three black pieces.

Unveiled Attacks

A corollary to the sudden closing of lines is the instant opening of others. The human eye and mind can get just as used to certain diagonals and files being closed as they can to their being open. And that leads to surprises in situations like this:

KUIJPERS – JONGSMA
Amsterdam 1968

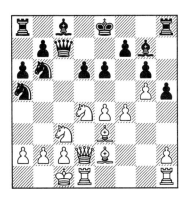

White to move

White was lost within two moves. How is that possible?

The position looks like a typical Sicilian Defense middlegame in which White gains the upper hand by way of a standard sacrifice: He puts one of his knights on b5 and after it's captured he retakes with the other knight, followed (after a retreat by the black queen) by ♘xd6+ or ♕xd6. In terms of material, he may get only two pawns for the piece, but experience has shown that it is very difficult for Black to extricate himself. What can be wrong with that?

> 1.♘db5?   axb5
> 2.♘xb5   ♘b3+!
> 0-1

The opening of the queenside files (3.axb3 ♖a1#) doesn't seem possible in the diagram. But it happened.

SEIRAWAN – KUDRIN
U.S. Championship 1981

1.c4 ♘f6 2.♘c3 e6 3.e4 c5 4.e5 ♘g8 5.d4 cxd4 6.♕xd4 ♘c6 7.♕e4 d6 8.♘f3 dxe5 9.♘xe5 ♗d7 10.♘xd7 ♕xd7 11.♗g5 ♘f6 12.♕e3 h6 13.♖d1 ♕c7 14.♗f4 ♕a5 15.♗e2 e5? 16.♗f3 ♖c8 17.0-0 ♗b4 18.♘d5 ♗c5 19.♕e2 ♔f8 20.♗d2 ♕xa2??

Black had a bad game but this removes all doubts. What he has overlooked is the sudden opening of...

> 21.♘xf6   gxf6
> 22.b4!

...the second rank. Now 23.♗xh6+ and 24.♕xa2 is the main threat, and Black had to choose between allowing that and 23.bxc5, e.g. 22...♘xb4 23.♗xb4.

A more elaborate example befell White in this promising position.

LANE – VELIKOV
Toulouse 1990

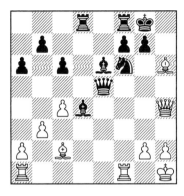

White to move

White has a dangerous attack directed at h7, and with 1.♗g5 the threat of 2.♗xf6 and 3.♕xh7# virtually forces 1...♖fe8. Then 2.♖ae1 leaves White with a substantial initiative.

But White thought he had a more immediate trick, based on the same idea of capturing on f6.

1.♖xf6

This looks decisive. All the reasonable replies by Black seem to lose:

a) 1...♕xf6 2.♗g5, hitting the queen and threatening 3.♕h7#;
b) 1...gxf6 2.♗g7! and mates soon;
c) 1...♗xa1 2.♗xg7!, threatening mate on both h7 and h8.

However, Black actually wins in two of these lines. After 1...♕xf6 2.♗g5, he has 2...♗f5! 3.♗xf6 ♗xf6. And 1...♗xa1 2.♗xg7 is beaten by 2...♖d1+! 3.♗xd1 ♔xg7.

Nevertheless, Black found a more elegant refutation of 1 ♖xf6:

251

1... ♗f2!

By unveiling the threat of 2...♕xa1+ as well as attacking the queen, Black effectively ends the contest. White didn't bother to play out 2.♕xf2 ♕xa1+ 3.♕f1 ♕xf6 or 3...♕xf1+ 4.♖xf1 gxh6. **0-1**

The Retained Image

Nikolai Krogius, a Russian grandmaster and psychologist, analyzed in some detail another kind of mental trick that we calculators play on ourselves. Krogius called it the "retained image" – the retention of certain incorrect, out-of-date information about a position during the course of a calculated sequence.

In some cases our minds will simply not allow us to "see" what is evident.

GALLAGHER – MAIER
Swiss Team Championship 1991

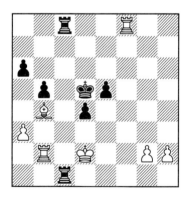

Black to move

Black has some drawing chances if he can eliminate a few more white pawns. With that in mind he tries:

1... ♖g1??

And was embarrassed into resignation after:

2.♖xc8   1-0

We can understand the confusion in Black's mind. In the diagram, the c1-square is controlled by one black rook and occupied by another. It is a square White can only dream of occupying some day. So 1...♖g1 threatens not just to win a pawn but to win the b2-rook with 2...♖xg2+.

It never occurred to Black that 2.♖xc8 ♖xg2+ 3.♔c1! was possible. He retained the image of a piece still occupying that square.

In the following game, White could have resigned after move 14 because he failed to visualize the sudden appearance of an enemy rook on e2.

CHRISTIANSEN – EPISHIN
New York 1990

1.c4 e5 2.♘c3 ♘f6 3.g3 ♗b4 4.♗g2 0-0 5.e4 ♗xc3 6.bxc3 ♖e8 7.♘e2 c6 8.♕b3 b6 9.0-0 ♗b7 10.f4 exf4 11.d3 d5 12.♗xf4 ♘bd7 13.exd5?? ♖xe2 14.♗f3 ♕e7 15.♕d1 ♖e3 16.dxc6 ♖xf3 17.♕xf3 ♕c5+

White soon resigned. What did he overlook at move 13? He counted on regaining his sacrificed piece favorably with 14.dxc6 – not seeing 14...♖xg2+! until it was too late. In his mind, the rook was still on e8.

Let's move on to an example involving two former world champions:

SPASSKY – KARPOV
Belfort 1988

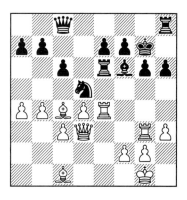

White to move

White has reason to believe he is close to a win and correctly begins his search for the winning combination. Equally correctly, he comes up with the idea that Black is most vulnerable at g6. He concludes he can mate by sacrificing on that square.

1.♖eg4		♖e1+
2.♔h2		♖xc1

And here White **resigned**. He had seen this far, of course. But he was counting on playing 3.♖xg6+ fxg6 4.♕xg6+ ♔f8 5.♗xh6+ ♖xh6 6.♕g8#.

Only when the position after 2...♖xc1 appeared on the board did White realize that 5.♗xh6+ would involve a piece that no longer existed. **0-1**

Once White played 1.♖eg4? in the last example, there was no backing out. But more often a player can correct a faulty analysis by rechecking his variations along the way. Black's failure to spot a retained image in the following game cost him dearly.

EHLVEST – ANDERSSON
Belfort 1988

1.e4 c5 2.♘f3 e6 3.d4 cxd4 4.♘xd4 ♘c6 5.♘c3 a6 6.♗e3 ♕c7 7.f4 ♘xd4 8.♕xd4 b5 9.♗e2 ♗b7 10.0-0-0 ♖c8 11.♕d2 ♘f6 12.♗f3 ♗e7 13.♖hd1 0-0 14.e5

Here Black thought for a long time trying to choose between two move orders. He did not intend to retreat the knight in either case. As an experienced Sicilian Defense player, Black knew that he should meet e4-e5 with ...b5-b4.

14...	**♗xf3?**

The first mistake. If Black plays the correct 14...b4, the desperado line 15.exf6 bxc3 16.fxe7 cxd2+ 17.♖xd2 ♖fe8 offers White nothing (18.♗xb7 ♕xb7 19.f5 f6!; or 19.♕xd7 ♖xe7 20.♕d8+ ♖e8).

In fact, White's best answer to 14...b4 is 15.♘a4, after which 15... ♗xf3 and 16...♘d5 is excellent for Black.

15.gxf3	**b4?**

This compounds the error. Now was the time for Black to recheck his previous analysis based on the new position after 15.gxf3. He would likely have noticed that the g-file is now partly open. And he would have cut his losses by way of 15...♘e8! 16.♕xd7 ♗b4.

16.exf6	**bxc3**
17.♖g2!	

After retreats by bishop (and queen), the easiest move to overlook is the lateral shift of a rook or queen. Black could have resigned here (17... ♗xf6 18.♕xf6) but continued until...

17...	**♕b7**
18.♖xg7+	**♔h8**

19.♖g8+!   **1-0**

White can now capture on e7 with discovered check (19...♔xg8 20.♖g1+ ♔h8 21.fxe7+; or 19...♖xg8 20.fxe7+ ♖g7 21.♖g1! ♕xb2+ 22.♔d1 ♕b1+ 23.♗c1 ♖g8 24.♖xg7 and wins).

Optical Illusions

The most humiliating oversights are those, similar to retained images, that involve surprises such as this:

ZAPATA – M. GUREVICH
Manila 1990

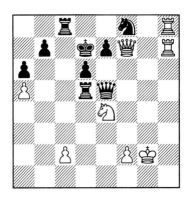

White to move

In time pressure, White saw the idea of a fork on f6 in connection with a capture on d5. So on the final move of the time control he could have played 1.♘f6+, after which Black would probably have resigned in view of 2.♘xd5.

But it was White who ended up resigning: He played **1.♕xd5??** first, only then realizing that the knight was pinned after 1...♕xd5. With more time on the clock, White would have rechecked his variation more thoroughly.

Too often we make oversights because we think too logically. Logic can be a powerful ally in the generation of ideas, the inspiration stage of calculation. But in the counting-out stage and particularly in the rechecking process, it can't be relied on.

SHERWIN – BENKO
U.S. Championship 1966

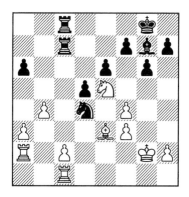

Black to move

Black has a better position on the kingside, queenside, and center. He can win easily with 1...♖xc2+, for example (2.♖cxc2 ♖xc2+ 3.♖xc2 ♘xc2 4.♗c1 ♗xe5! 5.fxe5 ♘e1+ and 6...♘d3 is a won endgame).

But Black decided that he could shorten the game quite a bit with:

1...   ♘e2

Makes excellent sense. Now after the attacked rook moves, Black can capture on c2, he thinks. Isn't it better for Black to have a rook on the seventh rank and threaten all sorts of discovered checks than (as after 1...♖xc2+) to trade off all the rooks?

2.♖e1   ♖xc2??

Failure to recheck! With 2...♘c3 and 3...♘a4, Black is still winning.

3.♖xe2!

Of course. It was all a mirage, and Black must lose a piece.

It's a Big Board

As we mentioned in Chapter 2, players tend to calculate by focusing their attention on grids, that is, on chunks of 16 to 20 squares, rather than the entire board. Usually this is sufficient to understand the key elements of a position. But there are costly exceptions.

Even the greatest players overlook the simplest moves because they don't look at the other side of the board.

KASPAROV – PETROSIAN
Moscow 1981

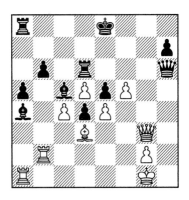

White to move

1.♖xa4??   ♛c1+!

The future world champion explained that Black's winning move, crossing from one side of the board to the other, "simply escaped my field of vision." He resigned shortly after 2.♔f2 ♛xb2+.

In our minds we tend to divide the board into two wings and to assume that matters on one wing cannot normally affect the other. This is what hurt White in the following game:

MALANIUK – HECTOR
Politiken Cup 1992

1.d4 d5 2.c4 c6 3.♘f3 ♘f6 4.e3 ♗f5 5.cxd5 cxd5 6.♕b3 ♕c7 7.♘c3 e6 8.♗d2 ♘c6 9.♖c1 a6 10.♘e5 ♗d6 11.♘xc6 bxc6

White now saw a forcing four-move combination that seemed to win at least a pawn.

12.♗xa6?	**♖xa6!**
13.♘b5	**♕b8**
14.♘xd6+	**♕xd6**
15.♕b7	

This is the point. The attacked rook cannot retreat or be protected by the nearby queen. But here's what White overlooked at move 12:

15...	**♗d3!**

So simple. White went through the middlegame motions with **16.♕c8+ ♕d8 17.♖xc6 0-0,** but was already quite lost.

There is no simple remedy for this malady except to remind yourself periodically that there are (at least) two wings on the board. In the previous example, White lost "mental sight" of the f5-bishop due to his focus on the queenside.

A comparable error is to forget that your own pieces can swing from one side to the other.

SHORT – PIKET

Wijk aan Zee 1990

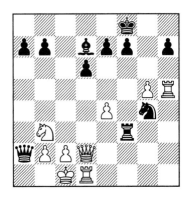

White to move

Black has just captured on a2 in what is shaping up as a traditional battle of wing attacks. Who will break through faster – White on the kingside, or Black on the queenside?

The answer should be, "White on the queenside!" White played the logical and consistent **1.♖xh7??** and only drew after **1...♗c6 2.♕e2 ♖xb3!.**

Afterward, a grandmaster-spectator asked why he didn't play 1.g6. White replied that he rejected the move because the black knight covers the h6 square and therefore 1...hxg6 2.♖h8+ ♔g7 was perfectly playable (3.♕h6+?? ♘xh6).

No, no, the spectator said. The main point of 1.g6 is to threaten 2.♖a5!, trapping the queen. (Black is, in fact, lost after 1.g6 even after 1...♗a4 2.♕d4 or 1...♖xb3 2.♕d4).

Summing up, we've found there are several factors that lead us to miss good moves: discounting the strength of retreats; focusing on only part of the board; retaining images of a position that no longer exists; and so on. Aside from being aware of these dangers, there is no simple way of avoiding oversights except this: Recheck everything.

Chapter 9

RECHECKING

"Mistrust is the most necessary characteristic of the chessplayer."
—*Siegbert Tarrasch*

Even after you've worked out the general features of a calculated line, whether two moves deep or 10, and you're certain of the evaluation and move order, you're still not done. In a game of speed chess or a coffee-house game, you might stop there and make your move. But in a more serious situation, such as a tournament game, you should check over your analysis.

There are several methods of verifying your work. The checklist of questions to ask yourself includes:

1) Am I somehow making a crass error, like mentally making two moves in a row or moving a piece illegally?

2) Am I certain of what the final position looks like? Where are the pieces? Did I make a mistake in visualization? For example, am I still seeing that bishop on b3 in the final position when I've sacrificed it on my second move?

3) Is there, in fact, a better way of using the basic ideas? Can I improve matters with the insertion of an intermediary move?

4) In looking for my opponent's weak spot, have I overlooked my own Achilles' heel, something that will short-circuit my intended sequence?

The benefits of rechecking variations should be obvious. Yet it is shocking how often a player will plunge into a high-risk variation, even with plenty of time on his clock, after only a cursory inspection of the main lines, a once-over for the entire tree.

BERNSTEIN – LASKER
St. Petersburg 1914

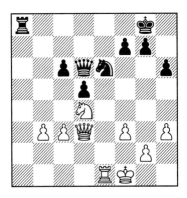

Black to move

Here is one of the most famous examples of bad rechecking. In what was arguably the greatest tournament held up to that time, world champion Emanuel Lasker nearly failed to qualify for the finals because of this game.

With an advantage as Black, he seeks a way to exploit White's kingside, either with 1...♕h2 or 1...♕g3, followed in either case by 2...♘f4 or even 2...♕xg2+.

The two queen moves are similar, but not exactly alike. After either one, White will probably capture on e6. But 1...♕g3 2.♘xe6 fxe6 3.♖xe6 ♖a1+ would win for Black, and so would the improved version with the *Zwischenzug* 2...♖a2!. (White could play 2.♘e2, of course, but then 2...♕h2 is very strong.)

1...   ♕h2?

$$2.\unicode{x2658}xe6 \qquad \unicode{x2656}a2$$

This threatens mate on g2 and h1. Clearly White has one reply and clearly Black must have counted on it when he considered the diagram position.

$$3.\unicode{x2656}e2 \qquad \unicode{x2656}a1+$$
$$4.\unicode{x2654}f2$$

This move was obvious. Yet Lasker completely missed it. According to an eyewitness (Siegbert Tarrasch), the world champion said afterward that he believed somehow White would now be mated on e1. But there is no mate, and after 4...fxe6 5.♕g6! he had to play the ending a pawn down, and eventually lost.

Walkthrough

Whether beginning a combination or simply defending a difficult position, before playing a move that requires serious calculation it always pays to walk through the variation mentally one more time, *slowly*. The mind can play all sorts of tricks on the calculator who rushes.

Mikhail Tal liked to recall how in his first serious match he rejected a simple defensive idea that would have left him a rook ahead, and began to analyze instead "a fantastically beautiful" combination. He decided to play it. But, after several moves had been made, he "discovered the whole point of my combination lay in the move ...♗f8-g5(!!!).

"And since bishops don't move that way, I had to resign."

Something similar happened to David Bronstein in his most important event when, after lengthy thought, he came up with "a wonderful combination." But he then passed up both a chance to walk through his analysis – and paid the price. It began when, as Black, he initiated an early queenside attack:

BOTVINNIK – BRONSTEIN
World Championship (9) 1951

1.d4 e6 2.c4 f5 3.g3 ♘f6 4.♗g2 ♗e7 5.♘c3 0-0 6.d5 ♗b4 7.♗d2 e5 8.e3 d6 9.♘ge2 a6 10.♕c2 ♕e8 11.f3 b5!

This looks like a blunder because of...

12.♕b3!   ♗c5

Black forges on. He can bail out with 12...♗xc3 13.♘xc3 bxc4 14.♕xc4 ♕f7, with a fine game positionally.

13.cxb5

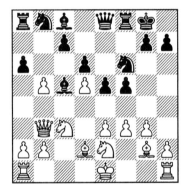

Now with 13...axb5 14.♘xb5 ♕f7!, attacking the d-pawn, Black can obtain a solid initiative for his sacrificed pawn: 15.e4 fxe4 16.fxe4 ♘g4; or 15.♘bc3 c6.

But, as Bronstein explained many years later, he had intended a much more elaborate continuation of the sequence he began at move 11. His idea was to allow White to queen a pawn in such a way that the new queen would become trapped and would lead to a material edge for Black.

However, once the sequence began Bronstein was afraid to recheck his variations because he might be frightened off by some nonexistent refutation. "How many times has precisely that happened with me!" he added.

13...   ♗**d7?**

Black saw that 14.bxa6 ♘xa6 was risky, e.g. 15.0-0 f4 16.gxf4 exf4 17.♘xf4 ♗xe3+!, winning a piece. So he guessed White's next move.

14.♘a4!   ♗**a7**

Black can also cut his losses here with 14...axb5 15.♘xc5 dxc5.

15.b6   ♗**xa4**

Black is consistent: he's not so badly off after 15...cxb6 16.♘xb6 ♗xb6 17.♕xb6 ♘xd5 18.♕xd6.

16.b7!   ♗**xb3**

A remarkable position. Here Bronstein turned pale and his "head began to spin," he recalled. In his calculations back at the diagram position, he had counted on playing ...♗b6 here, and after White plays bxa8♕, he wins the queen back with ...♗xd5.

White would then have to give up his second queen and emerge from the complications with only a rook for it.

17.bxa8♕   ♗**b6**

...but it was not Black's turn to play, but White's. Bronstein had blundered into a bad line by mentally making two moves in a row. Play continued:

18.axb3   ♕**b5**

And having lost the exchange, Black was in serious trouble. (But he later drew.)

265

A more contemporary example reveals an even stranger aberration.

HJARTARSON – SALOV
Barcelona 1989

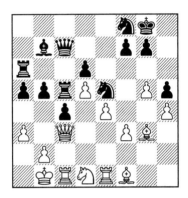

White to move

Black has just played the blunder ...♖c5, and White knows why it is a blunder. He quickly calculated the winning reply. But then decided on **1.♗e2?** instead, realizing his error only when he pushed his clock.

Where is the win? It starts with 1.♗xe5 dxe5, which removes the pawn support for the c5-rook. Then 2.b4! axb4 3.axb4 traps the rook in the middle of the board.

Why did White reject that? Because he convinced himself that the variation failed to 3...cxb3 (that is, *en passant*) 4.♕xc5 ♕a5 with a mating attack. Of course, a thorough review of the variation would have shown him that the *en passant* capture is not legal.

The reason we make such errors is that often when we calculate we add and subtract moves to the trees very quickly in order to consider the maximum number of candidates. Inevitably, a few things are overlooked. So, before choosing a final move, we should take an extra minute to re-examine those trees. Among the questions we should ask are:

Where Are the Pieces?

Spectators are often surprised by the moves of the greatest players. But virtually everyone, amateur or grandmaster, who watched the ninth game of the 1990 world championship match unfold were struck dumb by this:

KARPOV – KASPAROV
World Championship (9) 1990

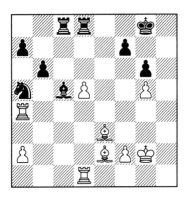

White to move

Anatoly Karpov, with an excellent position – even with mating chances along the h-file – and with thirteen minutes to play nine moves, took three minutes before selecting:

1.♗d2??

When the move appeared on a huge electronic demonstration board, Valery Salov, among others, was sure there had been a mechanical error. "Here I am, a well-known grandmaster, and I couldn't explain to the spectators what White intended to do in answer to 1...♖xd5," he recalled.

There was no answer. Karpov later explained that he had calculated 1.♗f4, with its threat of 2.♗e5! with ♖h1-h8#. He concluded that 1...♗d6 was forced, and then 2.♗d2! would win material (2...♘b7 3.♖xa7; 2...♗c7? 3.♗c3).

Since that might have been a winning position, good calculating technique required White to walk through his line once more and ask about the end positions: "Where are the pieces?" Had Karpov done this, he would have seen **1...♖xd5,** which (luckily for him) led only to a draw, and might have found the improved idea, 1.♗c1! (1...♗f8 2.♗b2 ♗g7 3.♗f6!), which might have won.

Rechecking where the pieces are is most important in forcing and sacrificial variations because typically there is more to lose if you mentally misplace material.

SASIKIRAN – SHORT
Skanderborg 2003

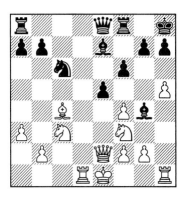

White to move

White had an inspired thought based on a familiar mating pattern: He calculated 1.♘h4 ♗xe2 2.♘g6+.

The pattern comes into view after 2...hxg6 3.hxg6+. Black's king has no moves. White must have seen that the forced move 3...♗h5 can be answered by 4.♖xh5#.

What else was there to calculate? Well, White had to make sure that after 1.♘h4 there was no way for Black to avoid both 2.♕xg4 and 2.♘g6+.

And, yes, there *was* something else. White went ahead with **1.♘h4** and Black met **1...♗xe2 2.♘g6+** with **2...♕xg6.**

White retook, **3.hxg6,** and threatened 4.♖xh7# as well as taking the bishop on e2. He may have an edge after 3...h6 4.♘xe2, for example.

But if he could visualize that the black bishop was at e2 in that line he should have been able to see that Black had a much better move, **3...♗xc4!.**

White is suddenly two pieces down and, after **4.♖xh7+ ♔g8,** he resigned – because he didn't check where the pieces were. **0-1**

It's embarrassing when you lose sight of pieces in the course of a game. It's humiliating when you do it in print:

PKHAKADZE – FRIDINSKY
USSR 1972

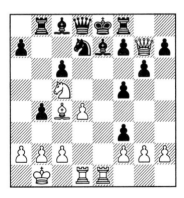

Black to move

This comes from a game analyzed in a Soviet magazine by Black, a master, and also by grandmaster Eduard Gufeld. Their comment at this point was: "If 15...♘xc5 16.dxc5 ♕c7, then 17.♖d6! White's initiative is sufficient for a draw.

"For example, 17...fxg2 18.♕xh7 g1♕ 19.♗xf7+ ♖xf7 20.♕g8+ ♖f8 21.♕xg6+ with perpetual check."

That's a long variation, but it's worth trying to visualize it out to the end. Do this in your head and try to think of where all the pieces are. Then play the position out on a board, and you'll see what the annotators missed: There's a black queen on g1 that can move backward and simply capture that white queen on g6!

That was a long and difficult variation to walk through. But even in short variations – as short as two moves in length – it's wise to take time before initiating a line of play by mentally picturing what the board looks like at the end of your calculations.

SAIDY – MAROVIĆ
Málaga 1969

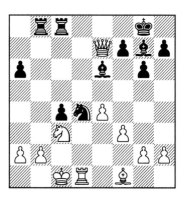

Black to move

Black has sacrificed his queen for rook and bishop, and a bit of an attack. With 1...♘b5, for example, he can obtain considerable long-term counterplay against the king (2.♘a4 c3!; 2.♘xb5 axb5 3.a3 ♗f8 followed by 4...b4).

But Black's position also suggests he may have something quicker. The tactical idea that has caught his eye is to catch the white king in the corner at a1, where something like a smothered mate can occur after ...♘c2+.

How to get there? Well, 1...♗h6+ 2.♔b1 ♖xb2+ is a start. After 3.♔xb2 ♖b8+ 4.♔a1 ♘c2 we have the mate. White can avoid this with 4.♔a3 or even with 4.♘b5. But the knight move is too risky because of 4...♗g7! (better than 4...♘xb5 5.♖d8+, or 4...♖xb5+ 5.♔c3!).

Therefore the main line seems to be 1...♗h6+ 2.♔b1 ♖xb2+ 3.♔xb2 ♖b8+ 4.♔a3. Now there is no ...♘c2 mate. But Black's tactical eye has spotted the possibility of winning back the queen with ...♗f8. The immediate 4...♗f8 fails to 5.♕xf8+ and 6.♖xd4, after which Black is a piece down with nothing left to fuel his attack.

So Black takes one last look. And there it is: After 4.♔a3, he can play 4...♘c6, attacking the enemy queen and removing the knight from capture with a gain of time. Then, regardless of where the queen moves, Black will play 5...♗f8+! and emerge with at least material equality.

1...	**♗h6+?!**
2.♔b1	**♖xb2+?**
3.♔xb2	**♖b8+**
4.♔a3	**♘c6**
5.♕c5!	**♗f8**
6.♖d6	

Black completely missed this defense. He missed it because he failed to ask himself where the pieces were after 4...♘c6. Had he asked, he would have seen that the rook was available for blocking the bishop's diagonal.

6...	**♘e5**

Black tries to use tricks to make up for what he failed to do with solid calculation. White avoided 7.♕xe5?? ♖b6! and won with **7.f4! ♘d3 8.♗xd3 exd3 9.♕d4 ♖e8 10.♔b2 1-0.**

One further example illustrates faulty calculation by both players, but only one of them is punished. White fails to visualize where his rook and king will be after three moves and allows what should have been a winning fork. But it all works out well in the end.

BENI – SCHWARZBACH
Vienna 1969

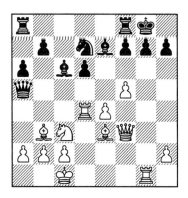

Black to move

Black played **1...♗f6,** not so much to attack the rook as to defend g7. The move also leaves the d-pawn hanging and it must have occurred to White that a trap was being set.

What happens on 2.♖xd6?, he asked himself. Black can play 2... ♗xc3 3.bxc3 and then what? On 3...♕xc3, Black seems to be both attacking and defending. But he's given up his dark-squared bishop, and that suggests some kind of trick such as 4.♗d4! (attacking the queen and g7) 4...♕xf3 5.♖xg7+.

So White continued:

2.♖xd6!?!	**♗xc3**
3.bxc3	**♕a3+**

This is what White overlooked. He didn't see that his rook was unprotected at d6, that White's b-pawn was now on c3, and that this now-possible check was a fork.

4.♔b1   ♛xd6

End of sad story? No, because even though it was not intended, White has a winning position after all. Black, who had almost certainly seen the 4...♛xd6 position when he played 1...♗f6, has made another of our rechecking errors: He stopped too short.

5.♗d4!!

Now g7 can be defended by 5...g6, but then 6.♛h5! is a killer (6...♘e5 7.fxg6 ♘xg6 8.♛h6, for example). And 5...♘e5 6.♛g3 or 6.♛g2 is fairly deadly.

Black actually played **5...♛h6** and allowed the wonderful windmill combination **6.♛h3! ♛xh3 7.♖xg7+ ♔h8 8.♖xf7+ ♔g8 9.♖g7+ ♔h8 10.♖xd7+** and mate next. (Yes, he overlooked the immediate 10.♖g8#).

Remember to Remember

There's a story about Richard Réti and the day in 1925 when he set a new world record in São Paulo by playing 29 blindfold games simultaneously. On his way out of the playing site, an Argentine fan rushed over to Réti to bring him his beloved portfolio.

"Thank you very much," Réti replied. "I always forget it. I have a terrible memory."

Our ability as players to visualize incredibly complex and lengthy variations – and then to forget something relatively simple – is something we have to live with. Often you'll hear this refrain in postmortem: "I saw the combination, but then I forgot what move makes it work."

Sometimes what we overlook isn't even a two-mover.

GUNSBERG – CHIGORIN
Match (10), La Habana 1890

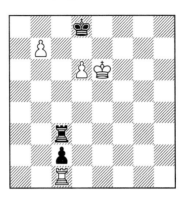

Black to move

These two players were world championship challengers and they played well – up to a point:

1...	♖e3+!
2.♔d5	♖b3
3.♔c6	♖c3+!
4.♔b6	♖b3+
5.♔c6	♖c3+
6.♔d5	♖b3
7.♔e6	

Now 7...♖e3+! would repeat the position following Black's first move above. But Black saw a new idea, forgot how easily the checks would draw, and played...

7...	♖xb7??
8.♖h1!	

And Black had to resign or be mated.

A more modern example proved just as costly:

YUSUPOV – TIMMAN
Candidates' Match (9) 1992

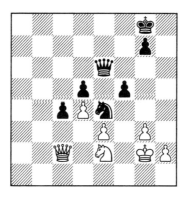

Black to move

Here Black found the winning plan 1...♘f6 followed by 2...♘g4 – even if White plays 2 ♘f4. There followed:

1...	**♘f6!**
2.♘f4	**♛e4+?**

Played after 15 minutes' thought. Black saw that 2...♘g4! 3.♘xe6 ♘xe3+ 4.♔f3 ♘xc2 is a win (5.♔f4 c3) but simply forgot about it.

You can often forget your original intention when you see an appealing alternative line, particularly one that seems to win.

3.♛xe4	**dxe4**
4.♔f2!	**♘g4+**
5.♔e2	**♘xh2**
6.♘g6	

But it doesn't win, and after **6...c3 7.♘e7+ ♔f7 8.♘xf5 ♘f1 9.♔d1 ♔f6 10.g4 g6** a draw was agreed.

Ideally, we could prevent forgetfulness the way postal players do, by recording our analysis on a sheet of paper. Unfortunately, that is quite illegal in over-the-board play.

A good, *legal* alternative remedy for this and similar calculating maladies is to stop before making the first move of a calculated sequence and explain your train of thought to yourself as if to a stranger. Black, for example, would have said back at the diagram: "Okay, first I'm going to play 1...♘f6, after which 2...♘g4, winning the e-pawn, cannot be prevented. In fact, I can even meet 2.♘f4 with 2...♘g4!"

With this device, it becomes much harder to forget what must be remembered.

Ghosts

That procedure would also help deal with ghosts, another of the common pitfalls that befall calculators. These are flashbacks to ideas, variations, or other bits of analysis that occurred in the calculator's mind earlier in the game.

Rather than recheck his thoughts, the calculator often relies on past work. In the Chigorin rook ending, this would have saved Black. But that's because the position was almost exactly the same in the diagram as six moves later. In most games, the positions don't repeat exactly:

LARSEN – SMYSLOV
Hastings 1988-89

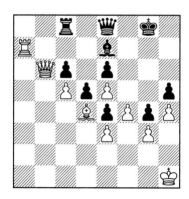

White to move

This was the kind of position in which we say White can calculate "without an opponent." He has been slowly improving his position for many moves and decides the time is right for:

1.f5!   **exf5**
2.♕b7??   **♚f7!**

And White can no longer win (3.♕b1 ♚e6 4.♕f1 ♖a8, etc.).

Afterward White wondered how he could have missed the winning 2.e6!, the necessary prelude to 3.♕b7, which then wins.

He answered the question himself: White had earlier calculated a similar variation with the white queen on c7. Then ...♚f7 was no defense because the pawn advances to e6 with check. This bit of information remained in his consciousness in a misleading form and he mistakenly believed that ♕b7 would be a winning move as soon as Black played ...exf5.

Here's a more elaborate example.

SILMAN – ROOT
Los Angeles 1990

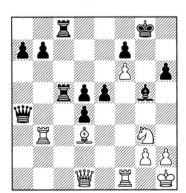

White to move

In this complex, sacrificial position, White played:

277

1.h4!

...which was based on 1...♗xh4 2.♕g4+ ♔f8 3.♕g7+ ♔e8 4.♖xb7 and wins.

What happens if Black blocks with 2...♗g5, you may wonder? Then White counted on penetrating to h7 with 3.♕f5 e4 4.♘xe4!. For example, 4...dxe4 5.♕xe4 ♔f8 6. ♖xb7! and wins.

But, as Silman commented later, this last variation "actually contributed to my defeat since I soon tried to reconstruct it in a completely different situation." Amid deepening time pressure, play continued:

1...		♖c1
2.♕f3	e4	

And now the relatively simple 3.♕g4 and 4.hxg5 must win, as White intended when he played 2.♕f3. But as Silman recalled in *Inside Chess:*

"After Black played ...e5-e4 I stared at the clock and saw that I had a couple of minutes left. I looked at the board and my brain went dead. ... Panic! ... Then I remembered..."

3.♘xe4??

White recalled only the key idea in the 1.h4 ♗xh4 variation. This "ghost" cost him the game:

3...		dxe4
4.♕xe4	♖xf1+	
5.♔h2	♗f4+	

White resigned as soon as the time control was reached: **6.♔h3** ♕d7+ 7.g4 ♖h1+! 8.♕xh1 ♕e6 9.♖xb7 ♕e3+ 0-1.

Throughout this book you've been confronted with diagrams showing complicated positions, and it probably took you a good deal of time to recognize the key elements in each new position. But if you had been playing the game in question, you could have reached certain conclusions much faster.

That is because you would have visualized the diagram position, or an approximation of it, earlier in the game and made certain assumptions about it. For example, you might have concluded previously that such a position is very favorable to you; that you should try to trade queens if given the opportunity; that your first positional priority is creating a passed c-pawn; and so on.

Those assumptions stay with you and may become unwelcome ghosts. So, when making a major decision in a game, it always pays to question your assumptions. Let's see how:

ALEKHINE – KASHDAN
Bled 1931

Black to move

Facing the world champion, a young American master (Black) used his extra pawn brilliantly:

1... **g4!!**

The point was revealed after...

2.♕xh5 **♕d4+**

Now White sees that, after 3 ♔g2, Black can exchange queens and win: 3...♕d2+ 4.♔g1 ♕e3+ 5.♔h2 ♕f2+ 6.♔h1 ♕f1+ 7.♔h2 ♕xh3+! 8.♕xh3 gxh3 9.♔xh3, and now 9...♔d5 10.♔g4 ♔c4 11.♔g5 ♔xb4 12.♔f6 a5 13.♔xf7 a4 14.g4 a3 15.g5 a2 and queens.

Play continued:

3.♔e2 ♕e4+ 4.♔d1 ♕d3+ 5.♔c1 ♕f1+ 6.♔d2 ♕g2+ 7.♔d1 ♕f1+ 8.♔d2 gxh3 9.♕c5+ ♔e6 10.♕c8+ ♔f6 11.♔e3 ♕e1+ 12.♔f3 ♕e6 13.♕c3+ ♔g6 14.g4

Black can nurse his passed pawn home with careful but simple play: 14...♕d5+ 15.♔g3 ♕g2+ 16.♔h4 h2, and there is no perpetual check (17.♕d3+ ♔g7 18.♕c3+ f6! 19.♕c7+ ♔g6).

But Black now suffers a delusion. He believes he can get the same kind of king-and-pawn ending that would have won for him in the 3.♔g2 variation mentioned above. After all, 14...♕f6+ forces queens off the board and brings the black king closer to the queenside, whereas White's king will have to spend time winning the h-pawn before it can go after the f-pawn.

14...	**♕f6+?**
15.♕xf6+	**♔xf6**

What he should have done at move 14 is to visualize this position and ask himself, "Does my a-pawn still win the race against the g-pawn?"

The answer would have been: "No! I'm two tempi behind the other variation."

16.♔g3	**♔e5**
17.♔xh3	**♔d4**
18.♔h4	

And here Black saw nothing better than to accept White's draw offer. He had become yet another victim of a ghost. ½-½

Lasker's Law

One of the easiest ways to improve your tournament results is to learn to sit on your hands.

KHARITONOV – DAUTOV
Kaliningrad 1986

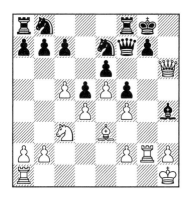

Black to move

White has sacrificed a piece to develop a virulent attack along the g-file (♖ag1 and ♖xg7+). Defensive measures such as 1...♗f6 2 exf6 offer little hope of salvation. Black tries a different tactic: confusion.

1...   **g5!?**

Clearly hoping for something like 2.fxg5?? ♘g6, clogging the attacking lanes. But there can't be anything wrong with 2.♕xh4, can there?

2.♕xh4?

What's wrong with this seemingly obvious move is that there was a much better one.

2...   g4!
3.f3   ♕h7
4.♕xh7+?!   ♔xh7

And after **5.fxg4 fxg4 6.♖xg4 ♘f5,** Black had survived the worst and had real drawing chances.

But after 1...g5 the game would likely have ended within five moves, not 20, if White had continued 2.♖ag1!. For example, 2...g4 3.♖xg4+! fxg4 4.♖xg4+; or 2...♘g6 3.♖xg5! ♗xg5 4.♖xg5, winning the queen in either case.

White failed to heed Emanuel Lasker's sage advice: When you see a good move, don't make it immediately. Look for a better one.

There's a logical basis for this. Winning moves do not come about because of the brilliance of the players but because of the soundness of their position. A powerful position can generate more than one tactical idea. And often that idea can be improved a bit.

PANNO – BRAVO
Fortaleza 1975

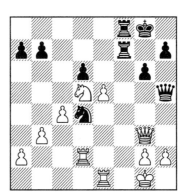

Black to move

It's Black's move and he surely must see 1...♘e2+. The fork of king and queen forces 2.♖dxe2, after which 2...♕xe2! appears to win the exchange (3.♖xe2?? ♖f1#).

But there are two things wrong with this picture. László Szabó, the Hungarian grandmaster, recalled that he began to improve his calculation when he reminded himself of this motto: After you're finished calculating, calculate one move further.

Following Szabó's advice, we look at the position after 2...♕xe2. Since Black is threatening 3...♖f1+, we should be looking for something forceful by White. That suggests a check: 3.♘e7+ works if Black takes the knight (3...♖xe7?? 4.♖xe2), but not if he finds 3...♔h8!. On the other hand, there is 3.♘f6+!, which forces 3...♖xf6 4.exf6 when Black has lost his material and positional advantages.

But if we apply Lasker's Law, we succeed in finding a better move: It's **1...♕e2!**. Black threatens 2...♕xd2 as well as 2...♖f1+ or 2...♕f1+. And 2.♖dxe2 ♘xe2+ 3.♖xe2 ♖f1 is mate. White resigned after **2.♖dd1 ♕xd1** (3.♖xd1 ♘e2+ 4.♔h1 ♖f1+ and mate next). **0-1**

The superior move you should look for need not be the first one of a sequence but may come two or three moves later. For instance, in the following diagram the potential tactical idea should occur readily: It's the last rank.

CROUCH – SPEELMAN
Hastings 1992-93

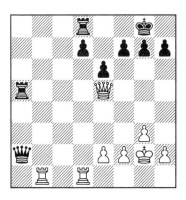

White to move

Once White sees that idea, several candidate moves occur to him, including 1.♖xd7, 1.♕c7, 1.♖b8, and even 1.♕b8 (1...♖xb8?? 2.♖xb8#).

They all appear to be easily met by 1...♖aa8. So White, who is a pawn behind, regained his material with **1.♖xd7** and then drew after **1...♖f8!** and **2.♖b2 ♖xe5.**

But there is a win, and the method is 1.♖b8 ♖aa8 and now 2.♖a1!!, since 2...♕xa1 3.♖xd8+ ♖xd8 4.♕xa1 costs a queen, as does 2...♖dxb8 3.♖xa2 (3...♖xa2?? 4.♕xb8#).

In the next example, the move to find is actually a spectacular third move in the sequence. At first, White sees that with 1.♘e6+ ♗xe6 2.♕xd3 he can trade off Black's pesky knight and get closer to an ending. But in that ending his exchange may be no better than Black's pawns.

PORTISCH – FORINTOS
Hungarian Championship 1971

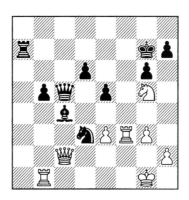

White to move

A further look shows him that 1.♕xd3(!) ♗xd3 2.♘e6+ and 3.♘xc5 reaches another endgame but one that doesn't seem nearly as good. Before abandoning this position, White employs Lasker's Law at the third move.

$$\begin{array}{ll} \textbf{1.♕xd3!} & \textbf{♗xd3} \\ \textbf{2.♘e6+} & \textbf{♔h6} \end{array}$$

Forced, since other king moves permit 3.♖f8#.

3.g4!!

A terrific finesse. By creating the threat of 4.♖h3#, White forces...

3...	**g5**
4.♖f6+	**♗g6**
5.♘xc5!	

Now we have a much superior endgame to the ones considered back at the diagram. After **5...dxc5 6.♖xb5,** Black had only a pawn for the exchange, and he eventually lost.

A graphic example of grasped – and missed – opportunities like this was the following. Set this one up on a board and consider all the calculating mistakes:

BRONSTEIN – R. SHERBAKOV
Lloyds Bank (London) 1992

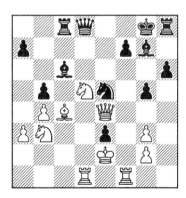

White to move

White has sacrificed two pawns to place his rooks and two minor pieces on superior squares. Black's last move (...b7-b5) appears to refute the attack, but White finds:

1.♘d4	**bxc4**
2.♘f5!	

White's original intention was likely 2.♘xc6 ♖xc6 3.♘f6+, but it would not have taken him long to see that 2...♕xf6 3.♖xf6 ♗xf6 is a winning material edge for Black.

But after 2.♘f5 White threatens two good knight checks on e7, and the black queen has no easy escape (2...♕e8 3.♘d6 and then 3...♕e6 4.♘xc8 ♗xd5 5.♖xd5 ♕xc8 6.♖xe5 with unclear results). To keep an edge, **Black has to find the queen-sacrificing 2...♖c7! 3.♘de7+ ♕xe7 4.♘xe7+ ♖xe7.**

2...	**♗xd5**
3.♖xd5	**♕c7??**

In time trouble, Black misses his chance to transpose into the last note with 3...♕e8 4.♘d6 ♕e6, and should now lose.

4.♖c5!	**♕d7!**
5.♖xc8+	**♗f8!**

Now, with a material edge but a far from clear position, White's best is 6.♖xf8+! ♔xf8 7.♕a8+! ♕e8 8.♕xa7 and 9.♕c5+ with a nearly winning position. But again White played a good-looking, second-best move.

6.♖xf8+!	**♔xf8**
7.♕xe5??	

White mars his fine play by missing 7.♖d1!, e.g. 7...♘d3 8.♘xe3 ♕e8 9.♕xe8+ ♔xe8 10.♘xc4 and wins.

7...	**♕d3+!**
8.♔f3	**♕xf1+**

And now White should have conceded a draw, which was still available via 9.♔e4! ♕d3+ 10.♔f3 because of 10...e2+ 11.♔f2! e1♕+ 12.♔xe1 ♕b1+ and perpetual check.

But he actually played **9.♔g4??** and was lost after **9...♕d1+ 10.♔h3 ♕h5+ 11.♘h4 g4+!** and **12...♕xe5.**

Improving the Breed

Often a sequence can be improved by the insertion of an intermediary move at its very start. An illustration is this opening trap: 1.e4 c5 2.♘f3 d6 3.d4 cxd4 4.♘xd4 ♘f6 5.♘c3 g6 6.f4 ♗g7 7.e5 dxe5 8.fxe5 ♘d5? 9.♗b5+! ♔f8 10.0-0 ♗xe5.

A Soviet opening manual several years ago claimed that White wins with 11.♘xd5 ♕xd5 12.♘f5, with the idea 12...♕xd1 13.♗h6+ ♗g7 14.♖axd1 and a winning attack.

However, after 12...♕c5+ 13.♗e3 ♕c7 14.♘h6, Black has some hope of surviving with 14...f5!.

Russian amateurs then tried to save the analysis by examining 14.♗h6+ (instead of 14.♘h6) 14...♔g8 15.♘xe7+ ♕xe7 16.♖xf7!?, with immense complications.

But, as so often happens, the easiest way to improve a sequence lies at the beginning, not at the end. Here it is quite simple: White plays 12.♗h6+! first instead of 12.♘f5. Black cannot interpose (12...♗g7 13.♗c4! ♕c5 14.♖xf7+!). Therefore 12...♔g8 follows, and then White can begin his sequence in improved form: 13.♘f5! ♕c5+ (forced) 14.♗e3 ♕c7.

We now have the same position as in the opening manual, but with one significant difference: The black king is on g8 instead of f8. White exploits this difference with 15.♘h6, which is now a decisive check.

Or you can improve a variation with a tempo-gaining move that pushes your opponent's pieces onto bad squares:

KASPAROV – KAMSKY
Linares 1993

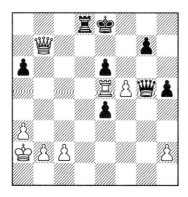

White to move

At first it seems that White's choice is between 1.♖xe6+ and 1.fxe6. The former is the most forcing, but after 1...♔f8 the only reasonable follow-up (2.f6, threatening 3.♕e7+) allows 2...♕d5+ and a trade of queens.

The pawn capture also has a major point, since 1.fxe6 ♕xe5?? allows mate on f7. Clearly, White stands well after 1...♕e7 2.♕c6+ and 3.♖xh5. But does he have better?

He does with one minor addition:

1.h4!

Black could have resigned here since the queen now has no way of watching both e7 and d5. The game ended with:

1...	♕xh4
2.♖xe6+	♔f8
3.f6	**1-0**

Because 4.♕xg7# as well as 4.♕e7+ are threatened.

So far we've examined forcing moves inserted at the beginning or middle of a sequence. But often the move that improves a sequence is exceptionally quiet:

SERPER – PĘDZICH
European Junior Championship 1989

1.c4 g6 2.♘c3 c5 3.g3 ♗g7 4.♗g2 ♘c6 5.a3 a6 6.♖b1 ♖b8 7.b4 cxb4 8.axb4 b5 9.cxb5 axb5 10.♘f3 e5 11.d4!? exd4 12.♘d5 ♘ge7 13.♗g5 ♗b7

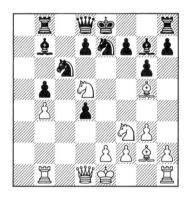

Here White went into a long think about what he called the "natural" combination 14.♘xd4 ♗xd4 15.♕xd4! ♘xd4 16.♘f6+ ♔f8 17.♗h6#!. (It's natural because it works in a lot of similar opening traps.)

On further inspection, though, he questioned his assumption that Black must play 14...♗xd4. What, he wondered, do I do on 14...♘xd4! and then 15.♗xe7 ♕xe7! 16.♘xe7 ♗xg2 17.♖g1 ♗b7. The e7-knight is lost.

So White decided that the best combination in the position was none of the above.

14.0-0!

Whatever Black does now will result in an edge for White.

14...	0-0
15.♘xd4!	f6

Or 15...♗xd4 16.♘xe7+ ♘xe7 17.♕xd4 with a positionally won game. As the game proceeded, White's edge was clear following **16.♗f4 ♘e5 17.♘xb5 ♘xd5 18.♗xd5+** and he won in seven more moves.

The slight but decisive improvement of a sequence was a prime feature in one of the finest combinations played in the early twentieth century:

BREYER – ESSER
Budapest 1917

1.d4 d5 2.c4 c6 3.e3 ♘f6 4.♘c3 e6 5.♗d3 ♗d6 6.f4 0-0 7.♘f3 dxc4 8.♗b1?! b5 9.e4 ♗e7 10.♘g5 h6 11.h4!? g6 12.e5 hxg5 13.hxg5 ♘d5

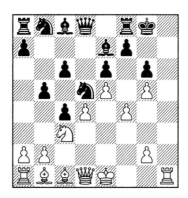

White has a strong attack for his sacrificed knight. The natural follow-up is to get the queen to the h-file (at h8 or h7) as soon as possible. Gyula Breyer, one of Hungary's greatest chess talents, saw that 14.♕g4 virtually forces 14...♔g7 (with the idea of 15...♖h8).

Then White can begin a long but forcing sequence: 15.♖h7+! ♔xh7 16.♕h5+ ♔g7 17.♕h6+ ♔g8 18.♗xg6! fxg6 19.♕xg6+ ♔h8 20.♕h6+ ♔g8 21.g6 looks very strong. In checking over his sequences, however, Breyer noticed the flaw. At the very end, Black has the defense 21...♗h4+ and 22...♕e7!, covering the h7 mating square.

But before giving up on this wonderful sequence, White began to appreciate how bound up Black is. Black's only defensive idea is 14...♔g7 (and 15...♖h8). And that can be met by 15.♖h7+ ♔xh7 16.♕h5+, transposing into the line given above. So, he looked for an improvement on 14.♕g4.

14.♔f1!!

An amazing move. The threat is 15.♕g4, as we'll see.

14...   ♘xc3

As brilliant as White's play is from move 16 on, he can win more quickly with 15.♕g4 and then 15...♕xd4 16.bxc3 ♕xc3 17.♔e2! followed by ♕h4. But Breyer remains true to his original idea.

15.bxc3   ♗b7?

Hopeless, in retrospect. Black should reinforce g6 with 15...♕e8.

16.♕g4   ♔g7
17.♖h7+!

Now the sequence works because of White's 14th move. Play continued **17...♔xh7** (17...♔g8 18.♕h4) **18.♕h5+ ♔g8 19.♗xg6 fxg6** (19...♖e8 20.♕h7+ and mates) **20.♕xg6+ ♔h8 21.♕h6+ ♔g8 22.g6.**

Now since there is no saving ...♗h4+, Black has to accept the consequences of **22...♖f7 23.gxf7+ ♔xf7 24.♕h5+.** White **would only have perpetual check after 24 ... ♔g8!. But Black lost instead after 24...♔g7? 25.f5 exf5 26.♗h6+ ♔h7 27.♗g5+ ♔g8 28.♕g6+** (and would have lost faster had White played 27.e6!).

In the endgame such gains of time are often not significant. In fact, many endgame positions can be improved by the loss, rather than the gain, of a tempo. For example:

KARPOV – ANAND
Linares 1991

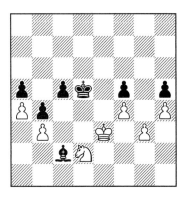

Black to move

Clearly Black has a big advantage, close to decisive. But he needs a passed pawn or an entry for his king to win. Obvious moves yield nothing here, so Black must try to work with the ideas in the position.

What are they? Well, one is the mock sacrifice ...c5-c4. The other is the serious sacrifice ...♗xb3. Black probably considered the pawn sac first, with a main line such as 1...c4 2.♘xc4 (2.bxc4+? ♚c5 and 3...♗xa4) 2...♗xb3 3.♘xa5 ♗xa4, and Black has excellent winning chances.

He probably also examined the flashy 1...♗xb3?! 2.♘xb3 c5 3.♘xa5 b3 before rejecting it as either unsound or unclear. But then he found the best move, a tiny but very significant improvement on both ideas:

1...   **♗d1!!**

White can resign here. He clearly cannot move the knight, since 2.♘c4 ♗xb3 3.♘xa5 ♗xa4 gives Black a pawn more than in the 1...c4 tree.

And king moves are terrible. On 2.♔f2 ♚d4 and 3...♚c3, Black wins as he pleases. What is more important is that 2.♔d3 now loses – thanks to White's loss of tempo – to 2...♗xb3! and 3.♘xb3 c4+. Black's little finesse saved him a lot of work.

Once you learn to sit on your hands, you'll realize how often you used to play second-best moves that looked fine at the time. Or, as in the following, even third-best.

LAUTIER – CHRISTIANSEN
Biel 1991

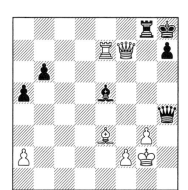

Black to move

Despite the material equality, Black is in very poor shape and would be close to losing after, say, 1...♗f6 2.♖e8. So Black goes in for...

1...   ♗xg3!?

White no doubt considered the natural 2.fxg3 ♖xg3 + 3.♔f1 ♕h1+ 4.♔e2 and may have concluded that he had good chances.

2.♖e8

Good enough. Black got a few checks – **2...♕h2+ 3.♔f1 ♕h1+ 4.♔e2** – and resigned a short time after **4...♖xe8 5.♕xe8+ ♔g7 6.♗d4+**

♔h6 7.♕e6+. But if White saw enough to realize that 2...♕h2+ was not a serious threat, he should have looked further and found 2.♗g5!, which would have ended the game almost immediately (2...♕xg5 3.♕xh7#; 2...♕h2+ 3.♔f1 ♕h3+ 4.♔e2 ♕g4+ 5.f3).

One final example, a full game in which White repeatedly passes up one candidate move for a slightly improved one:

SHIROV – HAUCHARD
Paris 1990

1.d4 ♘f6 2.c4 c5 3.d5 b5 4.cxb5 a6 5.b6 d6 6.♘c3 ♘bd7 7.a4 ♕xb6 8.a5 ♕c7 9.e4 g6 10.f4 ♗g7 11.♗c4 0-0 12.♘f3 ♖e8 13.0-0 e5 14.dxe6 fxe6 15.♘g5 ♘f8 16.f5 h6

White can safely offer a piece here with 17.fxg6 hxg5 18.♗xg5 threatening 19.♗xf6. Then 18...♘8d7 19.♘d5 (or the more adventurous 19.♕f3) is more than enough compensation for White.

But on rechecking 17.fxg6, White probably saw 17...♘xg6! and if 18.e5 then 18...♘xe5, with no problems for Black.

So...

| 17.e5! | dxe5 |

On 17...hxg5 White has 18.exf6 ♗xf6 19.♘d5!, and if 19...exd5 20.♗xd5+ forks king and rook.

| 18.fxg6! | hxg5 |

Now we see the improvement provided by his 17th move. If Black tries the 18...♘xg6 idea now, he finds it fails to 19.♖xf6! ♗xf6 20.♕h5 and a ♘e4 move (20...♕g7 21.♘ge4 ♗g5 22.♘xg5 hxg5 23.♗d3! and White wins).

19.♗xg5	♘8d7
20.♕f3!?	♖a7
21.♖ad1	♕b7
22.♕h3	♕c6

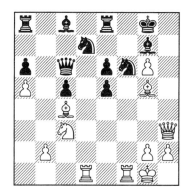

Now White sees another opportunity to employ the same ♘d5 idea that has been in the position since move 17. He would like to play 23.♘d5 exd5 24.♗xd5+ ♕xd5 25.♖xd5 "and wins."

But this is a false end position. The real one is 25...♘b6!, after which it is not at all clear that White is winning. So White improves again on a sequence.

23.♘d5!	exd5
24.♖xd5!	

This is based on 24...♘b6 25.♖d7+! and now 25...♘fd5 26.♕h7 is mate. The most complex line is 25...♘xc4 26.♖xf6! ♕xf6! 27.♕h7+ ♔f8 28.♗xf6 and White wins.

24...	♔f8
25.♕h7	♖e6!

Otherwise 26.♖xd7! or 26.♗h6! wins quickly.

26.♗h6	♔e8

$$27.\text{♛xg7} \qquad \text{♞xd5}$$

Now 28.♗g5! wins.

$$28.\text{♛h8+?} \qquad \text{♔e7}$$

One more finesse. White would love to finish with 29.g7 and queen next move. But 29...♖xh6 30.g8♛ ♖xh8 is unclear enough for White to ask if he has yet another improvement on an idea.

$$29.\text{g7} \qquad \text{♖xh6?}$$

Black's turn to miss a win: 29...♗b7!.

$$30.\text{♖f7+!}$$

And, by finding a forcing method, White convinced Black to give up after **30...♔xf7 31.g8♛+ ♔e7 32.♛d8+** because it is mate next move. **1-0**

Achilles' Heel

Even when you have rechecked a variation using all of the previous procedures, there are times when one final precaution is useful. If you are considering a forcing line in which you hold the initiative, stop: Stop calculating in terms of moves and think in general terms about your own vulnerability.

If you had to put it into words, what is the worst thing you could say about your position tactically?

POPOVYCH – KAVALEK

U.S. Championship 1972

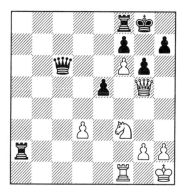

White to move

White has sacrificed the exchange to establish the dangerous pawn at f6 and the ♕h6-g7 mating idea. He wants to play 1.♕h6, but that allows 1...♕xf6.

1.♘h4??

With 1.♘d2, White accomplishes pretty much the same thing (uncovering rook protection of f6, safeguarding g2) and enables himself to play ♘e4 in key lines such as 1...♔h8 2.♕h6 ♖g8 3.♘e4 ♕a8, when now the quiet move 4.♖g1! prepares ♘g5 and mate (4...♕f8 5.♘g5!!).

But White is too optimistic. He doesn't want to allow 1.♘d2 ♖xd2 with equal material.

1... ♖fa8

Only now does White realize that his first rank is just as vulnerable as his g2 square. On 2.♕h6, Black has 2...♕xf6! 3.♖xf6 ♖a1+ and mates. With the knight on d2, White could have played 4.♖f1.

2.♕xe5 ♖f2!

Again exploiting the weakness White failed to appreciate. Now 3.♖xf2 ♕c1+ again mates. White played **3.♔g1 ♖xf1+ 4.♔xf1,** but the handwriting **(4...♖e8 5.♕b2 ♕d6)** was on the wall.

One of the psychological causes of this kind of mistake is that we recognize only the ways in which our position will improve as a result of our intended move and blot out the ways in which it may be compromised.

UBILAVA – SERPER
Manila Olympiad 1992

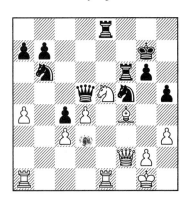

White to move

White appreciates that he has at least a slight edge, but to prove this he must either break the blockade on squares such as f5 or find a way to use his own outpost at e5 effectively. He finds the correct way to begin:

1.g4!　　　　　　**hxg4**

Here 2.♘xg4! would be strong, e.g. 2...♖fe6 3.♗e5+ ♔f7 4.♘e3!, or 3...♔h7 4.♘f6+; or 2...♖xe1+ 3.♖xe1 ♖f7 4.♗e5+ ♔f8 5.♕f4 and ♘h6.

But White sees something more appealing. After 2.hxg4, Black appears to be completely lost, because 3.♗h6+ meets any knight move.

2.hxg4??　　　♖h8!

It probably never occurred to White when considering the position in the diagram that he could be mated on h1, because at that point his king was shielded by pawns at g2, h3, and h5.

3.♘f3　　　♖h3
4.♘h2

White gains a large advantage with 4.gxf5! ♕xf3 5.♕xf3 ♖xf3 6.♗e5; while 4...♖xf3 5.♖e7+ ♖f7 (5...♔f8 6.♖ae1! ♖xf2 7.♗h6+!) 6.♗e5+ ♔f8 7.♖xf7 ♔xf7 8.♕h4 leads to a decisive advantage for White.

4...　　　　　♘g3

White was so shaken by his oversight that he missed his best defensive chances (5.♕xg3! ♖xg3+ 6.♗xg3) and fell apart immediately with **5.♕f3?** ♖xf4!. He resigned after 6.♗e7+ ♖f7 7.♕xf7+ ♕xf7 8.♖xf7+ ♔xf7 9.♔g2 ♖xh2+! 10.♔xh2 ♘e2 0-1.

As a rule of thumb, when a candidate move appears as decisive as 2.hxg4, it calls for the utmost rechecking. That's the hallmark of the practical calculator, as we'll see in the final chapter.

Chapter 10

THE PRACTICAL CALCULATOR

"He was a pitiful sight to behold. Over and over he calculated and recalculated the variations, and couldn't understand how I could save myself. Of course he couldn't – he was looking for something that wasn't there."

> –Anatoly Karpov on a Candidates' Match game he managed to draw from a lost position against Lev Polugayevsky

Among the crucial questions you face in every game is how much you must calculate. Or, rather, when you must calculate, and when it's simply not worth it.

There are two distinctly different points of view here. The perfectionists believe you should always try to find the best move because otherwise you settle for too many second-rate choices that let superior positions slip into draws and equal positions deteriorate into losses.

The pragmatists, on the other hand, believe that the search for the best move is worthwhile only a few times a game because only then is there a *significant* difference between best and second best. And even when there is an objectively "best" move, sometimes it takes too much effort to find it.

Neither side is completely right. Let's see what happens in a classic struggle between a perfectionist and a pragmatist:

KARPOV – KORCHNOI
Candidates' Match (6) 1974

1.e4 e5 2.Nf3 Nf6 3.Nxe5 d6 4.Nf3 Nxe4 5.d4 d5 6.Bd3 Be7 7.0-0 Nc6 8.Re1 Bg4 9.c3 f5 10.Qb3 0-0 11.Nbd2 Kh8 12.h3 Bh5 13.Qxb7 Rf6 14.Qb3

Viktor Korchnoi had already spent 39 minutes on his 11th move and now went off on another enormous – and to spectator Alexander Kotov "incomprehensible" – thinking binge. By the time he had decided on his next move, Black had only 10 minutes of his original two and a half hours left, and shortly after that only seconds to reach the time control at move 40.

"What is the reason for Korchnoi's record irrational expenditure of time?", Kotov asked. "Obviously the first impression is the desire of the creative mind to work out the details of the position.

"However, in this particular case, this is the decisive error. It should be noticed that the variations that arise are so numerous that this task is out of the question."

Remember, these words are coming from an outspoken advocate of deep calculation. But here Kotov was quite right. The game continued **14...Rg6 15.Be2 Bh4? 16.Rf1 Bxf3 17.Nxf3 Bxf2+? 18.Rxf2 Nxf2 19.Kxf2 Qd6 20.Ng5!** (a move Black either overlooked or vastly underestimated) **20...Rf8 21.Qa3.** When he forfeited on time at move 31, Black had been lost for several moves.

One obvious conclusion to draw from this is that it's wrong to spend a lot of time and then make bad moves. But it can also be wrong to invest time lavishly on the best moves. Here's a corollary game, Kavalek–Toth, Haifa 1976:

It followed the same moves as Karpov–Korchnoi until White varied with **9.c4.** There followed **9...♘f6 10.cxd5 ♕xd5!? 11.♘c3 ♗xf3 12.♘xd5 ♗xd1.**

Here White sank into thought. He quickly saw there were only two candidates to consider seriously, 13.♘xe7 and 13.♘xc7+. The only other move to avoid losing a piece, 13.♘xf6+, leaves Black a safe pawn ahead after 13...gxf6 14.♖xd1 ♘xd4 15.♗c4 ♘e6, or 15.♗e4 0-0-0!.

White first looked at the natural 13.♘xe7 ♘xe7 14.♖xd1 and concluded that, after 14...♘fd5 15.♗c4, he had a small edge because of his two bishops. Looking a bit further, he could see no clear plan after 15.♗c4. So he turned to his second candidate. Let's trace his thoughts:

**13.♘xc7+!　　♔d7
14.♗f4**

To decide on his 13th move, White needed to calculate 14...♘h5 in great depth because if the bishop retreats, he remains way behind materially.

Anticipating 14...♘h5, he considered the candidates 15.d5 and 15.♗f5+. He gave up on the former because of 15...♘d4 16.♗e5 and now 16...♗c2!, saving the bishop.

But White found that 15.♗f5+ ♔d8 16.♗e5 was good (16...f6 17.♘xa8 fxe5 18.♖axd1 exd4 19.♗e4 ♗f6, and now 20.b4!). This was one of many points that had to go into the decision to play 13.♘xc7+.

14...	**♗g4**
15.d5	**♘d4**
16.♘xa8	**♖xa8**

White also invested some time back at the diagram considering what would happen on 16...♗d6!?. He concluded he could take advantage of Black's centralized knight with 17.♗e3! ♗f5 18.♗f1 and then 18...♘c2 19.♗b5+ and ♗xa7, returning the exchange but holding a material edge.

17.♗e5	**♗f5**
18.♗f1!	

After finding this fine move in his analysis at move 13, White was confident of gaining the advantage (18...♗c5 19.♖ad1 ♘c2 20.♗b5+ ♔e7 21.d6+ ♔f8 22.♖e2, for example).

Black actually played **18...♘c2** and more material was whisked off the board: **19.♗b5+ ♔d8 20.d6 ♘xe1 21.♖xe1! ♗e6** (21...♗f8?? 22.♗xf6+ and 23.♖e8#) **22.dxe7+ ♔xe7 23.♗d4:**

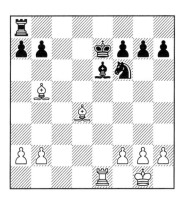

This is one of the many end positions White examined at move 13. Other end positions in his mind went at least ten(!) moves further. White has the two bishops and so Black's queenside pawns will remain vulnerable for some time.

But that's not the entire story. To calculate this morass of tree limbs, White spent 90 minutes in selecting his 13th move. He felt exhausted but confident that his analysis was absolutely correct when he chose 13.♘xc7+. And he was correct in his analysis.

But the decision to work it out to the end position was disastrous. White quickly found himself in severe time trouble, began to make second-best moves, and soon lost control: **23...b6 24.a4 g6 25.a5 bxa5 26.♖a1 a6 27.♗e2 ♖d8 28.♗c3 ♘d5 29.♗d4 ♘b4 30.♗c5+ ♔e8 31.♗d1 ♖d2! 32.♗a4+ ♗d7 33.♖e1+ ♔d8 34.♗b6+ ♔c8 35.♖c1+ ♔b7 36.♗xd7 ♔xb6!.**

White resigned on the 52nd move.

What should White have done on move 13? The practical calculator would have seen quickly that neither 13.♘xc7+ nor 13.♘xe7 leads to a decisive advantage. So he would have to choose between two moves that lead at best to modest edges. This would have forced him to budget his time.

White would start with the quieter and easier line: Once he had concluded that 13.♘xe7 leads to a small but certain edge, he would know that no matter what he found in 13.♘xc7+ he would have a very playable fallback. At that point he would have allowed himself a reasonable amount of time to gauge 13.♘xc7+.

But once White saw that 14...♘h5 and 16...♗d6 had to be calculated out to a safe degree of certainty, he would have to come to a decision. Either he would give up on 13.♘xc7+ at that point – because sufficient certainty would be almost impossible to achieve. (We saw Aron Nimzowitsch reason this way in his game with Tartakower in Chapter 6.) Or, as Mikhail Tal often did, he would get the gist of several possibilities and play 13.♘xc7+, taking the risk that his intuition about his resources in the later tree limbs would pan out.

"Enough wasted time!" Nimzowitsch once commented after spending 25 minutes calculating a sub-variation that never occurred. "The game of chess is a struggle, not a mathematical exercise," he said.

And just because you can control your impulse to calculate doesn't mean you won't win a pretty game nevertheless.

SZABÓ – BÖÖK
Saltsjöbaden Interzonal 1948

1.♘f3 d5 2.g3 ♘f6 3.♗g2 e6 4.0-0 ♗e7 5.e4 0-0 6.d4 e6 7.♘e3 b6? 8.♘e5 ♗a6 9.exd5 exd5 10.♗f4 ♘fd7?

White had reason to believe that Black had erred at least once so far, and this encouraged him to consider a sacrifice on d5. He saw that 11.♘xd5 exd5 needed a better follow-up than 12.♗xd5 ♘xe5, so he searched and found 12.♘xf7!? ♖xf7 13.♗xd5, after which 13...♘c6 14.♗xc6 looks good.

But then he saw that 14...♘f6 15.♗xa8 ♛xa8 had to be carefully rechecked. (Are the evaluations correct? Are these true end positions? Are there *Zwischenzugs?*) White concluded it would take just too much calculation to be certain. Instead, he played the routine **11.♖c1.** But this did not deny him the chance for brilliancy. In fact, he won with an even prettier combination: **11...♘xe5 12.♗xe5 b5 13.e4! b4 14.♘e2 ♛a5 15.exd5 exd5 16.♘f4! ♗xf1.** Here he rejected the two candidate captures on d5 in favor of **17.♛g4! g6 18.♗xd5** and, with the threat of 19.♘xg6 hxg6 20.♛xg6#, won in a few moves.

The practical calculator knows that once an idea arises in a game – particularly one with a blocked center – it is likely to remain for several moves. He doesn't have to leap into complications by using the idea the first time he notices it:

SHORT – LJUBOJEVIĆ
Amsterdam 1991

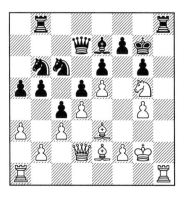

White to move

After several moves of preparation on opposite wings, both players have by now noticed a key idea here: the possibility of a breakthrough by White along the h-file with ♘h7!?, which threatens ♘f6 or ♗h6+.

White examined the immediate 1.♘h7 here with the continuation 1... ♖xh7 2.♖xh7+ ♔xh7 3.♖h1+ ♔g8 4.♗g5. This looked strong; only 4...f6 held out defensive hope. Furthermore, he saw that 5.exf6 ♗f8 and now 6.♕e3 followed by ♖h4 and ♕h3 was very dangerous. But he also saw that after 6...♖b7! the sacrifice begun by 1.♘h7 was far from clear.

1.♗f4!?

So he makes the practical choice. The ♘h7 idea isn't going away.

1...	♖bf8
2.♕e3	♕d8
3.♘h7!	

Now is the time to pull the trigger. Black threatened to solidify the kingside with 3...♖xh1 4.♖xh1 ♖h8.

3...	♖xh7

4.♖xh7+   ♔xh7
5.♖h1+   ♔g8
6.♕h3   ♗h4
7.♗h6!

Better than 7.g5 ♔g7! and Black defends with 8...♖h8. The text threatens 8.f4 and 9.♗g5, and after **7...g5 8.f4** White soon had a winning position.

When You Must Calculate

There are, of course, occasions when you must calculate, when the price of not examining variations in detail is just prohibitive. The trick is recognizing these occasions.

The simplest rule here may seem obvious: You must calculate when you suspect there is a move available that forces a concrete result. (As opposed to the solid but relatively small advantage White obtained in Kavalek–Toth.)

You must think twice when these concrete opportunities arise because you may not get a second chance. Naturally, there are three kinds of concrete results: a win, a draw, and a loss. The one we should be most pleased to calculate should be a win:

SHIROV – KIR. GEORGIEV
Manila 1992

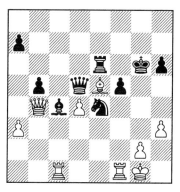

White to move

White has more material and the safer king, and here he decides to go for the knockout. His last move was ♕b2-b4 and it isn't hard to see that 1.♕f8 contains numerous threats and bears all the appearances of a winning move.

$$1.♕f8??\qquad ♖xe5!$$

If it were as good as it looked, it would have ended the game in a few moves. When you have a move that looks that strong, take the natural precaution of spending a little extra time to make sure. Avoid a lot of extra, unnecessary calculation that will get you into time pressure. If 1.♕f8 really was a knockout, there would have been no further time pressure.

As it turned out, White, already short on time, blundered again (3.♔h1 would have drawn) and lost with:

2.dxe5	♕d4+
3.♔h2	♕xe5
4.g3??	

4.♔g1 can still hold.

4...	♕b2+
5.♔g1	♕xc1+
0-1	

The same rule applies to drawable positions, such as when you are offered a draw or when you can deliver perpetual check or exchange queens down to a dead-drawn endgame. When you have a forced draw, that is precisely the moment to take as much time as necessary to re-check.

YUSUPOV – LJUBOJEVIĆ
Bugojno 1986

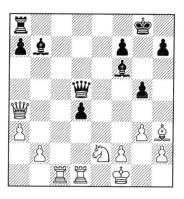

Black to move

1...	g4!
2.♗xg4	

2.♔e1!? gxh3 3.♖xd4 offers some survival chances.

2...	♕h1+
3.♘g1	♕g2+
4.♔e2	♕e4+

Here White sees that his king cannot escape via 5.♔d2 because of 5...♗g5+ 6.f4 ♕e3+ 7.♔c2 ♗e4+. So...

5.♔f1	♕g2+

If Black had any winning hopes he would play 5...♕xg4. Now the onus is on White. But is it an onus? He sees that 6.♔e2 virtually forces 5...♕e4+ with an almost certain draw by repetition.

6.♔e1??

A particularly impractical decision. White had only two minutes for more than 10 moves to reach the time control, and this is precisely the type of position that you don't want to play with so little time. And if you can't calculate with accuracy and thereby find something better than a draw, you must play 6.♔e2.

6...	**♕xg1+**
7.♔e2	**d3+!**

This is probably what White overlooked (counting instead on 7...♕g2? 8.♖xd4!). The game ended with **8.♔xd3 ♕xf2 9.♖c7 ♕xb2 10.♖d2** (10.♗c8! was the final chance) **10...♕b6 11.♖xb7 ♕xb7 12.♕b4 ♕c6 13.♔e2 ♗c3** and **0-1**.

And, of course, there is a third possible result in a game: a loss. When you see your hand about to make a move that you know is going to lose, you must search for alternatives.

You say, "Nobody makes moves they *know* will lose"? But experienced players will tell you it happens. In fact, they will tell you it has happened to them.

ŞUBĂ – CONQUEST
London 1991

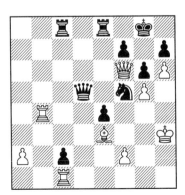

White to move

In mutual time pressure, White found:

1.♗d4

And a paralyzed Black responded:

1...	♕xd4??
2.♖xd4	♖c3+
3.♔g2	♖d3
4.♖c4	e3
5.♖1xc2	1-0

Now that the time control has been reached, Black has the first opportunity in some moves to recognize how lost he is. But it must have been obvious at the diagram that 1...♕xd4?? was a losing move. In situations like this, the practical calculator must look for an alternative. If it doesn't exist – and you forfeit on time – then it won't cost you anything.

But if a defense does exist (such as 1...♔f8! 2.♕h8+ ♔e7 3.♕f6+ ♔f8 here), then your search will have paid off. In fact, if White had then repeated the position (4.♕h8+) Black would have had good reason to play for a win (4...♔e7 5.♕f6+ ♔d7!?).

Getting Fancy

These last three examples present extreme, though hardly unique, situations. They occur in almost every game: You see an apparently decisive move and have no time to decide whether to play it or not.

But compare that with the following:

BENKO – DOMÍNGUEZ
Las Palmas 1972

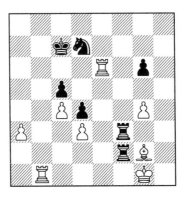

White to move

White has an extra pawn and can add the exchange with 1.♗xf3. He was not in time trouble. But he begins to wonder how difficult it would be to win the ending after 1.♗xf3 ♖xf3 (2.♔g2 ♖xd3 3.a4? ♖a3, or 3.♖a1 ♖c3).

So he searches for something better. And he finds:

**1.♖b7+??   ♔xb7
2.♖e2**

Very cute. Now 2...♖xe2 3.♗xf3+ leads to a won bishop-vs.-knight endgame because Black is forced to dedicate a piece to halting the a-pawn's advance. But instead Black finds:

2...   ♖xg2+!

And White, having made what he called "my traditional rook oversight," **resigned**.

White's blunder was understandable. There is a natural human desire to polish off a well-played game with some sparkling move or dramatic gesture. But it's better to make sure of the full point by calculating accurately.

YUSUPOV – LJUBOJEVIĆ
Linares 1990

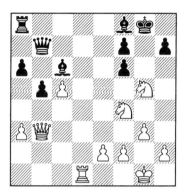

White to move

This position is the result of a fine combination begun four moves before when White offered a knight sacrifice by capturing a pawn on e6. Now White continued:

1.♘f3

A simple move that deserves no comment and that led to other simple moves and victory in less than ten moves: **1...♗xc5 2.♘h5 ♗xf3 3.exf3 ♕c6 4.♔g2 ♗xf2 5.♕b2!.**

But White admitted afterward that he was strongly tempted to finish in the style of his previous play, with 1.♘ge6. But after examining 1... fxe6 2.♕xe6+ ♔h8 3.♕xf6+ ♔g8!, he didn't see anything for White. Rather than search further for a thematic continuation, White opted for the less pretty – as he put it, "definitely saner" – retreat.

Beware Understandable Moves

When you were beginning to play chess, you learned that you should try to figure out the point of your opponent's last move: Did he threaten something? Did he anticipate a threat of yours?

ANAND – TIMMAN
Linares 1991

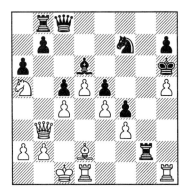

White to move

You still perform this task today – at least you should – although it is by now so routine that you may not do it consciously.

Here, out of a sharp opening, the position has clarified a bit and both sides have good practical chances. White now played:

1.♕c3

With plenty of time on his clock and some quite reasonable candidates (1...♕d8, 1...♕h8), Black responded:

1... ♕d7??

...which cost him the game. He hadn't performed the elementary beginner's task of asking himself what was the point of his opponent's last move. Had he done so he would instantly have seen:

2.♗xf4+ 1-0

Sometimes a move by your opponent may be so subtle that it doesn't seem worth considering.

VASIUKOV – POPOVIĆ
Vršac 1989

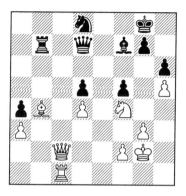

White to move

1.♔g1!

Black apparently misread this move as a useless "pass." In fact, he himself should now pass with something like 1...♖a7, maintaining control of his second rank.

1...	♘e6?
2.♕xf5	

Were the king still on g2, Black could respond 2...♘xf4 (with check) 3.♕xf4 ♗xh5.

2...	♘xf4
3.♖c8+!	

This was the second thing Black overlooked. After **3...♗e8 4.♕xd7 ♖xd7 5.♖xe8+,** he **resigned** since he would be a piece down.

There is a trap we create for ourselves when we incorrectly guess the reason for an opponent's last move. We think it contains the positional threats A and B, when in fact the main threat, C, is a mate in one.

"One should be wary of easily understandable moves," warned Richard Réti.

BAREEV – KARPOV
Tilburg 1991

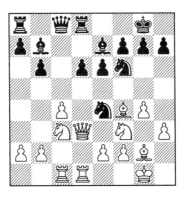

Black to move

White's pieces are clearly more actively placed. Black chose:

1...   ♘xc3

White may have thought to himself: "This makes sense. He's probably afraid of 2.g5 and then if 2...♘xc3 I have 3.gxf6 ♘xd1 4.fxe7, winning material. He also captures on c3 so he can gain time, such as with 2.♕xc3 ♘e4. So I'll play a bit differently, with 2.♖xc3, and if 2...♘e4, then 3.♖c2 so I can later double rooks."

All very logical. However:

2.♖xc3?   **e5!**

The point of Black's first move was not so obvious. He now wins a piece because of the coming pawn fork on e4. The pin 3.♕e3 exf4 4.♕xe7 fails to 4...♖d7!, trapping the queen. And **3.g5 ♘h5 4.♗c1 e4,** as the game went, was hopeless.

And one should also be wary of obviously bad moves:

FRIDJÓNSSON – McKAY
Stockholm 1969

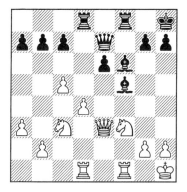

Black to move

1...	♗c2

This is the type of time-loser that beginners play. It attacks a rook that can go to a useful square (d2), and later White will be able to double rooks. But White should know that in a world junior championship, which is what this event was, there are no beginners.

2.♖d2?	♗g5!

0-1

White evidently had so little faith in his opponent's skill that he assumed he would play such a move as bad-looking as 1...♗c2. The flip side of this error is...

Believing Him

Players have to have trust in chess: They must believe in their own calculations. Korchnoi once said that another veteran grandmaster, Yefim Geller, was a good attacker "but he calculates variations badly."

Geller, he said, "wastes a lot of time, and often does not believe himself."

You know players like Geller: They check and recheck their variations, and then play something entirely different because they don't trust their own analysis. But in competitive chess there is another question: Should you trust your opponent?

This matter received widespread attention after a game in the 1965 Candidates' Match between Mikhail Tal and Bent Larsen. With the score tied, it began **1.e4 ♘f6 2.e5 ♘d5 3.d4 d6 4.♘f3 dxe5 5.♘xe5,** and now the Dane played **5...♘d7!?.**

This was apparently a new move, and it was sufficiently rare to intrigue Tal. His instinct instantly led him to a tactical idea. He later wrote that had it been a simultaneous exhibition, he would have played 6.♘xf7 ♔xf7 7.♕h5+, after which Black's king must step into a dangerous center to protect the knight.

But then Tal began to wonder why such a worthy opponent as Larsen, in an opening he had obviously prepared, would allow such a dangerous idea. At this point it was his natural intuition ("The sacrifice must be sound!") fighting his competitive doubt ("He couldn't have overlooked this, could he?").

Tal decided to resolve the matter by calculating everything out to mate if possible. After spending 50 minutes he concluded it wasn't possible and played **6.♗c4,** after which **6...e6** led to a balanced, double-edged game and an eventual draw.

Tal's decision provoked years of second-guessing by annotators who tried to show that the sacrifice would have won and that he had been the victim of a psychological trick: He trusted his opponent, and his opponent was bluffing.

Here is the opposite side of the coin *(see diagram next page)*:

KARPOV – SPASSKY
Candidates' Match (3) 1974

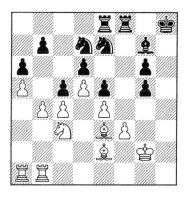

Black to move

In this difficult position Black tried:

1...   ♘**f5!**

With 11 moves to go before the time control, White examined 2.exf5 and saw that the most likely candidate reply was 2...e4. Was it a sound knight sacrifice?

Karpov took the practical approach: It might be sound or it might not be, but in the time remaining it would be difficult, if not impossible, to reach a definite conclusion. Also, he probably reasoned, a definite conclusion is not necessary because I have a perfectly good alternative that I can clearly see leads to an advantage. Since 2.exf5 e4 fails the test of leading to a concrete result, the pragmatic Karpov responded:

2.♗xg5!

Played after only four minutes' thought. Now 2...♗h6 runs into 3.exf5 ♗xg5 4.♘e4, with a large edge.

2...   ♘**d4**
3.bxc5   ♘**xc5**

319

4.♖b6

And White won without risk.

This is the dilemma of believing your opponent: If you insist on calling your opponent's bluff, you had better calculate everything correctly. If you take his word, your alternative had better be good.

KASPAROV – LARSEN
Bugojno 1982

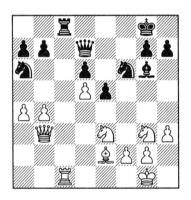

White to move

The dangers of bluff-calling are illustrated by the following:

1.♖c6!

A splendid move – for psychological reasons. It contains a threat to win a pawn (2.♗xa6) and also the minor positional threat of 2.♗g4 ♘xg4 3.♖xc8+ and 4.hxg4, reaching an endgame with superior minor pieces.

But the greatest effect of 1.♖c6 is to drive Black, a player known for his stubbornness, into using up 20 of his remaining 25 minutes. Instead of the quiet retreat of the knight to c7 or b8, he plays:

1...	bxc6?
2.dxc6+	♕f7
3.♗c4	

This much Black had to expect. Now the calculations of both players were realized on the board:

3...	d5
4.♘xd5	♔h8
5.♘b6!	♕c7
6.♘xc8	♕xc8

Black saw this far and assumed that 7.♗xa6 ♕xa6 would follow.

7.b5!	♘c5
8.♕a3	

The knight must move and the c-pawn will advance after 8...♕f8 9.c7 ♘fd7 10.♗e6; or 8...♘ce4 9.♕e7 ♘xg3 and now 10.fxg3, winning in either case. The game was shortened a bit when Black's flag soon fell.

Toward the end of a time control, major decisions like Black's 1...bxc6 are made. One of the psychological traps you can set for yourself is to say, "Well, I've already spent 15 minutes on this and I haven't come to any firm conclusion. But if I decline the sacrifice, then what have I got to show for those 15 minutes?"

The same trap often occurs when you're offered a draw in time trouble and, after lengthy thought, feel compelled to accept because you've taken so much time that continuing the game would be too risky. On the other hand, you can calculate a lot and decline the risks – and still make a losing move:

DOLMATOV – SPEELMAN
Hastings 1989-90

1.e4 c6 2.d4 d5 3.exd5 cxd5 4.c4 ♘f6 5.♘c3 e6 6.♘f3 ♗b4 7.♗d3 dxc4 8.♗xc4 0-0 9.0-0 ♘bd7 10.♗g5 ♗xc3 11.bxc3 ♕c7 12.♗d3 ♕xc3 13.♖c1 ♕a5 14.♘e5 ♘xe5 15.♖c5 ♕a3 16.dxe5! ♕xc5 17.♗xf6

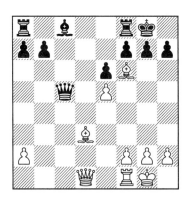

Black has enough extra material – and also enough kingside dangers – to believe that his next move will determine whether the game ends in a win, a draw, or a loss. He must also deal with the immediate threat of 18.♗xh7+ ♔xh7 19.♕h5+ ♔g8 20.♕g5 g6 21.♕h6 and mates.

After considerable thought, he decides to clear a square for his queen to defend g7.

17... ♖e8?

Black made two mistakes here.

The first was concluding that the bishop can't be taken. The natural line is: 17...gxf6 18.♕g4+ ♔h8 19.exf6? ♖g8 20.♕h4.

While Black was thinking about his 17th move, White rechecked his intended sequence (20...♖g6 21.♗xg6 fxg6 22.♕h6) and suddenly realized that Black can improve substantially with 20...h5! and probably win.

White, in fact, had decided that if the sacrifice was accepted he would continue 18.♕g4+ ♔h8 19.♕h4! f5 20.♕f6+ ♔g8 and then draw by perpetual checks on g5 and f6.

Black, in his calculations back at the diagram, saw the possibility of a draw but also felt that the position after 20...♔g8 left him too passive. If White could improve at move 21, he might very well win, he felt. For example, Black saw the idea of 21.♖e1 followed by 22.♖e3 and 23.♖g3+.

Actually, Black is probably quite secure after giving back material with 21...b6 22.♖e3 ♕xe3! 23.fxe3 ♗b7, since White has no way of adding fuel to his attack.

18.♗xh7+!

This is Black's other mistake. The attack is much stronger now (18...♔f8 19.♕g4 gxf6 20.exf6 and mates).

18...	♔xh7
19.♕h5+	

This was good enough to win after **19...♔g8 20.♕g5 ♕f8 21.♖d1 b6 22.♖d4 ♗a6 23.♖g4,** and Black kept matters going with **23...♗e2! 24.♗xg7 ♗xg4 25.♗xf8+ ♔xf8.** Black conceded on move 68.

But White failed to apply Lasker's Law: With 19.♕d3+! ♔g8 20.♕g3 ♕f8 (not 20...g6 21.♕h3 and mates) 21.♖d1, we get the same kind of position as in the game but it's a bit better after 21...b6 22.♖d4 ♗a6 23.♖g4 and ♖xg7+ (or 23...g6 24.♖xg6+) with mate following.

Summing Up

As we've seen, a chess game can go wrong in many ways. But it can also go right in many ways. There are, in fact, many different – and equally successful – methods of calculating.

Some calculators scan a wide range of candidate moves, while others intuitively examine only one and usually end up playing it. Some players decide on sacrifices only after examining 10-move, multi-branched trees while others develop a sense that allows them to be confident about a sacrifice's success after considering only a few variations. Some try to reach a clear judgment about every tree. Others avoid lengthy, perfectionist searches and rechecking of variations, believing that quick, second-best moves are more practical than time-consuming, optimum moves.

The goal of every calculator should be to find the method most comfortable – and successful – for them. Calculation should be the key that unlocks the inner game of chess, and each person's key is different.